A DISCOURSE ON PROPERTY

John Locke and his adversaries

D1520700

A DISCOURSE ON PROPERTY

✦

John Locke and his adversaries

✦

JAMES TULLY

Associate Professor of Political Science
McGill University

CAMBRIDGE UNIVERSITY PRESS

CAMBRIDGE

LONDON   NEW YORK   NEW ROCHELLE

MELBOURNE   SYDNEY

Published by the Press Syndicate of the University of Cambridge
The Pitt Building, Trumpington Street, Cambridge CB2 1RP
32 East 57th Street, New York, NY 10022, USA
296 Beaconsfield Parade, Middle Park, Melbourne 3206, Australia

First published 1980
First paperback edition 1982

Printed in Great Britain at the
University Press, Cambridge

Library of Congress catalogue card number: 79–15989

British Library Cataloguing in Publication Data
Tully, James
A discourse on property
1. Locke, John – Political science
2. Property
I. Title
330′.17′0924   JC153.L87
ISBN 0 521 22830 1 hard covers
ISBN 0 521 27140 1 paperback

FOR ERIN AND CYNTHIA

Contents

Preface

My major aim in this book is to recover the meaning which John Locke intended to convey in his theory of property in the *Two Treatises of Government*. Such an exercise seems to me to require situating the text in two contexts. One is the range of normative vocabulary and conventions available to Locke and in terms of which his theory is written. This intellectual matrix is constituted by the seventeenth-century natural law and natural rights 'discourse' to which Locke is a contributor. Therefore, I have sought to use other natural law theories to throw light on Locke's work by illuminating their similarities and dissimilarities.[1] By this method it is possible to make explicit the conventions normally employed in natural law writing and to answer three sorts of questions. First, it enables us to see which aspects of Locke's analysis of property are conventional; where he wishes to endorse or to reassert prevailing beliefs and assumptions. Second, it provides a framework against which to gauge where Locke diverges from the norm and presents his audience with something new and different. Third, this method furnishes the means of isolating the intersubjective beliefs which his audience had no reason to doubt and which thus could function as public criteria for justifying arguments.[2] The second context is the group of social and political issues Locke addresses in the *Two Treatises*. To understand his intentions, and so his meaning, it seems essential to ask what Locke is doing in deploying the normative vocabulary in the way he does; what social and political action he wishes to condone or to condemn. In this concern, as well as in the former, I am indebted to the methodological writings of Quentin Skinner and John Dunn.[3]

The study extends, in the same manner, beyond the confines of the natural law discourse to include Locke's major opponent, Sir Robert Filmer, who is not a natural law writer. This in turn affords the opportunity to ask and to answer the question why Locke should choose a natural law argument to discharge his main ideological task: the refutation of Filmer's *Patriarcha*. In adopting natural law Locke rejects, as Skinner points out, 'one of the most widely accepted and prestigious forms of political reasoning available to him': an 'appeal to the alleged prescriptive force of the ancient English constitution' (1978: 1, p. xiv). Locke gives reasons for his commitment, and he appeals to his historically minded audience by grounding natural law in more widely held beliefs. By tracing this line of Locke's argument it is possible to reconstruct the constitutive and regulative elements which underpin his theory of property. The central epistemological and theological premises are embodied in a conceptual model of the relation between God and man which I call the workmanship model. In Chapters One and Two I explore this dimension and attempt to bring to light the connections between the *Essay* and the *Two Treatises*.

In a letter to Richard King in 1703 Locke gave his assessment of his explanation of property: 'property, I have found nowhere more clearly explained than in a book intitled, *Two Treatises of Government*' (1823: x, p. 308). This uncharacteristically immodest appraisal was not shared by his contemporaries; the work met with either silence or abuse.[4] Since the early nineteenth century, however, Locke's theory of property has played a major and contradictory role in western political thought. The early English and French socialists took it as the major philosophical foundation of modern socialism: the workers' right to the product of their labour and possession regulated by need.[5] In the twentieth century the tables were turned; Locke became the spokesman for limited private property and, more recently, for unlimited private property.[6]

What I have attempted to do in this study is to replace Locke's argument in its context and to recover its original meaning. His analysis is fashioned within a discourse constituted by many conventions and assumptions we no longer share; and aimed to encourage and discourage forms of social action no longer our own. Indeed, the term 'property' itself has a meaning different from ours. Locke's theory is neither socialist nor capitalist; our modern dichotomy of private and common has no place in it. The mutually exclusive concepts of common and private property divide the modern world into two spheres. By coming to understand a way of thinking about rights in which our opposed concepts do not exist, we can begin to see what is contingent and what is necessary in our predicament.

Acknowledgments

I am greatly indebted to those friends who gave their assistance at various stages in my research and in the writing of this book. Ed Hundert first kindled my interest in the topic and his erudition and unreserved assistance have been at my disposal ever since. John Yolton has read various drafts, bringing to bear his unsurpassed understanding of Locke and helping me immeasurably in tracing the conceptual connections between the *Essay* and the *Two Treatises*. Keith Tribe has helped to guide me through the intricacies of the history of economic discourse in a series of discussions and letters. Alan Ryan has read the whole manuscript, making numerous suggestions and aiding me in making my arguments clearer. To three friends I owe a special word of thanks. One is Richard Tuck, whose unparalleled knowledge of the history and philosophy of rights, as well as his companionship, has assisted me throughout. Quentin Skinner has helped to supervise my work, offering his wealth of knowledge and kindness to guide my research and writing. To John Dunn I owe most of all. He has supervised from the beginning, read innumerable drafts, and given criticism, encouragement and support at every stage. His unexcelled interpretation of Locke has served me as a model of scholarship. I should also like to thank Cathy Duggan who typed the manuscript with unfailing efficiency and courtesy. Finally, I should like to offer my thanks to Anndale Goggin who checked quotations and grammar with unlimited patience.

Note on the text

I have used the author–date system to give the reference of quotations. At the end of each quotation, or preceding an indented quotation, the author's name, date of publication and page number appear in brackets. If the author is mentioned in the sentence, his name is omitted from the bracket. There are exceptions to this rule. First, in the case of Locke's *Essay*, all quotations are from the Nidditch critical edition and only the book, chapter and section numbers are placed in brackets. I have used the Laslett critical edition of the *Two Treatises* and the treatise and section numbers appear in brackets. When the quotation is from a manuscript in the Lovelace collection, the manuscript reference is given and this is followed by a reference to a modern text in which it has been republished. Also, if more than one quotation in a paragraph is from the same author and page or section I have given the reference after the first quotation only, thus avoiding undue clutter.

Many of the early modern works cited are available in several editions. To make the quotations as readily identifiable as possible to readers with different editions at hand, I have cited chapter and section numbers rather than page numbers. In the case of well-known authors, such as Aristotle and Aquinas, I have used the conventional abbreviations to facilitate reference. In addition, when an author is first cited the full title and date of publication is given; and all further references are to that work unless otherwise specified. I have translated all titles into English in the text and given the title in the original language in the bibliography. I have not been able to do away completely with notes. In a few places, where the reference has been too lengthy to place in brackets or the point has been inappropriate for the body of the text, I have placed a note at the end of the chapter.

One of the most important and interesting difficulties which Locke faced is a problem of translation. Property had been discussed in a highly technical manner by the Latin authors; a complex set of linguistic distinctions had been developed to deal with the Latin concepts of *ius*, *proprietas*, *suum* and *dominium*. To deal with these issues Locke developed a set of English locutions to translate the Latin terms. To understand

Locke's meaning, it is indispensible to read his English terminology in the light of the Latin equivalents. I have adopted two methods to achieve this goal. First, I have used a seventeenth- or early eighteenth-century English translation of a Latin author whenever one is available. This provides the means of reading Locke's text in the light of other attempts to translate Latin terms into English, and thus render his prose less quaint and untoward than it otherwise would be. Much of the misunderstanding of Locke on property stems from wrenching his argument out of its linguistic context and reading it in the light of our quite different vocabulary. Second, to clarify the conceptual distinctions involved in a quotation from a Latin author I have inserted the Latin terms in the quotation and discussed their meaning in the body of the text. Although this method is somewhat cumbersome, it seems essential if Locke's meaning is to be recovered. No doubt Locke's terminology would have been clear to his audience with their classical education; however, it is quite possible that Samuel Johnson, in his extensive use of Locke in his dictionary, was one of the last persons to understand and record the meaning of Locke's rich array of distinctions and technical phrases.

J.H.T.
McGill University, Montreal

PART ONE

Philosophical Underpinnings

CHAPTER ONE

The contribution of the *Essay*

i. From the *Two Treatises* to the *Essay*

1

Locke begins the chapter in the Second Treatise entitled 'Of Property' with two propositions which, as we shall see, are established in the First Treatise. Scripture reveals that the world is a gift given to mankind in common and natural reason teaches that men have a right 'to Meat and Drink, and such other things, as Nature affords for their Subsistence' (2.25). This, in turn, leads to an *aporia* or difficulty: 'this being supposed, it seems to some a very great difficulty, how any one should ever come to have a *Property* in any thing'. Locke sets himself to solve this difficulty of individuating the common gift within the constraints of each man's right to it: 'I shall endeavour to shew, how Men might come to have a *property* in several parts of that which God gave to Mankind in common'.

'Locke wants to explain', writes Yolton, 'how particularisation of the common is possible' (1970: p. 187). It is not, as Day assumes, a 'justification of private property' (1966: p. 207). It is an attempt to work out this problem of the natural distribution of common property (Dunn, 1969: p. 67n.4). To understand the nature of Locke's 'great difficulty', and his solution, it is necessary to trace the two propositions which give rise to it back to their basis in the law of nature. This is especially necessary in light of Nozick's potentially misleading claim that Locke 'does not provide anything remotely resembling a satisfactory explanation of the status and basis of the law of nature in his *Second Treatise*' (1974: p. 9).

Locke calls the right which all men have to the things necessary for subsistence 'property' and this is, in some sense, distinguished from 'property in' some thing which a person 'comes to have' in the process of individuation of the common gift (1.23, 24, 86, 87; 2.25). The right or property that all men have to things necessary for subsistence is said to be a consequence of the right which all men have to their preservation, derived by what Locke calls 'natural reason' (2.25). Locke consistently uses 'reason' in two senses, in the *Essays on the Law of Nature* (pp. 111, 149) the *Essay* (4.17.1) and in his second reply to Edward Stillingfleet

(1823: IV, pp. 366–7): to stand for either the object of search or the rational means of search (the discursive faculty). This is common in natural law writing and we also employ this linguistic practice when a kind of knowledge stands in a means–end relation to its object; for example, 'logic', 'politics' and 'art'. Locke writes here of reason in the sense of the discursive faculty. This is known by the fact that when he wishes to characterise what the reasoning faculty discovers in morals and politics, other than by 'reason', he calls it natural law (1.101; 2.6; 1823: VII, p. 11).

Since the two rights, to preservation and to the means of subsistence, are discovered by natural reason, they are, *ipso facto*, derived from natural law. Locke derives the right to preservation from the fundamental law of nature that mankind ought to be preserved (1.86; 2.8, 25, 149). This logical series can be traced back one step further. In the *Essay* Locke argues that each natural law is a normative proposition and, as such, has itself a reason from which it follows as a consequence: '*there cannot any one moral Rule be propos'd, whereof a Man may not justly demand a Reason*. . .the truth of all these moral Rules, plainly depends upon some other antecedent to them, and from which they must be deduced' (1.3.4; cf. 1.3.12). The primary duty to preserve mankind, and its corollary duty to respect 'what tends to the Preservation of the Life, the Liberty, Health, Limb or Goods of another', follows immediately from a special relation between God and man: 'For Men being all the Workmanship of one Omnipotent, and infinitely wise Maker; All the Servants of one Sovereign Master, sent into the World by his order and about his business, they are his Property, whose Workmanship they are, made to last during his, not one anothers Pleasure' (2.6).

It is not easy to understand the meaning of this conceptual model of God as maker and man as his workmanship, nor of God as master and man as his servant. Nor is the implicatory series from this workmanship model (as I shall call the relational model of man and his maker) to the law of nature and so to the two natural rights pellucid. If one looks for clarification one sees that the workmanship model is a fundamental feature of all Locke's writing. (Indeed, on the basis of a content analysis alone the workmanship model can be seen to be a common theme uniting the *Essay* and the *Two Treatises*.) In the *Essay* he states that it is the 'Foundations of our Duty and Rules of Action' from which 'the measures of right and wrong might be made out' (4.3.18). (Measures of right and wrong are either natural laws or norms inferred from them (2.28.8, 13).) In his many uses of this conceptual model Locke makes it clear that it is the ground of property relations as well as of many political relations. Since Locke's theory of property takes its start from this description of God and man, I begin with an investigation of it. It is discussed extensively in the *Essay* and in the *Essays on the Law of Nature* and so to these we turn for enlightenment.

2

In using the *Essay* to assist in understanding Locke on property I am deliberately following an historical precedent. The three natural law writers whom Locke recommends are Richard Hooker (1554?–1600), Hugo Grotius or Huig de Groot of Delft (1583–1645) and Samuel Pufendorf (1632–92).[1] Hooker, the famous defender of Anglicanism, wrote the *Of the lawes of the Ecclesiastical Politie* (1593–1648). Grotius was a leading Dutch statesman, scholar and jurist whose single most important contribution to natural law political theory is *The Laws of War and Peace* (1625). Pufendorf, a German jurist, historian and political theorist, is famous for his major study, *The Law of Nature and Nations, or, a general system of the most important principles of morality, jurisprudence and politics* (1672). Jean Barbeyrac (1674–1744), a French legal theorist, annotated a Latin edition of Grotius' *The Laws of War and Peace* (1735) which was translated, with notes, into English by W. Innys and R. Manby in 1738. He annotated and translated into French Pufendorf's *The Law of Nature and Nations* (running to six editions by 1750) and this, in turn, was translated, with notes, into English by Basil Kennett and Carew (1729). Included in the English translation of Barbeyrac's annotated edition of Pufendorf is an account of natural law writing by Barbeyrac entitled 'An historical and critical account of the science of morality, and the progress it has made in the world, from the earliest times down to the publication of this work'. This study in the history of natural law political theory by Barbeyrac makes explicit the links between Locke and Grotius and Pufendorf on one hand, and between the *Two Treatises* and the *Essay* on the other.

Barbeyrac corresponded with Locke three times between 1702 and 1704, informing him of his intention to translate Pufendorf and asking his advice (MS. Locke, c.3, fo. 140). He learned English in order to read Locke in the original and offered criticism to Pierre Coste for his second French edition of the *Essay* (1729: 'Avis au lecteur'; Axtell, 1968: p. 92). 'No man in the early eighteenth century', Laslett notes of Barbeyrac, 'was in a generally better position than he to know about the relationship of his [Locke's] writings with the natural-law jurists and with the whole tradition of social and political theory' (1970: p. 306n). He was also the first to agree in print with Locke's claim that his is the best available explanation of property (1729: 4.4.3n.2).

Both Grotius and Pufendorf begin their work with a discussion of the kinds of concepts used in natural law theory, of the method appropriate to it and of the degree of certainty obtainable (see below, pp. 30–2). Their substantive political theory is underpinned by the conclusions which they reach in this field. Barbeyrac's notes on this section in Pufendorf refer to Locke's *Essay* for both a clarification and a better treatment of the issues involved (1.1.2n.2). When Pufendorf comes to discuss property he states that his theory rests on his epistemological and methodological conclusions (4.4.1). In his commentary on Pufendorf's discussion of property Barbeyrac refers his reader to the *Two Treatises* for the definitive analysis of the topic (4.4. *passim*).

Barbeyrac strengthens the connection between the *Two Treatises* and the *Essay* in his 'historical and critical account of the science of morality'. He argues that the superiority of the seventeenth-century natural law writers rests on their reconstruction of political theory on the basis of a new epistemology introduced by Francis Bacon (p. 79). He adds Richard Cumberland (1631–1718), the Bishop of Peterborough, to the list of political theorists involved in this new wave of natural law writing (p. 87). Cumberland wrote *A Treatise of the Laws of Nature* (1672) to refute the political theory of Thomas Hobbes (1588–1679) and Barbeyrac brought out a French edition of Cumberland's treatise in 1744. Cumberland reinforces Barbeyrac's reconstruction argument, adding John Wallis, the Savilian Professor of Geometry in Oxford, and Locke's close friend, to those responsible for providing the conceptual tools necessary to revolutionise natural law theory (1727: pp. 183–5).

Although I am using Barbeyrac's excellent essay to situate Locke's writings in the correct *intellectual* context, it is important to note that Cumberland's treatise can be seen to be a constituent element of it by another means. In 1679–81 Locke renewed his interest in natural law, worked in close association with his friend James Tyrrell (1642–1718) on critical notes to *The Mischief of Separation* (MS. Locke, c.34), and probably composed major parts of the *Two Treatises* (for the date of composition of the *Two Treatises*, see below, pp. 53–4). Tyrrell wrote his *The Patriarch un-monarched* (1681) in this period and later went on to write an English version of Cumberland's work, entitled *Disquisition of the Law of Nature* (1691). Although Locke neither owned nor cited Cumberland's treatise, it cannot seriously be doubted that he read it, either independently or through prompting by Tyrrell in 1681 (von Leyden, 1970: pp. 14, 55, 66; Gough, 1976). It is also worth noting that Pufendorf inserted several quotations from Cumberland's treatise into the second edition of *The Law of Nature and Nations* (1688).[2]

Barbeyrac states that Grotius 'introduc'd in the last Age, the methodological Study of the Law of Nature' (p. 36), and Cumberland and especially Pufendorf brought about the revolution in natural law theory (p. 81). However, Barbeyrac grants Locke the honour of completing the theoretical reconstruction in a definitive manner and opens his historical account with several sections of the *Essay* quoted in full. The *Essay* is said to prove the superiority of the moral sciences over the natural sciences in terms of the certainty of knowledge obtainable (pp. 1–9). As all these authors make clear, the term 'moral sciences' is a synonym for 'natural law theory' signifying works such as the *Two Treatises*: 'I [Barbeyrac] mean by this [the Practical Science of Moral Actions], and the Term *Morality*, not only what is commonly so call'd, but also *The Law of Nature, and Politicks*: In a word, all that is necessary for the Conduct of a Man's Self, according to his Estate and Condition' (p. 1n and see below, pp. 27–34).

Barbeyrac isolates three main lines of the *Essay*, all dealing with the epistemological foundations of moral knowledge, which are both analyses of problems in seventeenth-century natural law theory and underpinnings of Locke's own political theory. First, he takes Locke's workmanship model to be the ground of natural law theory in general and of a limited natural rights theory in particular. Second, Locke's work on modes and relations is said to be propaedeutic and necessary in understanding natural law political theory. Third, Locke's analysis of real essences is responsible for putting political theory definitely on a superior footing (pp. 4–5, 10–13).

The aspect of Locke's political theory of which these lines of the *Essay* are supportive is Locke's theory of property (p. 5; 1729: 4.4.2n, 4.4.3n, 4.4.6n, 8.1.3n). Barbeyrac includes in his references Locke's discussion of property in the *Letters Concerning Toleration*, as well as the *Two Treatises* and the *Essay*. To speak of Locke's theory of property is to speak of Locke's theory of rights: 'Mr. Locke means by the word 'property' not only the right which one has to his goods and possessions, but even with respect to his actions, liberty, his life, his body; and, in a word, all sorts of right' (p. 4).

Therefore, Barbeyrac presents two major investigative aids: three parts of the *Essay* are essential in understanding Locke on property in context and Locke's term 'property' means 'right' of any sort. These are the same two points derived above from the initial textual analysis, reinforced with contextual detail. This lends historical justification to the decision to begin, as Barbeyrac himself suggests, with the former (p. 84).

3

This approach may appear to contradict Laslett's claim that the *Two Treatises* and the *Essay* exhibit no philosophical links. 'None of the connecting links is present' (p. 84). 'It was written for an entirely different purpose and in an entirely different state of mind' (p. 83). I think, however, that the apparent contradiction is not irreconcilable. Laslett's primary intention in this section is to disabuse the reader of the notion that Locke's political theory might be a logical deduction from his philosophy, as, for example, Hobbes' theory is (pp. 85–90). With this I wholeheartedly agree. Laslett goes on to suggest that there might be some sort of looser, 'open' relationship between the *Essay* and the *Two Treatises* (p. 87). It is this sort of relationship which is explored in this chapter, although I agree with Dunn that Laslett's description of it as a 'Lockeian attitude' as opposed to a 'Lockeian philosophy' is an unhappy one (1969: p. 199n). The following three introductory points serve to illustrate my basic agreement with Laslett. First the relationship suggested both by textual analysis so far and by Barbeyrac holds between only certain parts of the *Essay* and the *Two Treatises*. Second, the nature of the relationship is much looser than formal logical demonstration. I have tried to suggest this by using 'implicatory series', 'supportive', 'ground' and 'underpinning' to express, tentatively, the kind of connection. Yolton has shown that even when Locke uses the term 'demonstration' he normally means something less formal than logical deduction: 'demonstration meant primarily for Locke just the uncovering of conceptual connexions' (1970: p. 92; cf. Dunn, 1969: pp. 24n.3, 191). Third, Barbeyrac clearly thought there was an important link between the two works. This provides the historical justification, which Laslett seems to imply is missing (p. 83), for an attempt to make the link explicit. Finally, Yolton has already broken turf in this area with his excellent discussion of Locke's theory of property as an application of the kind of conceptual analysis recommended in the *Essay* for moral concepts (1970: pp. 181–95).

The major block to seeing the connections between the *Essay* and the *Two Treatises* has been, as Dunn states, the predisposition to view the *Essay* as a contribution to empiricism or rationalism (1969: pp. 198–9; cf. Yolton, 1970: p. 14). Following Barbeyrac's lead and situating it in the wider intellectual context of seventeenth-century natural law writing provides a means of interpreting it in an historically more sensitive manner, and so of understanding the 'reasons internal to the positions argued in the *Essay* which determined the particular shape' of the *Two Treatises* (Dunn, 1969: p. 92).

ii. Mixed modes and relations

1

The three themes in the *Essay* which Barbeyrac singles out for attention are closely related. The workmanship model, which we saw to be bedrock for the analysis of property in the *Two Treatises*, is shown in the *Essay* to comprise two complex ideas: 'The *Idea* of a supreme Being, infinite in Power, Goodness, and Wisdom, whose Workmanship we are, and on whom we depend; and the *Idea* of our selves, as understanding, rational Beings' (4.3.18). Here Locke says the workmanship model, 'duly considered, and pursued', would afford the foundations of morality, as indeed it does in the *Two Treatises* (2.6). When he gives the idea a name he calls it *'the Notion of his Maker'* which, if ideas were innate, God would set 'on his own Workmanship, to mind Man of his dependance and Duty' (1.4.13). The fact that Locke calls the idea a 'notion' means that it is a special kind of idea: either a mixed mode or a relation (3.5.12; 1823: I, p. 540; Yolton, 1970: p. 161). A description of Locke's analysis of mixed modes and relations provides an understanding of the epistemological status of the workmanship model. As Barbeyrac writes, 'In a System of the Law of Nature an author ought, without Dispute, to begin with instructing his Reader in the Nature of Moral Entities or Beings' (p. 84). 'Moral entity' is Pufendorf's term for the object constituted by a moral concept. Locke standardly uses his own terminology of modes and relations but he reverts to Pufendorf's term at 3.5.12.

One of the things which an idea is is the meaning of a term in use which stands for the idea: 'The meaning of Words, being only the *Ideas* they are made to stand for by him that uses them' (3.4.6). A general idea is what a general term in use stands for (3.3.6). There are two fundamentally different kinds of general idea: ectype and archetype (2.31.12; omitting simple ideas). General ideas of substances are ectype (2.31.13). All general ideas, except those of substances, are archetype ideas (4.4.5). General archetype ideas comprise, therefore, all ideas of 'sorts of things' (3.3.12) which are, in some sense, constructed by man as opposed to substances, which are constructed by nature. Locke subdivides archetype ideas into two very general categories: modes and relations (2.12.4, 7).

Modes are general ideas which do not contain as part of their meaning the supposition of subsisting by themselves (as general ideas of substances do), 'but are considered as Dependences on, or Affections of Substances; such are the *Ideas* signified by the words *Triangle, Gratitude, Murther, etc*' (2.12.4). Pufendorf opens *The Law of Nature and Nations* with a similar distinction (below, p. 32). In the above definition 'substances' refers to men. Locke's meaning is that men construct triangles, feel or express gratitude and commit murder (3.6.42). Simple modes are composed of one kind of simple idea, such as 'a dozen', which is a combination of units (2.12.5). Mixed modes are composed of several ideas of several kinds, such as '*Theft*, which being the concealed change of the possession of any thing, without the consent of the Proprietor, contains, as is visible, a combination of several *Ideas* of several kinds' (2.12.5). Relations are general ideas which consist 'in a consideration and comparing one *Idea* with another' (2.12.7). Another way in which Locke makes the mixed mode relation distinction is to consider the word and its object. Words of relations, 'together with the thing they denominate, imply also something else separate, and exterior to the existence of that thing', whereas words of mixed modes do not (2.25.10).[3]

For the purposes of political philosophy there are three important kinds of relation. Natural relations are those in which two or more things are considered with reference to their origin or beginning, such as father, son, brother and countryman (2.28.2; cf. Pufendorf: 1.1.7). Instituted relations are those in which two or more things are considered with reference to an act, 'whereby any one comes by a Moral Right, Power, or Obligation to do something', such as citizen, governor, master and servant (2.28.3). They differ from natural relations in that they depend upon men's 'Agreement in Society' and 'in that they are most, if not all of them, some way or other alterable, and separable from the Persons, to whom they have sometimes belonged, though neither of the Substances, so related, be destroy'd' (2.28.3; cf. Pufendorf: 1.1.8–12). The workmanship model, for example, is a natural relation with respect to man but instituted with respect to God. A moral relation is a voluntary action's conformity to or disagreement with a rule. Sin and duty are the moral relations of a voluntary action to natural law, criminal and legal are the moral relations of a voluntary action to civil law, and virtue and vice are the moral relations of voluntary action to cultural norms (2.28.7; cf. Pufendorf: 1.2.5–6).

Mixed modes and relations, therefore, comprise an extremely large category of ideas. Many moral ideas (property, obligations, right) and all ideas of human artifacts, affections, actions and institutions are mixed modes. Any idea that we come to have by comparison is a relation. As Locke writes, '*to enumerate all the mixed Modes*. . .would be to make a Dictionary of the greatest part of the Words made use of in Divinity, Ethicks, Law, and Politicks, and several other Sciences' (2.22.12).[4] Relations too are the central ideas of political theory. The various relations under which men are picked out 'should be observed, and marked out in Mankind, there being occasion, both in Laws, and other Communications one with another, to mention and take notice of Men, under these Relations: From whence also arise the Obligations of several Duties amongst Men' (2.28.2).[5] As early as his Oxford lectures on natural law, *Essays on the Law of Nature* (1662), Locke stresses the central role of social relations in natural law theory: 'most precepts of this law [of nature] have regard to the various relations between men and are founded on those' (p. 197). Thus, there is a close connection between the *Essay* and the *Two Treatises* at this point. The epistemological aspects of these sorts of concepts are investigated in the *Essay* and the conceptual connections yielding duties and rights of various relations, with reference to natural law, are worked out in the *Two Treatises*. Indeed, this is the stated aim of the *Two Treatises* (2.2). Thus, a fundamental assumption of Locke's political thought is, contrary to common misunderstandings, not to treat man as an isolated individual but, rather, to treat him in his various relations with other men and with God.

The kind of knowledge appropriate to ideas of substances is knowledge of 'The Nature of Things, as they are in themselves, their Relations, and their manner of Operation'; φυσική or natural philosophy (4.21.1). The end of this kind of knowledge is 'bare speculative Truth' (4.21.2). The kind of knowledge appropriate to mixed modes and relations is knowledge of 'That which Man himself ought to do, as a rational and voluntary Agent, for the Attainment of any End, especially Happiness'; πρακτική or practical knowledge (4.21.1). Locke's redescription of practical knowledge shows that it includes, but is not exhausted by, morality as defined earlier in terms of the kind of knowledge which is founded on the workmanship model (4.3.18), and which is identical to Barbeyrac's definition of morality in terms of natural law and political theory (4.21.3):

Πρακτική, The Skill of Right applying our own Powers and Actions, for the Attainment of Things good and useful. The most considerable under this Head, is *Ethicks*, which is the seeking out those Rules, and Measures of humane Actions, which lead to Happiness, and the Means to practise them.

The end of practical knowledge is 'not bare Speculation, and the Knowledge of Truth; but Right, and a Conduct suitable to it'. The third branch of knowledge is the logic of the ideas used in either practical or natural philosophy; semiotics or the doctrine of signs (4.21.4).

The first point to note in Locke's classification of knowledge is that practical knowledge includes both making and doing. As he writes, 'things good [doing] and useful [making]; any end'. This accords with his classification of knowledge elsewhere (1967: pp. 245–7) and with his grouping of the ideas of the applied sciences and those of morality, divinity, politics and law into one category (archetypal) (cf. Cumberland, 1727: pp. 50–2; Barbeyrac, 1729: pp. 2–5). The distinction between natural and practical knowledge is Aristotelian (Joachim, 1970: pp. 1–18). Man's object in the natural sciences is to understand, to contemplate; in the practical sciences to live in a certain way and to make certain things; not to understand except to act.

The second point to note is that the distinction between natural and practical philosophy is not isomorphic with theory and non-theory. Both these categories have a theoretical and a 'prudential' or experimental component. The normal Scholastic classification, on the other hand, is between natural philosophy as theoretical and practical philosophy (economics, politics and ethics) as non-theoretical (Weisheipl, 1965: pp. 59–90). Francis Bacon is standardly credited with breaking the normal Scholastic classification by apportioning to each branch of knowledge a theoretical and a 'prudential' aspect (1874: IV, pp. 79, 373; see Jardine, 1975: ch. 4). The theoretical aspects of morality and politics is taken over by Grotius, as Barbeyrac notes (p. 79), and developed in various ways in natural law political theory or the 'science of morality' by Hobbes, Spinoza, Pufendorf, Cumberland, Leibniz, Locke and Vico.

2

All general ideas have a function: 'to be ideas of', 'to stand for', 'to represent' or 'to conform to' that of which they are ideas (2.30.1, 2.31.1; 3.2.2, 3.3.12; 4.21.4). Using ideas – speaking, writing, thinking – is an intentional activity. Ideas 'represent those Archetypes, which the Mind supposes them taken from; which it intends them to stand for, and to which it refers them' (2.31.1). The 'archetype' is that which an idea is intended to stand for (2.30.1). Ectype ideas, which are ideas of substances, are called ectypes (copies) because they are intended to stand for an archetype existing independent of our knowledge *in rerum natura* (2.31.13). Therefore the archetypes of ectype ideas are substances, 'existing without us' (2.30.5).

Archetype ideas, which are ideas of conventional (non-natural) things, are archetypes (originals) because the archetypes for which they are intended to stand are the ideas themselves. The idea is its own archetype (as the name suggests). These ideas are 'not intended to be the Copies of any thing, nor referred to the existence of any thing, as to their Originals' (4.4.5). An archetype idea 'is not designed to represent any thing but it self'; it 'contains in it precisely all that the Mind intends it should' (2.31.14). Thus ectype ideas copy their natural archetypes whereas archetype ideas are their own archetypes.

This theme of the *Essay* draws attention to the radical difference between the kind of knowledge of natural and of conventional things. Ideas of substances are intended to copy their object *in re*; the idea is *derived* from its object. The 'adequacy' of such knowledge is judged by comparing the idea to its object (2.31.1, 13). Knowledge of social or conventional reality is just the opposite. Here, the knowledge, not the object, is the archetype. The idea is normative; conventional things are judged for their adequacy by comparing the 'object' to its idea. '*Complex* Ideas of *Modes and Relations, are* Originals, and *Archetypes*; are not Copies, nor made after the Pattern of any real Existence, to which the Mind intends to be conformable. . .and so are designed only for, and belong only to such

Modes [and relations], as when they do exist, have an exact conformity with those complex Ideas' (2.31.14). 'And hence it is, that in all these sorts of *Ideas* themselves are considered as the *Archetypes*, and Things no otherwise regarded, but as they are conformable to them' (4.4.5).

Ectype ideas refer to natural reality and are dependent on that reality for their truth value (2.32.13). Archetype ideas refer to social or conventional reality and are independent of that reality for their truth value (2.32.17). Mixed modes and relations not only define their objects; they constitute the essences of the sorts of things for which they stand: they are 'Essences of Modes [and relations *qua* objects] that may exist' (2.31.14). They are normative and constitutive; social reality is constituted, ranked, denominated and judged in terms of them (3.5.12; cf. Yolton, 1970: pp. 138–59).

Locke investigates a primitive language game to explain his constitution theory of archetype ideas; to show the sense in which these ideas are normative and constitutive in addition to being descriptive. (The knowledge of mixed modes and relations man comes to have by tracing their conceptual connections is also knowledge of social reality but it falls outside the constitution theory as described here.) Adam has the use of language but he is in a country where many things are as yet unnamed. Adam observes that Lamech is troubled and, assuming that Lamech is jealous of his wife's adultery, he invents the Hebrew words *kinneah* (jealousy) and *niouph* (adultery) in order to discuss the matter with Eve (3.6.44). Adam later discovers that Lamech was troubled over something else (he killed a man). He discovers that Lamech's trouble is not as his idea of it prescribes. This, however, does not make him change his idea. His mistake is not one of knowledge, but of performance: he misapplied his ideas: 'His own choice having make that Combination, it had all in it he intended it should, and so could not but be perfect, could not but be adequate, it being referr'd to no other Archetype, which was supposed to represent'. His ideas of *kinneah* and *niouph* remain archetypes of what jealousy and adultery are. They remain norms to which 'he gave Names to denominate all Things, that should happen to agree to those his abstract *Ideas*, without considering whether any such thing did exist, or no: the Standard there was of his own making' (3.6.46).

Locke contrasts this with the way Adam comes to have an idea of a substance, using *zahab* (gold) as an example. Adam observes that a sample of 'glittering substance' is yellow, hard and heavy and he selects these three qualities as constitutive of the essence of *zahab* (3.6.47). In making his idea of *zahab* Adam takes 'the quite contrary course' to the case of the mixed modes jealousy and adultery (3.6.46). The archetype of his idea of gold is in nature and he puts no simple idea in his complex idea 'but what he has the Perception of from the thing it self'. His idea is intended to copy its object *in re* and he intends that 'the Name should stand for an *Idea* so comformable'.

The crux of Locke's distinction is that the use of ideas is an intentional activity and so Adam's intentions were different in the two cases. As Mackie writes, Adam 'intended *zahab* to stand for *that stuff, whatever properties and constitution it may turn out to have*; but he did not intend *kinneah* to stand for *the sort of trouble, whatever it may turn out to be, from which Lamech is suffering*, nor *niouph* for *whatever Adah has been up to lately*' (1976: p. 93). In the case of *kinneah* or *niouph* he intends his idea to be a standard prescribing what it is to be an object of such a kind. If Adam wishes to increase his knowledge of what gold is he observes his sample more closely (3.6.47). In contrast, no observation of instances of jealousy and adultery, picked out under these names, would increase his knowledge of what it is to be either: the idea furnishes normative knowledge.

Locke's argument is not that Adam could not learn anything about conventional sorts of things by observing their instances. Adam could study, say, workmen and their workmanship (two relations) and learn about this sociological phenomenon. He could compile evidence about how and why and under what conditions they work. However, none of this would change his ideas of what it is to be a workman or a piece of workmanship. His empirical studies necessarily would take place within, and presuppose, the normative ideas which constitute the essence of either and so define the objects of investigation. To use another of Locke's examples, suicide is the taking of one's life and empirical studies of it pre-suppose the idea as a normative framework. The necessity of necessary propositions, such as 'suicide is the taking of one's life', consists for Locke not in the fact that they are derived from reality but, rather, that reality is judged in accordance with them. It is a conventionalist thesis that an archetype idea tells us what kind of object any non-natural thing is (3.10.33, 3.9.7).

Locke uses his primitive language game to return to the normal situation of a person born into an established community of language users. '*Kinneah* and *Niouph*, by degrees grew into common use; and then the case was somewhat alter'd' (3.6.45). Adam's children had the same free-dom as Adam to make whatever ideas they pleased. However, language is for communication and it is not a sufficient condition of communication for words to stand for one's own ideas. To communicate men must use their words for '*Marks of the* Ideas *in the Minds also of other Men, with whom they communicate*: For else they should talk in vain, and could not be understood' (3.2.4). Strictly speaking, it is not necessary, to be under-stood, to know the idea for which a word stands. It is enough for persons 'that they use the Word, as they imagine, in the common Acceptation of that Language'. This connection of ideas to the intersubjective language in common use forms the linguistic behaviour of Adam's children. They found the words *kinneah* and *niouph* in 'familiar use', as the general words whose abstract ideas 'were the Essences of the Species distinguished by those Names' (3.6.45). Therefore, if they were to use their words to refer to conventional sorts of things 'already establish'd and agreed on, they were obliged to conform the *Ideas*, in their Minds, signified by these Names, to the *Ideas*, that they stood for in other Men's Minds, as to their Patterns and *Archetypes*'.

The archetype, therefore, to which a general term, which stands for a mixed mode or relation, refers in a language community is not one's own idea, as with Adam, but 'to the signification annexed by others to their received Names' (3.6.43). A general term is properly used only if it conforms to the idea 'to which, in its proper use, it is primarily annexed' (2.31.4). Archetype ideas constitute the essences of conventional things and these in turn receive their significance from how their names are standardly used in the common language. Therefore, in an established language community, social reality is constituted into sorts of things in the first instance by language (and, *eo ipso*, by ideas) and dependent for its existence on the continued use of the appropriate names (3.5.10; cf. Yolton, 1970: pp. 138–9). Mixed modes and relations, and so the objects of which they are the essences, are not subjective but inter-subjective; existing in the continued normative employment of their names in the language in common use (3.5.10; cf. Hacking, 1975: p. 47; Yolton, 1970: p. 159).

Locke asks his readers to imagine what happens to Adam's general term *zahab* in common use. If men were to refer *zahab* to the combination of qualities they were able to find in their own particular sample, each man would be speaking of a different species, since there is an endless number of qualities that can be found in any particular substance (3.6.48). All would be reduced to Babel (3.6.28). Therefore an agreement is made amongst Adam and his friends to count a few 'leading qualities' as essential to being a member of a natural kind and to constitute nature into kinds on this basis (3.6.49). The idea of gold, enumerating a few easily observable qualities is turned into a norm in accordance with which nature is ranked by the language community (3.6.51; cf. Boyle, 1660: pp. 199–200). Ideas of substances with names annexed to them are established 'as Patterns, or Forms...to which, as particular Things existing are found to agree, so they come to be of that Species, have that Denomination, or are put into that *Classis*' (3.3.13). As with mixed modes and relations, ideas of substances in a language community are closely connected to their names such that the primary reference in using the idea is the common use of the name; 'to the signification of their Names, as to the *Archetypes*' (3.6.43).

Therefore, language, or the common use of general terms, constitutes the intersubjective reality into kinds, both natural and conventional, for that community (3.3.13). The use of general terms, speaking anachronistically, plays a role similar to grammar in Wittgenstein's constitution theory of language (Wittgenstein, 1974: ss.371,373).[6] It is at this point that Locke's distinction between archetype and ectype ideas seems to lose its sharpness. However, there are substances in nature independent of how societies organise them into kinds, although man confronts this reality in light of the concepts available to him. There are no conventional objects independent of the archetype ideas in accordance with which they are constituted; no stabbing for example in a culture void of the idea of stabbing (3.5.11; cf. Yolton, 1970: p. 139). These things are made and done *simpliciter* in accordance with one's language. This epistemologically unique status of archetype ideas gives political philosophy, which treats of archetype ideas, its superior status with respect to natural philosophy. Locke brings out the implications of his constitution theory for political philosophy in his treatment of nominal and real essences and, in so doing, explicates the epistemological foundations of the workmanship model.

iii. The place of political philosophy

1

Locke says that there are two types of essence, nominal and real: what it is to be named a particular of a kind and what it is to *be* that particular thing (3.3.15). The nominal essence is that combination of features named in the complex idea, which we agree is essential for an object to be of this or that sort (3.6.2). He calls the nominal essence the 'artificial constitution' (3.3.15) because, although these factors are observed to 'go constantly together', it is man who selects a certain number of them and decides that what they constitute is to be named *a such and such*; a sort of thing (2.23.1).

Locke uses gold as an example. We name an object gold because it has such and such qualities. This combination of qualities 'which makes it to be *Gold*, or gives it a right to that Name,...is therefore its nominal *Essence*' (3.3.18). There is general agreement within a tolerable latitude that 'nothing can be call'd *Gold*, but what has a Conformity of Qualities to that abstract complex *Idea*, to which that Name is annexed'. The nominal essence is the explanation because of which an object is *named* a sort of thing.

The real essence is 'something quite different' (3.6.3). There are two criteria for a real essence. It is 'the very being of any thing, whereby it is, what it is', the traditional meaning of 'essence' or *essentia* (3.3.15). Second, it is that upon which its species properties 'depend' (3.3.6); 'the causal basis of the thing' (Yolton, 1970: p. 30). Although the real essence is not 'a "class" or "kind" feature of things', is not itself a sort, it 'relates to a sort' (Yolton, 1970: pp. 30–1; cf. 3.6.6). Thus, in being the causal basis of a particular thing it is also that in virtue of which it is the sort of thing it is, although we know it as a sort of thing in virtue of its nominal essence (3.3.13, 15; 4.6.11). Real essence kinds of substances are not available to us, but they perhaps would be for a superior intelligence (Yolton, 1970: pp. 32–3). He writes that the nominal essence (what is to be named a such and such) and the real essence (what is to be that thing and so, although this cannot be known by us in the case of substances, to be that sort of thing) are always the same in modes and relations (*qua* objects) and always different in substances (3.3.18):[7]

Essences being thus distinguished into *Nominal* and *Real*, we may farther observe, that *in the Species* of...*Modes*, they *are always the same*: But *in Substances, always quite different.* Thus a Figure including a Space between three Lines, is the real, as well as nominal *Essence* of a Triangle; it being not only the abstract *Idea* to which the general Name is annexed, but the very *Essentia*, or Being, of the thing it self, that Foundation from which all its Properties flow, and to which they are all inseparably annexed.

In making this statement Locke is focusing on another dimension of his ectype–archetype distinction and laying the foundation for the theoretical aspect of practical knowledge.

That the nominal and real essence are always the same in modes and relations is a direct consequence of the way in which these ideas and their 'objects', or social phenomena, are made. Locke's statement turns on his claim that there are no essences of modes and relations (*qua* 'objects') independent of the ideas which represent them (3.5.3, 3.10.33). When men make ideas of modes and relations they do not follow any pattern existing *in re*, as they do in making ideas of substances (3.5.6).

Man 'unites and retains certain Collections' of the ideas of social phenomena with definite features (3.5.3). At the same time he 'ties them together by a Name' so only social phenomena with these features bear the name (3.5.4). In this way a complex idea is made containing ideas of these features and annexed to a general term (3.5.5). Other social phenomena, 'that have altogether as much union in Nature, are left loose, and never combined into one *Idea*' (3.5.6). In this way, 'a Species be constituted' and a community's social reality constituted into kinds (3.5.5): 'these essences of the Species of mixed Modes, are the Workmanship of the Mind; and consequently,...the Species themselves are of Men's making' (3.5.4; cf. 3.5.6).

Although these ideas are of social phenomena existing *in re* (constituted by their ideas), they are independent of that reality for their truth value: man does not 'verifie them by Patterns, containing such peculiar Compositions in Nature' (3.5.3; cf. 2.32.11–12). For example, the ideas of mother, father, son, daughter and sexual intercourse are grouped together into a certain combination and given the general name 'incest' (3.5.6. This is also Pufendorf's example: 1.2.6). The idea cannot but be the real essence because it is the idea which determines what it is to be an act of incest. The idea is the archetype (3.5.14). These ideas are deposited in our common language and we judge reality in accordance with them (2.30.4, 2.31.4, 2.32.11).

Since these ideas are constitutive of social practices and relations, taken together they are constitutive of the 'manner of life' of a particular culture (3.5.8). Because they are constitutive of social practices these ideas change simultaneously with changes in social practices (2.22.7). Men learn to participate in a common reality constituted by their language and cultural norms by 'tacit consent' in learning their language (1.3.22; cf. 2.28.10; 3.2.8). If King Apochancana had been educated in England he might have been as knowing a divine or mathematician as an Englishman. 'The difference between him, and a more improved *English*-man, lying barely in this, That the exercise of his Faculties was bounded within the Ways, Modes, and Notions of his own Country' (1.4.12).

Thus, when Locke explains how modes and relations are made he is not thinking that we, individually, make them. He is explaining how the normative framework of intersubjectively available general ideas, in accordance with which a society lives, comes to be. The way in which an individual agent comes to know these ideas is through explanation or by observing the activity already constituted, such as fencing and wrestling (2.22.9). There is, however, one case where men make the idea and constitute reality in accordance with it: invention 'or voluntary putting together of several simple *Ideas* in our own Minds: So he that first invented Printing, or Etching, had an *Idea* of it in his Mind, before it ever existed' (2.22.9). The inventor is like the artificer who fashions his idea in matter (3.6.40).

Ideas of substance are different. In this case, the general ideas of substances in common use are the normative 'patterns' or 'forms' in accordance with which a culture constitutes nature into kinds of things. However, independent of this (and unknowable) 'there are certain precise Essences, according to which Nature makes all particular Things, and by which they are distinguished into *Species*' (3.10.21; although this need be neither an ontic nor a fixed kind claim). The ectype idea under which a natural substance is picked out is that under which it is called that substance (3.6.50). If we discover what, say gold is, we observe our samples, assuming here that our species of gold, constituted in accordance with '*obvious appearances'*, does mark a species *in re* (3.6.25). The ectype idea in common use is the nominal essence, the 'artificial constitution', because it is that in accordance with which we constitute natural phenomena into particulars of various kinds. It is not that because of which the phenomena are initially members of species, the 'real constitution', as is the case with archetype ideas of social phenomena (3.6.2). Locke has a pragmatic theory of the evolution of a culture's organisation of nature into kinds. The classification of nature was made long ago by rude and ignorant people on the basis of practical human interests, not by logicians and philosophers seeking real essences (3.6.25). Because social phenomena, on the other hand, are classified in the first instance in accordance with general ideas in common use, the real essence (not simply the nominal essence) can be discovered by coming to know the meaning or definition of the corresponding name as it is normally used (2.32.12):

> [T]he abstract *Ideas* of mixed Modes, being Men's voluntary Combinations of such a precise Collection of simple *Ideas*; and so the Essence of each Species, being made by Men alone, whereof we have no other sensible Standard, existing any where, but the Name it self, or the definition of that Name.

Further light can be shed on Locke's distinction between ectype and archetype ideas by focusing on his concept of constitution. He says that an idea which constitutes a kind, of either natural or social items, is the essence of that kind (3.6.2). He also argues that in being the essence of a kind it is also, and *eo ipso*, the essence of a member of that kind (3.3.12). This is so because there is nothing essential to an individual as such: essentiality presupposes an idea which determines what is essential to being a particular of a given kind (3.6.4; cf. Mackie, 1976: p. 104). The essence is not an element in a set of phenomena which we pick out under a general term; it is the constitution, arrangement or organisation *of* that phenomena.[8] We constitute bodily movement into human action, practices, institutions and so on, by describing certain arrangements of movement with ideas. These descriptions are deposited in our language and function as norms with which we act and live and so cannot but be real essences (2.31.14; 3.5.14). Our ideas of nature function in the same manner. The difference is that the natural world is arranged in a certain manner independent of our descriptive and normative use of ideas, and so our ideas are nominal, not real, essences.

Locke's second criterion for a real essence is that upon which its species properties depend (2.32.24; 3.5.14, 3.6.3, 3.11.22). In modes and relations it is the complex idea 'on which all the properties of the *Species* depend, and from which alone they all flow' (3.5.14). The key to Locke's meaning here is his frequent use of 'cause' and 'original' as synonyms for 'real essence', 'real constitution' and 'that upon which' (3.3.15, 18). He is not thinking of a Humean cause; a before–after relation. The causal relation of real essence to properties in mixed modes and relations is, for example, that of a triangle to its properties and an action to its moral property of being a sin or duty (2.28.4). 'Cause' in this sense is standard seventeenth-century usage and roughly equivalent to our colloquial use of 'cause' or 'because'. The cause explains the properties in virtue of being their constitution.

Locke uses a triangle, a mixed mode, to explain his theory but he claims that it would hold true for substances if we could know their real essences (4.6.11). We 'find out' conceptual connections which yield statements about certain properties of a triangle from our real essence idea of a triangle (plus axioms and definitions). And, if there is a triangle *in re* it will *have* the properties our statement asserts *because* its constitution *is* three lines meeting at three angles (the configuration or real essence the real essence idea asserts (2.31.3)). If the figure does not have the essential features it will not have the properties: 'Is it true of the *Idea* of a *Triangle*, that its three Angles are equal to two right ones? It is true also of a *Triangle*, where-ever it really exists' (4.4.6). The idea of a triangle is the ground from which statements of its properties are derived. The relation is one of ground to consequence; hypothesis to conclusion. As constitutive of an existing triangle, the three lines meeting at three angles are the 'cause' or that upon which the properties of the triangle depend (3.3.18). The hypothesis or idea of the real essence therefore explains the phenomena (properties) in so far as they are organised in accordance with the hypothesis. The reason that the logical relation is isomorphic with the ontological relation is that the arrangement of the object conforms to the idea from which the logical relations follow (4.4.6). The *explanantes* are the constitutions of the *explananda*. Grene has shown that this explanatory model, where there is taken to be a metaphysical cause existing *in re* and answering to the hypothesis, was used by several members of the early Royal Society (1963). As she writes: 'explanation succeeds in explaining because things are the way the explanation says they are. If an explanation is true, not only does the description of the phenomena follow logically from it, but the phenomena themselves are the effects of the state of affairs which the explanation asserts. Physical explanation becomes causal insofar as it is metaphysical; not through linking phenomena necessarily or invariably to one another in a time sequence but through tying all the phenomena together as consequences of things being really of a certain sort' (p. 153).

To give the 'cause', explanation or 'original' of something in this sense is just to say why it is the case: X because of Y; Y constitutes X, or is the cause of its being. For example, when Locke writes on the title page that the *Two Treatises* is a book concerning the 'original' of civil government he means that it explains what it is for government to be. Consent is said to 'constitute' political society (2.99). This is a political society because it is constituted by consent. What follows in the 'because' clause is the essence or cause of it being what it is. This is a lamp, for example, because it serves to give light.

Francis Bacon (1561–1626) introduced this sense of 'original' in his *Valerius Terminus* as a translation of *naturae notior* which, in turn, is a translation of Aristotle's technical term τῇ φύσει (VI, p. 60; see Kosman, 1964). τῇ φύσει means 'better known absolutely' and in the Latin authors it takes on the meaning of 'prior in', or 'better known to nature'. What is better known in an absolute sense is Aristotle's 'cause' (αἰτία or διότι); the *explanans* as opposed to the *explanandum* or ὅτι (*An.Po*: 71b 30–3, 72a 22–4). When these seventeenth-century practitioners search for the origin or reason of things they are not searching for historical origins but, rather, the explanation because of which a thing is what it is (cf. Barbeyrac, 1729: p. 1). René Descartes plays an important role in linking together these various terms. He connects 'essence' and 'cause' directly with Aristotle's αἰτία as that which both explains and constitutes the facts. He does this by equating αἰτία (the explanation) and τό τι ἐν εἶναι (the constitution). He then writes in his reply to the fourth set of objections, following Aristotle, that the essence or cause is that from which theoretical 'knowledge of any kind may be derived' (1967: II, p. 112). This Aristotelian model of theoretical knowledge served as the paradigm up to and including the seventeenth century. As Aristotle writes, 'we think we understand a thing *simpliciter* (and not in the sophistic manner incidentally) whenever we think we are aware both that the explanation because of which the object is is its explanation, and that it is not possible for this to be otherwise' (*An.Po*: 71b 10–13).

An archetype idea of a mixed mode or relation cannot but meet these criteria of theoretical knowledge. We know that the archetype is the explanation because of which the object is because the object is made or constituted in accordance with it: the object is the kind of object that it is if and only if it conforms to the archetype. Archetype ideas are the 'explanation because of which' precisely because they are archetypal. And so, 'we cannot but be infallibly certain, that all the Knowledge we attain concerning these *Ideas* is real, and reaches Things themselves' (4.4.5; cf. Yolton, 1970: p. 108). Locke has therefore shown that the kind of knowledge which man is capable of having of much of the subject matter of morals and politics – human actions, institutions and social relations – is archetypal and, as such, is the kind requisite for theoretical or scientific treatment (3.5.14).

Knowledge of the natural world is just the opposite, as Locke illustrates (3.6.2). Here man knows the properties (phenomena) but not the real essence upon which they depend. The real essence which both explains and constitutes them is not available to man (2.31.6) and so his task here, as a natural scientist, is to map correlations and regularities and to make hypotheses (4.12.12; cf. Yolton, 1970: pp. 44–104). Knowledge of the natural world is particular, not general, and hypotheses are probabilistic. To know the natural world in the way in which man is capable of knowing the social world would be to know the way in which substances are made or constituted. It would be to know the real, not the nominal essences; that is, to have the archetype ideas of substances. But, as with mixed mode and relation 'objects' which man can know because they are made or constituted in accordance with his archetype ideas, substances can be known only by their maker: God (3.6.3; cf. Yolton, 1970: p. 80):

And had we such a Knowledge of that Constitution of *Man*, from which his Faculties of Moving, Sensation, and Reasoning, and other Powers flow; and on which his so regular shape depends, as 'tis possible Angels have, and 'tis certain his Maker has, we should have a quite other *Idea* of his *Essence*, than what now is contained in our Definition of that *Species*.

2

In his quotation of *Ecclesiastes* 9.5 on the title page of the *Essay* Locke foreshadows his conclusion that man is not capable of theoretical knowledge of substances because he does not make them. He further reinforces this theme by using the term 'archetype' to describe the ideas man has of the things he makes: products, actions, institutions, practices, social relations and so on. Plato and most Christian philosophers normally use 'archetype' to designate the Divine ideas in accordance with which God makes substances. By designating man's knowledge of the world he makes as archetypal, Locke signals that this is the area in which man is, epistemologically, in a position similar to God.

This sort of theory of maker's knowledge is not unique to Locke. Indeed, it is taken by Arendt and Habermas to be a hallmark of modern epistemology (Arendt, 1973: p. 295; Habermas, 1974: p. 61). According to Aristotle, the real essence of substances can be known through *nous* (*An. Po*: 100b 5f). However, as Locke's friend Robert Boyle (1627–91) points out in *The Origin of Forms and Qualities* (1660), Aristotle's examples of real essences are primarily drawn from human artifacts where the archetypes in accordance with which they are made are said to be the essences (p. 145). Professor Kosman has shown that Averroes was a major and important writer to voice scepticism with respect to knowing the real essence of substances and his reason is similar to Locke's. The causes of substances are better known to nature than to man because she makes them, like the relation of artificer to artifact (Kosman, 1964). This sceptical tradition was continued by William of Ockham and Cardinal Bellarmine (against Galileo). Bacon intended his *Novum Organon* to be a new logic which would mitigate this scepticism by furnishing a method for working back to the causes of substances and so enabling man to produce the effects (Bacon, 1874: I, p. 281). Descartes argues that real essences of substances can be known but with Boyle, Locke and Newton the sceptical argument is revived and the natural scientist constructs the simplest hypotheses which describe the correlations amongst phenomena.

Locke's constitution theory of archetype ideas, or theory of maker's knowledge, can be seen as a generalisation of the traditional theory of practical or maker's knowledge. Aquinas writes in his *Summary of Theology* that 'practical reason...causes the things it knows...speculative reason...derives its knowledge from things' (I. II.3.5.1). Speculative (physical) knowledge is ectypal; practical knowledge is archetypal. The paradigm of practical knowledge is the knowledge that an agent, doer or maker, is said to have of that which he brings about. His knowledge is the archetype or form in accordance with which he makes or does something and judges the outcome. This Aristotelian model is used by many seventeenth-century writers: Suarez, Bacon, Hobbes, Pufendorf, Boyle, Newton, Vico as well as Locke (3.6.40; 4.11.7; 1.52–4). It is important to distinguish the two claims which are made for this sort of knowledge. First, the agent has special knowledge of what the outcome *ought* to be: normative knowledge. He does not have prior knowledge of what the outcome will be; prescriptive knowledge. Second, the special knowledge which the agent has can be used to *judge* the outcome.

Locke can be seen to generalise this model by showing, in his earlier example of Adam introducing new words, that it is contingent that the person who has the normative knowledge is the same person who makes or does something. It is not the making or doing which gives a person special knowledge but, rather, knowing the archetype in accordance with which what is done is done. Second, as we have seen, Locke argues that it is not only subjective cases of making and doing that are intentional activities, but the use of language and ideas as well. We intend our use of ideas to be the same as common use and thus we treat common use as a (variable) norm in accordance with which we proximately act and make our manner of life. Instead of a knowing subject making or constituting a product or action, Locke's generalised maker's theory is that of a tacitly knowing community constituting the actions, relations and products, which go to make up their manner of life, roughly in accordance with loose and variable archetypes in civil use.

Locke's generalisation yields the two conclusions that our ideas, and so our language, are descriptive and normative and that, with respect to the world which men make, our ideas enjoy archetypal priority. However, this extension of the traditional model of practical knowledge (both making and doing) seems to defeat the potentially theoretical status it had when predicated of individual agents such as geometers, architects and artificers. In these subjective cases the archetype ideas are clear and precise whereas Locke continually stresses the looseness and variability of archetype ideas in common use. One way to go on would be to ignore common use, make clear ideas with univocal definitions, draw various inferences using moral axioms, and then impose the resulting plan of a commonwealth on to society. This is of course Hobbes' infamous strategy as he outlines it in *Six Lessons to the Professors of the Mathematics* (1656) (1845: VII, pp. 183–4) and in the introduction to *Leviathan*, working from the traditional model of the knowing maker (cf. Child, 1953). However, Locke, in his extension of maker's knowledge to the constitutive role of ideas in common use and in his insistence that one must start with mixed mode and relation ideas as they are embedded in one's social reality, engages in a fundamentally different kind of philosophical approach (cf. Hacking, 1975: p. 6, for a similar contrast). In this respect Locke is in substantial agreement with the great natural law theorist and near-contemporary, Giambattista Vico (1668–1744). In *The New Science* Vico makes the strikingly similar claim about man's knowledge of the natural and social world. One 'cannot but marvel' at the fact 'that the philosophers should have bent all their energies to the study of the world of nature, which, since God made it, He alone knows; and that they should have neglected the study of the world of nations, or civil world, which, since men made it, men could come to know' (Vico, 1970: p. 96; cf. Hintikka, 1975: pp. 86–7; Pompa, 1975: pp. 77–9, 156–7). And from this he goes on to emphasise the necessity of beginning with the constitutive and regulative ideas of a given culture.

This hermeneutical dimension of Locke's thought, as Yolton terms it (1977: p. 10), is reiterated and employed in various places in the *Essay*. It also serves as the foundation for Locke's normative political theory in the *Two Treatises*, as well as being employed to explain man's attachment to the prevailing social structure (for example, 1.58; 2.223). The constitution theory of general ideas in common use is his philosophical explanation, as Dunn observes, of 'the extent to which Locke treats the social structures in which men live as data, as social facts, which cannot be explained as the immediate products of intentional actions and which cannot be effectively manipulated by individuals, which constitute in fact the context of their lives' (1969: p. 236). Dunn shows that the overlooking of this commitment is responsible for the misunderstanding of Locke as a philosopher of atomised and abstracted individuals (pp. 229–41).

Locke says that if man can come to have clear mixed mode and relation ideas, as geometers and tradesmen do, he will be able to find out their properties (3.11.10). The starting point for theoretical knowledge is the common or civil use of words (3.9.3, 8). This is the necessary starting point because it is civil use that is constitutive of the mixed modes and relations *in re* which the theorist wishes to discuss (4.4.8). Only with such a starting point will the knowledge be synthetic; that is, 'real knowledge' (4.4.9). This starting point is also entailed by the fact that an idea or action includes the idea of the 'circumstances' of the action (2.28.4). Thus, theorists '*must* also take care to *apply their Words,* as near as may be, *to such* Ideas *as common use has annexed them to*' (3.11.11). Using words as they are commonly used is a necessary condition of communication and a sufficient condition of civil conversation (3.10.22, 31). It is a necessary, but not sufficient, condition of what Locke calls the 'philosophical use' of words (3.9.3). This requires making clear the meaning of terms in common use: 'Propriety of Speech, is that which gives our Thoughts entrance into other Men's Minds. . .especially in the names of moral Words' (3.11.11).

Common use is 'a very uncertain Rule' (3.11.25). An idea in common use is generally confused, loose, indistinct and variable.[9] Locke does not think that it is possible to reform language, but he does think that it is possible to make common use precise enough for philosophical use (3.11.2). For this, it is necessary to make explicit the 'natural imperfections' of language (3.11.3, 27). This is one condition for knowledge with which people may know how 'to do what they ought' (3.10.13). In it lies the settling of 'Peoples Rights' and 'perhaps Peace too' (3.10.13, 3.9.21). The only way to make ideas more precise is to observe how they are properly used (3.11.11). Since most terms have more than one sense and are equivocal it is necessary to make clear the sense one intends to convey. This can be done explicitly but the normal practice is to make it clear from the 'import of the Discourse' (3.11.27).

Locke's underlabouring with common use to discover terms with enough precision to be used philosophically does not include coming to know all the various senses of a general term. The reason for this is the nature of Locke's 'Logick' or the way of ideas; what Yolton calls the tracing of conceptual connections (4.21.4). What is required is that the aspect or sense of the complex idea, on which the argument depends is isolated in the appropriate context (4.3.19). Other aspects of the idea may be left obscure: 'Our *complex Ideas* being made up of Collections, and so variety of simple ones, *may* accordingly *be very clear and distinct in one part, and very obscure and confused in another*' (2.29.13). The argument holds for the aspect in question (2.29.14; 4.17.3). For example, although the idea of a father includes many simple and complex ideas, such as love, the only part required for determining the rights and duties of a father with respect to his children is the act of begetting (2.25.4, 2.28.19; 1.50). Locke repeatedly stresses that the way of ideas does not

depend on clear ideas but on a clear perception of the agreement or disagreement between the relevant aspects of two or more ideas (4.1.2; 1823:
IV, pp. 116f).

This way of analysing conceptual connections is not only employed in
the *Two Treatises* in constructing his political philosophy, as Yolton has
shown (1970: pp. 160–96). It is used as well in his refutation of Filmer.
Locke argues that Filmer standardly makes the following illogical sort of
inference: (1) Filmer predicates a certain right or duty of one social
relation (father) in virtue of one aspect of the relation meeting the
requisite criterion; (2) he then draws on analogy with another social
relation (ruler) on the basis of another aspect of the original social relation; and (3) he then predicates the original right or duty of the second
social relation. The inference is faulty because the analogy which carries
the predication from (1) to (3) is based on a feature which, although
common to both social relations, is not the feature which exhibits the
criterion requisite for the initial right or duty (1.20). Locke calls this
illogical association of ideas exemplified in Filmer's work a kind of mad-
ness (2.11.13).

Having recovered the necessary mixed mode and relation ideas from
common use the ground is clear for theory (3.11.15). Not only is general
certain knowledge now possible, the resulting knowledge is 'real, and
reaches Things themselves' (4.4.5). Geometrical knowledge is based on
archetypal ideas and so it is theoretical, but it is real only if there are
objects *in re* conforming to the geometer's figures (4.4.6). Political and
moral theory, by starting with archetype ideas in civil use, treats of ideas
already constitutive of human action and association; 'the Truth and
Certainty of *moral* Discourses abstracts from the Lives of Men, and the
Existence of those Vertues in the World, whereof they treat' (4.4.8). Therefore, the general propositions the theorist is capable of formulating on
this basis are not only theoretical and certain, but synthetic: 'where-ever
we perceive the Agreement or Disagreement of any of our *Ideas* there is
certain Knowledge: and where-ever we are sure those *Ideas* agree with
the reality of Things, there is certain real Knowledge' (4.4.18).

In reaching this conclusion Locke has discharged one of the main ideological objectives of the *Essay*: to prove the potential certainty and
scientific status of moral and political knowledge and to illuminate its
superiority over knowledge of the natural world. The *Essay* opens with
the stated purpose of determining the certainty and extent of knowledge
and of demarcating certain knowledge from opinion (1.1.2, 3). Until man
knows where certainty is obtainable he will continue to flounder in 'the
vast Ocean of *Being*' (1.1.7). Before the project begins, however, Locke
states that man's primary concern is moral knowledge and action. 'Our
Business here is not to know all things, but those which concern our

Conduct. If we can find out those Measures, whereby a rational Creature put in that State, which Man is in, in this World, may, and ought to govern his Opinions, and Actions depending thereon, we need not be troubled, that some other things escape our Knowledge' (1.1.6). The happy conclusion which he reaches, as we have seen, is not only that morality is our business but also that it is epistemologically superior to other forms of knowledge. 'Perfect knowledge' is within man's reach in morality: knowledge of archetype ideas and their connections and, *eo ipso*, of actions and practises they constitute (3.11.16):

Upon this ground it is, that I am bold to think, that *Morality is capable of Demonstration*...Since the precise real Essence of the Things moral Words stand for, may be perfectly known; and so the Congruity, or Incongruity of the Things themselves, be certainly discovered, in which consists perfect Knowledge.

Morality is thus the science, in addition to the business of mankind in general (4.12.11; cf. 4.12.8). This real certainty, as he concludes, is precisely what he was searching for in writing the *Essay* (4.4.18). In fact, Locke fears that he may have elevated moral knowledge to such heights that he may have dissuaded his audience from engaging in the natural sciences (4.12.12).

The effort to assert and to establish the primacy of the moral sciences in the face of the growing preoccupation with the natural sciences in the seventeenth century is not restricted to Locke. It is a common theme uniting the natural law writers, especially Pufendorf, Cumberland and Vico. Barbeyrac opens his survey with a celebration of Locke's establishment of the epistemological foundations necessary to sustain this ideological movement, quoting the major passages of the *Essay* which I have examined (pp. 1–5).

iv. Theory and prudence

1

The way in which Locke achieves his objective entails a bifurcation of political knowledge. Locke lifts man, as the subject of morals and politics, into the realm of a theory by a move which Barbeyrac hails as the greatest revolution in natural law philosophy (p. 4). It is not necessary to know the real essence of man *qua* substance for the purposes of moral theory (3.11.16). It is sufficient only to discover what we standardly mean when we use the term 'man'. This functions as a norm in accordance with which we judge men to be men. It thus can be used as a logical criterion defining the subject of moral and political theory (3.11.16):

Natures are not so much enquir'd into, as supposed; *v.g.* when we say that *Man is subject to Law*: We mean nothing by *Man*, but a corporeal rational Creature: What the real Essence or other Qualities of that Creature are in this Case, is no way considered.

The qualities of rationality and corporeality are grouped together and a species is constituted. If a monkey happens to fit this archetypal description, it would be a man in this sense (3.11.16). Locke does not enquire into the cause of rationality or corporeality, which would be the case if this were an ontological claim. The theory applies only to men who make themselves, through education, conformable to this idea. The theory is, as he writes in the *Two Treatises*, '*grounded on* his having *Reason*, which is able to instruct him in that Law he is to govern himself by' (2.63). This is clearly an epistemological break from his earlier work, *Essays on the Law of Nature*, where the definition of man is ontological (p. 198). This normative criterion is, of course, necessary, since the real essence of man *qua* substance is not within man's knowledge. Locke's point is to repudiate the Scholastic assumption that 'rational animal' is the real essence of man, as he stresses in his first reply to Bishop Stillingfleet (1823: IV, pp. 73–9). Locke is also aware that conceptual change of this sort often distinguishes one culture from another (3.8.2).

2

The distinction between archetype and ectype idea provides Locke with a foundation on the basis of which he is able to make a definitive division between political theory and empirical political science. In '*Some Thoughts Concerning Reading and Study for a Gentleman*', he writes that 'Politicks contains two parts, very different the one from the other'. The one, containing the original of societies, and the rise and extent of political power; the other the art of governing men in society' (1823: III, p. 296). Locke's definition of the first and theoretical aspect of politics is a gloss on the subtitle of the *Two Treatises*. He includes in his list of works of political theory Hooker's *Laws of the Ecclesiastical Politie*, Pufendorf's *The Law of Nature and Nations* and the *Two Treatises*. The empirical part of politics 'concerns the art of government; that, I think, is best to be learned by experience and history, especially that of a man's own country'.

The two parts are the theoretical and empirical, or 'prudential', aspects of that part of practical knowledge concerned with politics. In making this distinction Locke is following the pattern set by Bacon (above, p. 12). In the former, the investigation of the conceptual connections amongst mixed modes and relations, and of their relation to natural, customary and civil laws, is undertaken. In the latter, as he writes in his draft letter to the Countess of Peterborough, 'an account of the actions of men as embodied in society' is given (1968: p. 394). For example, political theory treats of the father strictly as a begetter of children (a relation), and of the rights and duties he has with respect to natural law (1.50, 98). Political prudence treats of how particular fathers act, as a matter of fact, in a given historical context, and with the best way to enact laws on the basis of this empirical knowledge such that his moral rights and duties will be proximately actualised and protected (juris-prudence) (2.12).

Locke also makes this distinction in his journal entry of 26 June 1681 (MS. Locke, f.5, fos. 77–83; 1936: pp. 116–18). There are two kinds of knowledge, general and particular, founded on two different principles: true ideas and matter of fact or history. Geometry and moral and political theory are said to be examples of general knowledge:

[H]e that has a true idea of God of him self as his creature of the relation he stands in to god and his fellow creatures and of Justice goodness law happynesse &c is capeable of knowing moral things or having a demonstrative certainty in them.

In addition to asserting the theoretical nature of morality, Locke centres this normative enterprise on the conceptual model of God and man as His creation. As we have seen, Locke does this in the *Essay* (4.3.18) and in the *Two Treatises* (2.6). He goes on to stress that man could come to possess this sort of knowledge if he employed himself about it.

Political prudence, on the other hand, is of matters of fact and history. It is therefore particular. The conceptual tools appropriate to it are those employed in the natural sciences (which are also based on ectypal ideas):

The well management of public or private affairs depending upon the various and unknown humours, interests and capacities of men we have to do with in the world, and not upon any settled ideas of things physical, polity and prudence are not capable of demonstration. But a man is principally helped in them by the history of matter of fact, and a sagacity of finding out an analogy in their operations and effects. . .But whether this course in public or private affairs will succeed well, whether rhubarb will purge or quinquina cure an ague, is only known by experience, and there is but probability grounded upon experience, or analogical reasoning, but no certain knowledge or demonstration.

Prudential knowledge is of how men act and is based on their 'humours, interests and capacities'. This is knowledge of men as substances and so is particular.

Our knowledge of human action is archetypal because we know the normative ideas which are constitutive of it. To ask for the humours and interests which motivate men to act in certain ways is to ask about man's nature and so our knowledge here is ectypal (as in all natural phenomena). Viewing particular acts in this light, *ex post actu*, is like the natural scientist's perspective with respect to nature. Predictive knowledge of human behaviour will always be probable and uncertain. It is precisely at this crucial juncture that Locke notes his radical disagreement with Hobbes. Hobbes grounds his political philosophy on the claim that man's humours and interests are the causes of his actions and that these can be known (1650: 6.6). Locke repudiates this assumption by first noting the determinism involved (1823: x, pp. 255–6). In the *Two Treatises* he goes on to write that Hobbes' *Leviathan* is refuted by the very fact that man's humours and interests are unknowable to us in the *a priori* manner required by Hobbes' philosophy (2.98). Human action is contingent and free (2.21.51). It is not too much to say that the brief reference to Hobbes' *Leviathan* is Locke's decisive reply, since it follows from and is supported by his theory of knowledge in the *Essay*.

Political prudence is a part of politics because it is on the strength of this probabilistic knowledge of what usually correlates with what that legislators make laws. Natural law and its derivative rights stand as a general moral framework roughly in accordance with which lawmakers frame laws appropriate to the given circumstances (2.12, 135, 147, 152, 157f; cf. Habermas, 1974: p. 84; Dunn, 1969: pp. 227–9). However, this empirical component of politics plays no role in the *Two Treatises*. All Locke's statements on political theory conform to the content of the *Two Treatises* and he also classifies it as a work of theory in his letter to Richard King.[10]

3

In *The Law of Nature and Nations* Pufendorf criticises the distinction between political theory and prudence in Grotius' *The Laws of War and Peace* and reformulates it in a way which sets the stage for the doctrine we have seen in Locke. As Barbeyrac writes, of the nature of moral entities and natural laws, 'we meet with scarce any Thing in *Grotius*' (1729: p. 84). Grotius writes that natural law is theoretical yet consequences drawn from it, and applications of it, are necessarily prudential. This is so because one is treating of the contingent, variable and historical actions of men (prol. 31; 2.23.1). This is the way in which theory and prudence are distinguished in Thomist political writing (*ST*: II. 1.94.4). The justification for separating the two in this matter is, as Grotius points out, an analogy to mathematics: 'as Mathematicians consider Figures abstracted from Bodies, so I, in treating the Right, have withdrawn my mind from all particular Facts' (prol. 59). Here mathematical objects are conceived of in the Aristotelian manner as *ens re*, abstracted from matter; not as *ens rationale* or manmade, as we have seen in Locke.

Grotius starts, as does the mathematician, with the facts, and attempts to abstract universals. Whereas the mathematician is able to abstract exact universals, the moral philosopher is not. The human actions and relations

with which he begins are too variable. Thus, Grotius' concepts are in-
determinate and historical except for universal natural law and one real
and exact universal: man as a rational animal (1.1.10.1). Since the concepts of actions and relations are inexact and embedded in the situation
under consideration, moral science is inexact (2.23.1). Barbeyrac repri-
mands Grotius for relying too heavily on historical arguments (p. 84),
but this is a consequence of his explicitly Aristotelian view of the subject
matter.

The 'illustrious Samuel Pufendorf', as Barbeyrac calls him, is primarily
responsible for freeing moral science from its imprecision (p. 81). He
discusses the view held by Grotius in his chapter significantly entitled 'On
the Certainty of moral Science' (1.2). Aristotle's claim that morality is
incapable of certainty and precision (cited by Grotius) is presented as the
major opposing doctrine (1.2.1). Pufendorf's ingenious reply begins with
a denial of Aristotle's assumption that universal propositions need carry
existential import. Aristotelians hold that in a syllogism, 'the *Subject* of
the *Conclusion*, to which the *Predicate* was applied, ought always to be a
thing necessarily existent' (1.2.2). However, the subject of demonstration
in a syllogism is not one single term, but the entire proposition. The only
necessity involved is the logical entailment of conclusion by premisses. It is
contingent that the subject exist. It need be granted only that if the subject exists the predicate will be true of it: 'Where it signifies little, whether
or no the *Subject* of this demonstrable proposition necessarily exist; but
'tis sufficient, if granting its Existence such certain Affections necessarily
agree to it, and if it can be made out, that they do thus agree to it, by
undoubted Principles.' In the light of Locke's later work it is interesting to
note that the example used is, 'man is rational'.

Pufendorf, like Grotius, draws an analogy to mathematics, but now
the mathematician is understood to construct his figures and 'never
trouble himself to enquire, whether a *Triangle* be *necessary* or *contingent*'.
In a similar manner the moral theorist works with moral concepts that are
imposed on, not derived from, human action. For example, it is possible
to determine whether murder is a sin or a duty by comparing it to natural
law, irrespective of the existence of such an act (1.2.6; cf. Locke: 4.4.8).
And so, the rights and duties of men and of various relations can be
theoretically determined for hypothetical cases (1.2.5). In making this
move Pufendorf turns traditional moral and political theory on its head.
Instead of dealing with variable human actions and relations never quite
abstracted from practice, he begins with exact and hypothetical universals
and demonstrates their moral properties. Not only is natural law theoretical, but demonstrations from it are as well.

Pufendorf opens *The Law of Nature and Nations* with an analogy
similar to Locke's. God fashions chaotic matter into substances from which

follow various properties (1.1.2). Man in his turn fashions bodily movement and interaction into moral actions and relations. 'Our Business is, to
declare, how, chiefly for the direction of the *Will*, a certain kind of Attributes have been impos'd on Things, and their Natural Motions, whence
there springs up a peculiar Agreement and Conveniency in the Actions of
Mankind.' These attributes are '*moral Entities*'. Moral entities are 'Modes
superadded to natural Things and Motions by understanding Beings'
(1.1.3; cf. Locke: 3.5.12). Pufendorf has in mind here primarily our moral
concepts of right, property and obligation and the social relations of
which they are predicated (1.1.16–23, 4.4.1; cf. Barbeyrac: 1.1.5 n.2). God
imposes order by creation, man by 'imposition' (1.1.4).

The certainty of moral science is premissed upon Pufendorf's imposition
theory of moral entities and their moral properties. Although it is similar
to Locke's (and Vico's) constitution theory in many respects, it contains
three crucial dissimilarities. First, Locke's constitution theory consists in
human actions, institutions and productions, as well as moral concepts,
such as property, right and obligation, and relations. Pufendorf deals
almost exclusively with the latter and even here his analysis is cryptic and
patchy. The second concerns the role of the theorist in making clear
definitions. As we have seen, Locke begins with common usage and re-
covers one aspect of an idea necessary for the argument at hand. Pufendorf
sets out an elaborate method for coming to have a workable definition
from ordinary language (5.12), but he does not seem to employ this in his
demonstration. Like Hobbes, he makes univocal definitions. Third, Pufendorf sees demonstration as syllogistic. Locke launches a sophisticated attack
on the syllogism and develops his own non-deductive 'way of ideas'
(4.17.4–5; cf. Yolton, 1970: pp. 96–102).

Once Pufendorf has proved to his satisfaction the theoretical aspects of
morals, he proceeds to define its prudential component in a way similar to
Locke. Theory 'is concern'd' about the 'Rectitude of human Actions, in
order to Laws; the other [prudence] about the dextrous Government of
our own, and of other Mens Actions, for the Security and the Benefit of
ourselves, and more especially of the Publick' (1.2.4). The art of government is properly a matter of 'Prudence' and is equivalent to Aristotle's
phronesis (1.2.4). Thus there is the same latitude and variability as in
Grotius' realm of prudence, but now it is in the application of universal
deductions *to* practice; not in the attempt to draw *conclusions within*
practice (1.2.4, 9). Pufendorf stresses that his theory is compatible with
man's freedom. Our actions are free and their moral effects contingent,
'but when we have once determin'd which way to act, the Connection
between our Actions and the depending Effects is necessary and natural,
and consequently capable of Demonstration' (1.2.5).

4

Locke's maker's theory of knowledge provides the philosophical under-pinnings for normative political theory, thereby establishing its epistemo-logical superiority over the natural sciences. The price Locke pays for this hard-won victory is to place the knowledge of empirical correlations and analogies amongst contextual and historical social actions and states of affairs in an epistemologically inferior, yet practically equal, position. The normal mode of political discourse for Locke's English audience is historical: to argue from the prescriptive force of the 'ancient constitu-tion'.[11] In securing the theoretical dimension of politics in the way he does, Locke disassociates himself from the prevailing conventions of political discourse and situates political philosophy on a more rationalistic, natural law plane (Skinner, 1974: pp. 286–7). Therefore, once he has legitimated the importance of moral concerns with respect to the study of nature, by showing their epistemological primacy, he then goes on to show the epistemological preeminence of his sort of moral and political theory in comparison to the prevailing historical conventions.

The justification for this second ideological manoeuvre is already pro-vided by his distinction between theory and prudence. He stresses that knowledge of history, tradition and consensual norms is *important*: 'I would not be thought here to lessen the Credit and use of *History*' (4.16.11). As we have seen, it is the sort of knowledge essential to man in his everyday moral decisions and to legislators because natural law, and the theory developed with it, is not specific enough to function as a deter-mining guide in practice. However, historical knowledge of matters of fact and their analogies is ectypal and so cannot provide certain general truths. It is probablistic, not theoretical: 'the Probabilities...are only such as concern matter of fact, and such Things as are capable of Observation and Testimony' (4.16.12). The kind of truth available in this realm is thus based on persuasion, not certainty (4.5.11). The constant danger in this form of argument is that men do not assent to the proposition with the greatest probability but, rather, 'stick to a Party, that Education or Interest has engaged them in' (4.20.18).

The method which Locke proposes for moral theory is twofold: 'to display the conceptual connexions of concepts, and...to determine the measure of right and wrong' (Yolton, 1970: pp. 163–4). The first exercise consists in two types of case. One is to refer an action to a rule or principle, which is taken as given, in order to evaluate it morally (2.28.16). The Laws of God, of political society and of fashion are the three sorts of rule 'to which men variously compare their Actions: And 'tis by their Con-formity to one of these Laws, that they take their measures, when they would judge of their moral Rectitude, and denominate their Actions good or bad' (2.28.13). In exhibiting these connections men clarify the moral relations of sin and duty, legality and illegality, and virtue and vice respectively (2.28.4–12). Locke observes that quite often our action concepts are evaluative as well as descriptive and so this exercise serves to clarify these two elements (2.28.16).

Another type of case is the comparison of two things with reference to their origin or beginning, or an act which gives rise to natural and instituted relations, such as father and son, master and servant (2.28.2–3; see above, p. 10). The importance of these natural and instituted relations consists in their conceptual connections with obligations and rights. That is, to be a relation of a certain sort is to possess certain rights and duties: 'one comes by a Moral Right, Power, or Obligation to do something' (2.28.3). Our natural and instituted relations, we may say, unpack in terms of rights and obligations which, in turn, are founded on the 'origin' or 'act' which gives rise to the relation. A father, for example, has certain duties and rights because he is the begetter (1.51). Property, being 'a right to any thing' (4.3.18) is in this category, and, as a right, stands in need of clarification (4.5.4).

This latter type of case is closely connected with the second and more ambitious part of Locke's moral theory; determining the measures of right and wrong. The 'measures of right and wrong', or 'Duty and Rules of Action' (4.3.18) are God's laws or natural laws (2.28.8). The 'foundation' of these rules, from which they are capable of being demonstrated, is the relation of God to man as Maker to His workmanship (4.3.18). A natural law, as we have seen, is an 'ought' proposition asserting an obligation, and, as such, can be justified by reasons (above, pp. 3–4). According to Locke, the ground of these laws is the relation of Maker to workmanship (4.3.18). That is, the obligations (and rights) which man has, *qua* God's workmanship, are capable of being derived from the workmanship model, just as, say, a servant's obligation arises from his relationship to his master. The explanation because of which a relation (natural or instituted) is a relation is some beginning or act (2.28.19). From this real essence the moral properties follow as the properties of a triangle follow from its real essence (3.5.14).

This concludes the theme of maker's knowledge in the *Essay*. We have come full circle from our initial puzzle in the *Two Treatises*. There we were led from Locke's property right to the means necessary for preservation back to a natural law which, in turn, appeared to follow from the workmanship model. Now we have seen a major theme in the *Essay* which supports and underpins this implicatory series. This suggests that the relations of Maker and workmanship are the archetype ideas in common use from which Locke makes out man's natural obligations and rights.

CHAPTER TWO

The law of nature

i. God as Maker

1

Two conditions must be met if Locke is to employ the workmanship model in the way he suggests in the *Essay*. First, the archetype idea of our maker should be a normal description in common use; thus constitutive of the maker relation in seventeenth-century society. Second, there must be a God such that 'maker' is truly predicated of Him. This ensures that, although the terms we use to express the obligations (and rights) which follow from the relation, and the terms expressing the relation itself, might be culturally bound, they will be grounded in the nature of things and thus *natural* laws in this sense (cf. Dunn 1969: pp. 96–7).

Locke states in the *Two Treatises* that the locution 'our Maker' is the normal description under which God is picked out: 'one of the ordinary Appellations of God in Scripture is, *God our Maker*, and *the Lord our Maker*' (1.53). Although God is also described as 'our Father', this is not a problem since any object or person can bear several descriptions (2.25.7). What he wishes to show is that the relation idea of a maker is standardly used and that it can carry his argument in the way 'father' cannot (1.53). Locke's friend, Sir Isaac Newton (1642–1727), reserves the General Scholium of Book Three of the *Mathematical Principles of Natural Philosophy* to drive home the point that what normally 'we say' of the great Pantokrator is that 'God is a relative term' signifying 'the Maker and Lord of all things' (II, p. 544).

Locke's characterisation of God as a maker stands between two extreme views. The first is that of pantheism, reasserted in the late sixteenth century by Giordano Bruno (1548–1600) and promulgated by Locke's acquaintance John Toland (1670–1722). On this model 'God [is]...the soul of the universe' and the world His attributes (Toland, 1751: p. 17). There is an intimate relation between God and the world, including man, but, as Newton stresses in the *Opticks*, it renders God dependent on the world (p. 181). At the other extreme is the view held by Gottfried Leibniz (1646–1716), later embraced by Deist and Enlightenment thinkers, that God created the world in a manner similar to the making of a machine (1717: *passim*). In this case God is not dependent on the world but neither is there a continuing and intimate dependency of man on God. There is only the contingent fact that God made the world.

On Locke's model God is not dependent on the world, yet man is continuously dependent on God. God makes the world (in distinction to his creation of the material out of which He makes it) in a manner analogous to the way in which man makes intentional actions. Man is thus in a relation of continuous and intimate dependency on God in the way intentional actions are existentially tied to the agent who makes or performs them (4.10.19). Man is thus dependent on his maker for being brought into being and for his continuing existence. Locke's political philosophy hinges on this one-way dependency relation between God and man, and from which man's natural obligations follow (MS. Locke, c.28, fo. 141):[1]

The original and foundation of all Law is dependency. A dependent intelligent being is under the power and direction and dominion of him on whom he depends and must be for the ends appointed him by that superior being. If man were independent he could have no law but his own will no end but himself.

The concept of making which underlies and explains man's dependency on God is analysed by Locke in his discussion of causes. A cause 'is that which makes any other thing, either simple *Idea*, Substance, or Mode, begin to be' (2.26.2). Four activities are causal in this sense: creation, generation, alteration and making. When 'the Cause is extrinsical, and the Effect produced by a sensible Separation, or *juxta* Position of discernible Parts, we call it *Making*.' Thus, when Locke speaks of God as a maker he is focusing on His act of bringing man into being out of preexisting matter, not primarily on His continuous act of preserving. These two aspects are inseparable for God, who is outside time and always in the present tense; just as they are inseparable in intentional actions. Also in Locke's concept of making there is an analytical relationship between being a maker and knowing the description under which what is made is made. A maker constructs in accordance with his idea such that the idea is constitutive of the artifact (3.6.40). The object, whether artifact or action, is the idea 'in Matter' (4.4.6–7). This concept of a maker is commonly applied to God in natural law writing.[2]

2

The second condition to be fulfilled is that there is a God who makes man. Throughout his early *Essays on the law of Nature* and in some later writings Locke employs the argument from design to prove the existence of God (1823: III, pp. 244–5). Although he presents several arguments in his chapter in the *Essay* on our knowledge of the existence of God, his central proof is a cosmological argument. It is 'so fundamental a Truth, and of that Consequence, that all Religion and genuine Morality depend thereon' (4.10.7). He begins with a proof of the existence of man. Locke turns the table on the sceptics by stating that 'to doubt of it, is manifestly impossible' (4.10.2). Let the sceptic 'enjoy his beloved Happiness of being nothing, until Hunger, or some other Pain convince him of the contrary'. This anti-Cartesian move places the onus of proof on the sceptic, thus breaking with a long tradition which permitted him to set the conditions of the argument.

From here it is a simple matter of employing the law of sufficient reason twice: once ontologically, to a cause of every beginning thing, and once epistemologically, to the reason of beginning things (4.10.3–6; cf. 1931: p. 281). He denies of course that man can come to have a clear idea of the real essence of God (4.10.7). The description of God as a maker is not His real essence; it is simply a relation that God bears. He goes on to reject Aristotle's view that the world is uncreated, for 'it denies one and the first great piece of his Workmanship, the Creation' (4.10.18).

Locke says that God's act of creation is analogous to man creating bodily movement, in addition to making that movement into a particular action, by his will (4.10.19). This unexplained ability of the will to cause motion, involved in any act of making, is common to both God and man. Newton presents a similar argument in his early *Unpublished Scientific Papers*: 'God...created the World solely by an act of the will, just as we move our bodies by an act of the will' (1962: p. 107). Newton agrees with Locke in finding this element of making the key to 'moral philosophy': 'so far as we can know by natural philosophy the first cause, what power He has over us, and what benefits we receive from Him, so far our duty towards Him, as well as that towards one another, will appear to us by the light of nature' (1704: p. 182).

Therefore, the elements which comprise the concept of making are present in God's creation of man: the necessary creative act by which the will moves the body (in the case of man) and the essential act of arranging material into some pattern in accordance with reason. This composite act is the criterion for applying the term 'maker' and it gives rise to obligations and rights involved in this relation (2.28.3). It is worth noting at this point a feature of Locke's analysis which becomes important later (see Chapter Five). Due to the analogy between God and man as makers, anything true of one will be, *ceteris paribus*, true of the other. Since it is the explanation of God's dominion over man and of why man is God's 'property', it also explains man's dominion over and property in the products of his making: 'God makes him *in his own Image after his own Likeness*, makes him an intellectual Creature, and so capable of *Dominion*'

(1.30). That man's understanding is the reason why he has dominion over other creatures is one of the reasons Locke gives for writing the *Essay* (1.1.1).

We now know what our maker is, and that he is. In the manuscript that he intended to be the conclusion of the *Essay*, 'of Ethick in General', Locke points to the next step. 'This is God...whose existence we have already proved. The next thing then to show is, that there are certain rules, certain dictates, which it is his will all men should conform their actions to' (MS. Locke, c.28, fo. 148; 1830: II, p. 133; cf. von Leyden, 1970: p. 69; Dunn, 1969: p. 187).

ii. The argument from design

1|

By his proof of the existence of God in the *Essay* Locke is satisfied that he has shown God to be a '*cognitative Being*' (4.6.11). One way in which this cognitive element is employed is God's making of man in accordance with His knowledge (3.6.3). He can be said to have what I have called maker's knowledge. There is another sense of knowing with relation to making in addition to knowing what one makes. This is the sense of knowing why it is made; its reason or purpose. When God makes man and the world he knows both these elements. Hooker, Locke's recommended authority on natural law and constant reference in the *Two Treatises* (Laslett, 1970: pp. 56–7), expresses succinctly these two senses of making in accordance with reason: 'Neither have they [philosophers] otherwise spoken of that cause [God] than as an agent, which knowing what and why it worketh, observeth in working a most exact order or law' (1.1.2). That is, the 'maker of the world [is] an *intellectual worker*'.

The argument from design is deployed by Locke in his *Essays on the Law of Nature* to show that God made man and the world for certain purposes. That the universe is purposive is a regulative belief in all Locke's later writings (Yolton, 1970: p. 17; Dunn, 1969: p. 95). Since this early essay is his only sustained philosophical investigation of that belief, it is necessary to turn to it in order to understand its meaning. The Aristotelian concept of 'things known' functions as the starting point for his discussion: 'at all times every argumentation proceeds from what is known and taken for granted' (p. 149). What is known is that which is given in the perception of 'the objects of sense-experience'. What is given, in addition to their existence, is the order and regularity expressed in the objects of sense experience: 'this visible world is constructed with wonderful art and regularity, and of this world we, the human race, are also a part' (p. 151).

The growth of plants, motion of the tides and the revolution of the heavens about the earth are exemplary of this regularity (p. 109). Locke employs another 'no one can consistently doubt' argument, writing that it is not possible to speak of chance in these cases (p. 153).

An inference is then made from the observed order to the existence of a maker of that order. The only alternative that Locke considers is that the structured arrangement of man may have been made by man himself. This is rejected on the grounds that man can conceive of more perfections than he has and so would have included them if he had been the maker (p. 153). This unusual argument becomes clear in his refutation of Filmer (see below, p. 59). It is therefore safe to infer that the knowing maker, of the *Essay* and the *Two Treatises* (1.52–3), is responsible: 'He has Himself created the soul and constructed the body with wonderful art, and has thoroughly explored the faculties and powers of each, as well as their hidden constitution and nature' (p. 155).

It is said to follow from this that God 'has not created this world for nothing and without purpose. For it is contrary to such great wisdom to work with no fixed aim' (p. 157). In a way analogous to laws governing inanimate nature, God must be the author of 'certain definite principles of action' for man, which, when man chooses to act in accordance with them, realise God's purposes in making man (p. 111). Man cannot be made to be idle because he is made with an 'agile, capable mind', is capable of knowing, and has a 'body besides which is quick and easy to be moved hither and thither by virtue of the soul's authority' (p. 157). All this 'equipment for action' could not be furnished so man should be 'splendidly idle and sluggish'. Thus, 'God intends man to do something'.

2

This argument from design is intended to show that there is a lawmaker to whom we are 'rightly subject', and that He has made laws 'with respect to things to be done by us' (p. 151). These are two of the five criteria for a natural law. Natural laws also must be normative propositions, not commands, they must be promulgated and they must be backed up with rewards or punishments (pp. 111, 113, 157, 173, 197).[3] God's purposes for man are the Divine Laws, including the moral propositions in the Scriptures, promulgated by 'the voice of Revelation', and natural Laws, 'promulgated. . .by the light of Nature [reason]' (2.28.8; cf. 1.86, 2.59, 60; cf. Hooker 1.1.8). The reason required to come to know natural law is available to any diligent person (p. 187).

Locke's design argument satisfies the condition that there is a lawmaker, since it is said to establish that there is a God who acts for reasons and the reasons are his laws for man. Thus, natural law presupposes the existence of God and an immortal soul to which the rewards and punishments apply (p. 173). However, even if we could discover the principles which should regulate our moral lives, their existence would not entail that we are necessarily subject to them. Logical necessity does not entail moral obligation. It is often suggested that Locke confused, or failed to see, or did not discuss the distinction between the justification of a normative proposition and the justification of the obligation to act in accordance with it. Locke not only recognised this distinction, he devoted a part of the *Essays on the Law of Nature* and the First Treatise to its clarification. An answer to the further question of obligation is obviously presupposed in his use of the workmanship model in the *Two Treatises* (2.6) and in the *Essay* (1.4.13). In 'of Ethick in General' Locke prides himself on having resolved this puzzle (MS. Locke, c.28, fo. 152; 1830: II, pp. 122–33).

As we have seen, obligations and rights arise from the acts which constitute various relations. Locke shows that God as maker has a special right in man as his workmanship, and that this correlates with a positive duty or obligation on the part of man to God. Man's obligation is derived from 'the authority and dominion which someone has over another, . . .by natural right and the right of creation, as when all things are justly subject to that by which they have first been made and are also constantly preserved' (p. 185). Locke adds a second criterion for man's obligation: 'this obligation seems to derive partly from the divine wisdom of the lawmaker, and partly from the right which the Creator has over His creation' (p. 183). Goodness is suggested as well in the *Essay* (2.28.8). Nonetheless, the maker's right and correlative duty follow from the relation of existential dependency of man on his maker: 'we are bound to show ourselves obedient to the authority of His will because both our being and our work depend on His will, since we have received these from Him, and so we are bound to observe the limits He prescribes' (p. 183). On the other hand, it is said to be 'reasonable' that we should want to please Him who is most wise. When he comes to state from 'whence this bond of law takes its origin', wisdom and goodness disappear and he writes that, 'no one can oblige or bind us to do anything, unless he has right and power over us; and indeed, when he commands what he wishes should be done and what should not be done, he only makes use of his right' (pp. 181–3).

The sense in which man is subject to his maker and the sense in which God can exercise his right are taken to be undeniable by Locke. He uses an analogy to illustrate his point. God has 'right and authority' over man, 'for who will deny that clay is subject to the potter's will, and that a piece of pottery can be shattered by the same hand by which it has been formed?' (pp. 155–7). The clay is of course *de facto* subject to the potter's will whereas man is *de iure* subject to God's will. Locke is not punning on the equivocity of 'subject to'. He is employing the analogy between the way in which inanimate objects and man are subject to God's will. Inanimate objects are subject to God's will in a mechanical manner and thus can be seen to move in accordance with natural laws. Similarly, man fashions inanimate objects in accordance with his will and so they are subject to the artificer. Man is subject to God's will in a moral fashion. He uses his reason to discover natural law and chooses to act in accordance with it, thus participating in the divine order in the way appropriate to a rational creature.

Locke's solution to the problem of obligation is a compromise between the voluntarist (Ockhamist) and rationalist theories. According to the former view, natural laws are imperatives, accepted on faith, and are binding solely because they are an expression of God's will. The rationalist holds that natural laws are normative propositions, discoverable by reason, and are binding solely because they are rational. In this case, Grotius concludes in *The Laws of War and Peace*, natural laws are binding independent of the existence of God (prol. 12). Locke agrees with the voluntarist that God's will is the source of obligation, but rejects the inference that the test of the validity of natural law cannot be reason. He accepts the rationalist tenet that natural laws are discovered by reason, are wise and good by independent criteria, but he denies the inference that this is the source of their binding force (cf. Dunn, 1969: pp. 187–99; Yolton, 1970: pp. 167–9; Mabbott, 1973: pp. 105–28). Francisco Suarez (1535–1600), the Jesuit theologian and author of *The Laws and God the Lawgiver* (1612), takes a similar stance (2.6.5). His account of the role of God's will, as well as many other aspects of his theory, prefigures Locke's: 'just as our will controls our bodily members and imposes on them, by its command, the necessity of action, even so the Divine Will governs all created things and imposes necessity upon them, according to the varying capacity of each of these things' (2.2.10).

The act of making gives rise to the right in the product and this, in turn, confers a right over the product to use it in certain ways. Since God constructs man with reason, His right correlates with man's duty to act in accordance with the purposes for which he is made. The point of Locke's example is just to show that we in fact normally recognise this sort of right in everyday cases of making. In *A Treatise on the Laws of Nature* Cumberland uses a similar maker's rights analogy (1727: p. 320):

Before I had *universally* and *distinctly* consider'd the Original of *all* Dominion and Right whatsoever, I *us'd*, indeed, as most others do, to deduce the Divine Dominion intirely from his being the Creator: For I thought it *Self-evident*, That every one was Lord of his own Powers, which are little different from the *Essence* of any Thing, and that, therefore, any *Effect* must be *Subject* to him, from whose *Powers* it receiv'd its whole Essence, as is the case in *Creation*, by which the whole Substance of the thing is produc'd into Being.

God's maker's right and man's correlative duty is also explored by Pufen-dorf for similar purposes (1.1.4; 2.3.19). Cumberland's appeal to what 'most others do' and to the self-evidence of maker's right, help to buttress Locke's assumption that such a right would not be denied. Perhaps this helps to explain Locke's statement in the *Essay* that a proposition follow-ing immediately from the workmanship model would have to be self-evident (4.3.18). The reference cannot be to natural laws, since they are derived from something prior. What is clearly taken to be self-evident and undeniable is that a maker has a right in and over his workmanship.

In developing a theory of obligation to natural law Locke clarifies and presents his first natural right. To say that a maker has a right in his product is equivalent to saying that the product is his property: 'they are his [God's] Property whose Workmanship they are' (2.6). In the same manner that a person is proprietor of his products he is proprietor of his actions (2.44). In the *Essay* Locke says that a person 'owns' his actions (2.27.17). Richard Baxter (1615–91), the Presbyterian divine, uses this sort of language in a Holy Commonwealth, or *Political Aphorisms upon the True Principles of Government* (1659): 'God's kingdom is...constituted primarily by...His *right*, resulting immediately from His being our creator, and so our *owner*; our obligation is founded in our being His creatures, and so His *own*' (3.28). Although Locke repeats this theory of obligation in the First Treatise (1.52–4), he could count on his audience seeing this convention embodied in his use of the workmanship model in the Second Treatise (2.6). As Laslett writes, it 'is an existential proposition which men have not thought it worth while to question seriously until our own day' (p. 92).

3

Locke's specification of obligation in the *Essays on the Law of Nature* is compatible with his later argument in the *Essay* that the real essence of man is unknown and unknowable. Obligation is 'the bond of law where-by one is bound to render what is due' (p. 181). The obligation to natural law 'lies upon one to perform by reason of one's nature'. By 'one's nature', Locke means man's nature as an existentially dependent creature (p. 183). Whatever man's real essence is *qua* man, an essential feature of him as the bearer of the workmanship relation is his dependency (1.52). This was taken to be a feature of all natural things in God's universe. 'It does not seem', states Suarez, 'that it can be conceived, or exist, without a trans-cendental relation to that on which it depends' (2.5.15). The young Newton stresses this point and its intimate connection with morality. 'However we cast about we find no other reason for atheism than this notion of bodies having, as it were, a complete, absolute and independent reality in themselves. . .Philosophers are brought to a stand and lose their drift. . .when they try to form an independent idea of a thing dependent on God' (p. 144). It is interesting to note that Locke and Newton independently arrived at a similar interpretation of the relation between God and man. Pierre Coste mentions in his third French edition of the *Essay* that he wrote to Newton to seek illumination of Locke's analogy between God's acts of Creation and man's act of willing. Newton replied and mentioned that he and Locke met at the home of the Earl of Pembroke and discussed the matter (1735: p. 521n).

Locke goes on to distinguish two ways in which an obligation binds a person. Obligation binds 'effectively' in virtue of its imposition by a rightful lawmaker, and this is the 'formal cause' of obligation (p. 183). Secondly, a 'thing binds "terminatively", or by delimitation, which prescribes the manner and measure of an obligation and our duty and is nothing other than the declaration of that will [of the lawmaker], and this declaration by another name we call law' (p. 185). We are bound effectively by God, but His declaration of His will in natural laws delimits the obligation. Locke distinguishes four types of case. Some duties are binding absolutely and forever, such as not to commit murder or theft. Others bind absolutely and forever but relate sentiments enjoined by natural law: 'reverence and fear of the Deity, tender affection for parents [and] love of neighbours' (p. 195). The duties of charity arise out of the particular circumstances and thus are absolutely binding only when the requisite circumstances are present. Fourth, acts which express contingent preferences and which involve no direct obligations bind only with respect to the circumstances of the act. A man, for example, may speak of his neighbour if he pleases, but he has a duty not to lie and cheat in so doing (p. 195).

The fifth and final criterion for a law is that it has rewards and punishments annexed to it. This feature relates to the compulsion of law. Rewards and punishment do not function as the ground of obligation; if they did, we would be obligated to tyrants (p. 185). Rather, they act as psychological inducements to the man who does not control his desires with his reason (2.21.65). Logically, a law must be backed by either rewards or punishment different from the rewards or punishments which follow naturally in consequences of the prescribed act or the concept of law becomes meaningless (2.28.6).

iii. The natural laws

1

One manner of considering law is to distinguish between two ways of viewing the role law plays in relation to human action. We might acknowledge that the law normally forbids certain acts and prescribes others, but focus our attention on the area bounded by this, in which man is free to exercise his contingent preferences. If we take this area as primary, then our concept of law will be essentially negative; prescribing and proscribing are both classed as confining. Man is seen to act positively and in accordance with his will in that sphere where law does not function as a guide. This is the view taken by Grotius (1.3.1) and by Pufendorf (1.6.4). On the other hand, we might focus our attention on that area in which the law guides our action, where it enjoins certain kinds of action. If we see it here as directing us to our true interests and to what is good for us, then our attitude to law will be positive. Further, if we take law to be positive and see the exercise of contingent preferences as choosing between various specific courses of action which conduce to performing the generic duties enjoined by law, then we have Locke's view.

Locke defines law as 'that which prescribes to everything the form and manner and measure of working' (p. 117). This positive definition of law, which echoes Hooker's (1.1.2), is repeated in the *Two Treatises*: '*Law*, in its true Notion, is not so much the Limitation as *the direction of a free and intelligent Agent* to his proper Interest, and prescribes no farther than is for the general Good' (2.57). He goes on to state that the negative or restraining aspect of law should not even be thought of as confinement, since here it protects us only from 'Bogs and Precipices'. The '*end of Law* is not to abolish or restrain, but *to preserve and enlarge Freedom*'. Since man is placed in the world by God for certain purposes, it is not surprising that what is significant about law for Locke is its function to guide man in achieving them.

Locke's first move is to explore the 'form and manner' of acting which is appropriate to the performance of any particular duty enjoined by natural law. A 'manner of acting is prescribed to him that is suitable to his nature' (p. 117; cf. 2.4, 22). Hooker calls this the 'first law' (1.1.8). The method employed to discover it, as well as to discover the natural laws which specify its various ends, is teleological: 'what it is that is to be done by us can be partly gathered from the end in view for all things. For since these derive their origin from a gracious divine purpose and are the work of a most perfect and wise maker, they appear to be intended by Him for no other end than His own glory, and to this all things must be related' (p. 157). The other part of the inference is equally teleological. It is possible to 'infer the principle and a definite role of our duty from man's own constitution and the faculties with which he is equipped' (p. 157). Man's reason and equipment for action are to be used for acting in accordance with reason (rational principles) (p. 111). Thus, 'the proper function of man is acting in accordance with reason' (p. 113). 'Acting in accordance with reason' consists in rationally discovering objective moral norms and then using them as guides in acting. He quotes with approval Aristotle's conclusion that 'the special function of man is the active exercise of the mind's faculties in accordance with rational principle' (p. 113).

Thus, Locke's positive concept of law enables him to develop a positive concept of liberty. In the deliberative process man discovers the appropriate rules of action (natural laws or their implicates) and he works out a conformable course of action. In the explication of practical reasoning in the *Essay*, he explains that rational principles act as a guide in deliberation and, hence, as the direction in the consequent deliberate action (2.21.50). Contrary to a negative view of law, this is 'Not an Abridgment, 'tis the end and use of our *Liberty*' (2.21.48). Since God made man to engage in this form of activity it is his duty (2.21.52). It is a duty theory of positive liberty. Locke's account clarifies and specifies the meaning he wishes to attach to his description of men as both God's workmanship and 'rational Beings' (4.3.18).

To give this form of activity determination it is necessary to find the natural laws which guide and direct it. The solution is to uncover God's intentions in making man by seeing what purposes man's natural attributes embody; what ends man and other natural phenomena can be seen to be designed to serve. What these are will be natural laws. This teleological form of analysis is the answer to Locke's statement that natural laws are normative and, as such, have reasons which justify them (1.3.4). The reason for each law is that it is what a particular set of man's attributes are for. In discovering this we find out why God constructed man as He did.

2

The first and fundamental law of nature is that mankind ought to be preserved.[4] One derivation is directly from the workmanship model. Since God designed all men for some purposes, to do 'his business', the necessary conditions of men doing anything at all is that they are 'made to last' (2.6). To do His business men must go on living and so *'by the Fundamental Law of Nature, Man being to be preserved'* (2.16), it follows that 'Every one...is *bound to preserve himself*, and...when his own Preservation comes not in competition, ought he...to *preserve the rest of Mankind*' (2.6). That which *is* an end for man, 'being to be preserved', is turned into a normative proposition that he *ought* to be preserved. This is translated into an individual duty to preserve oneself, and to preserve others when one's own preservation is not in question. In extreme situations where some lives must be unavoidably sacrificed, 'the safety of the Innocent is to be preferred' (2.16). This is the distributive principle of preservation underlying the general formulation of the basic law of nature enjoining '*the preservation of Mankind*' (2.135). The proof which Locke presents at 2.6 is virtually an etymological argument. God has *authority* to decide what man is for because He is the *author* of his being. Man has a duty to preserve man's being, which belongs to God as His workmanship, and is therefore His servant. 'Servant' comes from *servare*, meaning to preserve.

Another way in which Locke argues for the primary natural law is to probe the purposive relationship of man to his natural environment. God 'furnished the World with things fit for Food and Rayment and other Necessaries of Life, Subservient to his design, that Man should live and abide for some time upon the Face of the Earth' (1.86). What clinches this interpretation of God's intentions is the implausibility of the opposite interpretation. God's purpose could not be 'that so curious and wonderful a piece of Workmanship by its own Negligence, or want of Necessaries, should perish again, presently after a few moments continuance'. Again, the finalistic nature of the facts proves the truth of the norm: 'Reason, *which was the Voice of God in him*, could not but teach him and assure him, that pursuing that natural Inclination he had to preserve his Being, he followed the Will of his Maker'.

Locke's reference in this section to man's natural 'inclination' or 'strong Desire' of 'Preserving his Life and Being' can lead to a misunderstanding. Macpherson suggests that Locke 'deduced' God's intention, and his moral principle, from man's desire (1975: p. 229). Macpherson might mean, by his use of the term 'deduction' to describe the relation between desire and right, that to seek one's preservation is right because man has the natural desire to preserve himself. This seems to be Macpherson's meaning since he further suggests that his interpretation entails that Locke is, in this respect, like Hobbes.

Clearly Locke wishes to show that there is a relationship between right and desire, but it is not this one. The criterion to which Locke appeals to justify natural laws is the way in which God made man, including a natural desire for preservation. But, since this is God's desire, and not man's, it is a rational desire and not just any of man's desires which, of course, could be irrational. Locke's point is twofold. First, man can have subjective desires and these will be rational, and therefore right, insofar as they are coincident with God's objective desires for man. God always has His desire under the control of his reason (2.21.49). Thus, to act in accordance with desires which are rational by this test is to act in accordance with God's reason, or natural law. As Locke says, reason 'teaches' man that in being motivated by such rational desires, 'he followed the Will of his Maker'. Not any desire which motivates man to seek preservation will meet this criterion, in contrast to Hobbes' view. The only rational desires are those which motivate man to seek preservation in a way conducive to the fulfilment of God's desire to preserve mankind. This is, as we have seen, precisely the preservation of mankind which natural law teaches.

The second point is a presupposition of the first. The relation between right and desire is, therefore, that what is right, 'natural law', is coincident with rational desire. This is to presuppose, against the Ockhamists, that rules of right are not completely divorced from what is desirable and convenient, without embracing the other, Hobbesian, extreme that whatever is desirable for me is therefore right. What is right is also convenient, but it is not right (nor obligatory) because it is convenient (cf. Yolton, 1970: pp. 145–7). Locke makes this point in the *Reasonableness of Christianity* (1823: VII, p. 142):

The law of nature is the law of convenience too: it is no wonder, that those men of parts, and studious of virtues. . .should, by meditation, light on the right, even from the observable convenience and beauty of it; without making out its obligation from the true principles of the law of nature, and foundations of morality.

The belief that we incline to natural law by our rational nature is an essential convention of rationalist theory of natural law. It stems from Aquinas' original presentation and analysis of self-preservation as the first law of nature (*ST*: I. II.94.2; cf. MacIntyre, 1974: pp. 117–18).

Natural laws are therefore known from the final causes or ends of things, not from their essences. Secondly, an end given by natural law, such as preservation, is not man's subjective goal. It is God's goal for all men. Thus, when man plots a course for his own preservation, he is under a natural obligation to ensure that this conduces to the preservation of all. Indeed, he is under an obligation to work for the preservation of others whenever this does not entail his own destruction. Natural law 'harmonises' human activity in such a way that the whole human community is taken into account and provided for (pp. 207–11). If, on the other hand, preservation were nothing more than the subjective goal consequent upon an individual's desire for self-preservation, no Lockeian moral theory would be possible. It would be impossible to generate the positive duty of preserving others and to discover a natural criterion of justice which could be used to define and delimit legitimate acts of self-preservation. In his essay *On Study*, written in the spring of 1677, Locke states that followers of Hobbes embrace this sort of egoistic moral theory and hence are unable to explain natural positive duties toward others: 'An Hobbist, with his principle of self-preservation, whereof himself is to be judge, will not easily admit a great many plain duties of morality' (MS. Locke, f.2, p. 128; 1830: I, p. 191). The point of grounding morality in man's relationship to God, and thus making him morally dependent on God's objective will, is to repudiate this subjectivism. In the *Essays on the Law of Nature* Locke asks, 'Is it true that what each individual in the circumstances judges to be of advantage to himself and his affairs is in accordance with natural law, and on that account is not only lawful for him but also unavoidable, and that nothing in nature is binding except so far as it carries with it some immediate personal advantage?' (p. 207). He immediately answers that 'It is this we deny.' This concern is stressed no less emphatically in the *Two Treatises* (2.22, 59).[5]

This type of natural law theory, in which 'all things must be related' to God's purposes is conventional within the Thomist tradition (*ST*: 1. II.93.1). The generic ends of human action are set by divine laws and man is free to choose from a range of possible specific goals which conduces to bringing about God's overarching intentions. Man is not free to deliberate about ultimate ends, but is free, and has a duty to deliberate on the various means available to realise them in his particular circumstances. Thus, just as in making civil laws in accordance with natural law, man acts within a realm of prudence where theory guides but does not determine a specific course of action. Locke offers a lengthy explanation of this 'latitude' between theory and practice in his letters to Dr Denis Grenville (1976: I, nos. 328, 374, 426; cf. Driver, 1928). Locke's conventional characterisation of Christian ethics stands between two extreme views which were both considered to be atheistic in the seventeenth century. An atheist is said to believe that either God has no intentions for man, and thus there are no objective moral rules, or man's action is causally determined, and thus there is no freedom (1.3.13–14; cf. Pufendorf, 6.3.7).

3

The second natural law is that each man is 'urged to enter into society by a certain propensity of nature, and to be prepared for the maintenance of society by the gift of speech and through the intercourse of language' (p. 157). The obligation to preserve society is stressed in the *Essay* (1.3.10) and the *Two Treatises* (2.134–5, 195). This natural law is expressive of man's existential dependency on the society of other men. In his journal entry of 15 July 1678, 'Lex Naa', Locke writes (MS. Locke, f.3, fos. 201–2; von Leyden, 1956: pp. 34–5):

If he finds that God has made him and all other men in a state wherein they cannot subsist without society and has given them judgment to discern what is capable of preserving that society, can he but conclude that he is obliged and that God requires him to follow those rules which conduce to the preserving of society?

Since man has a duty to preserve mankind, and since man cannot exist without the society of other men, the duty to preserve society follows immediately. 'God. . .[has] designed Man for a sociable Creature' (3.1.1). He not only designed man dependent on society for his material needs, but also 'fitted him with Understanding and language to continue and enjoy it' (2.77). The assumption that man is dependent on both God and society for his existence and enjoyment is conventional in natural law writing (Suarez: 3.11.7; Pufendorf: 2.3.20).

Therefore, as Lamprecht noted as early as 1918 in *The Moral and Political Philosophy of John Locke*, Locke never considers a congeries of presocial and isolated individuals (p. 132). He cannot, because society is an irreducible datum of man's existence. Since norms for the preservation of society and its members are constitutive of society, Locke's analysis always presupposes men organised into a unified community. Without these norms, including promise-keeping, every community 'falls to the ground. . .just as they themselves fall to the ground if the law of nature is annulled' (p. 119). The Second Treatise therefore opens with a statement of this dual supposition (2.4). Individuals outside of society are not men, but 'wild Savage Beasts' (2.11). Dunn points out the radical difference between the basic assumptions of Locke and Hobbes (1969: p. 79):

Hobbes's problem is the construction of political society from an ethical vacuum. Locke never faced this problem in the *Two Treatises* because his central premise is precisely the absence of any such vacuum. It was a premise which he emphatically shared with Filmer and this is why he could simply assume that part of his position which immediately controverts Hobbes.

In addition to norms for the preservation of itself and its members, society is also constituted by the institution of promising. Locke follows Grotius and Pufendorf in making promise-keeping a natural law precept (prol. 15; 3.4.1). 'These compacts [promises] are to be kept or broken. If to be broken their making signifies nothing if to be kept then justice is established as a duty' (MS. Locke, c.28, fos. 139–40). If compacts are broken then they signify nothing because to make a compact is to commit oneself not to break it. Since making a promise is to create the obligation to keep it, it might seem superfluous to ground it in natural law. However, as Locke goes on to show, his point is the following. Once a promise is made it is always possible to ask why we should continue to keep it through time. If, for example, our reason for making promises is self-interest, then it would be permissible and indeed right to break that promise if it were no longer in our self-interest to keep it. The institution therefore requires a ground outside of itself if it is to have binding force and preserve society. Otherwise, everyone 'will be subjected to the force and deceit of all the rest' and it would be 'impossible for any man to be happy unless he were both stronger and wiser than all the rest'. Therefore, promise-keeping must be grounded in, and a precept of, the natural duty to preserve society. Since no society could exist without it, it is one precept of natural law which enjoys universal consent within, but not between, societies (1.3.10). The actual practice of all societies is, in this case, 'coincident with Divine law' (2.28.10). In the *Two Treatises* he stresses its fundamental importance in stating that even God is not exempt (2.195).

These two natural laws, derived from investigating and interpreting God as a maker and man as his workmanship, provide the objective foundation for Locke's theory of natural rights. As Dunn neatly summarises, the 'theological matrix functions...as an interpretative axiom' (1969: p. 98). The third law expresses the duty man has to 'praise, honour and glory' God (p. 157). This is the basis for individual Christian living and does not play a direct role in determining man's rights.

PART TWO

Natural Rights

CHAPTER THREE

Inclusive natural rights

i. The political context

Armed with the key epistemological and theological theories supportive
of Locke's political philosophy, we are now in a better position to return
to and to understand his theory of rights, or property, in the *Two Treatises*.
The leading issue to which Locke responds in the *Two Treatises* is
arbitrary and absolutist government. He mounts a blistering attack on its
most popular justification: the political tracts of Sir Robert Filmer (1588–
1652). In its place Locke reasserts a radical constitutionalist theory of
popular sovereignty and an individualist theory of resistance (Dunn,
1969: pp. 87–187).[1] Filmer's treatises were written as a Royalist defence of
absolute monarchy between 1638 and 1652, and originally published in
1648, 1652 and 1653. These were republished in 1679 and again in 1680.
Patriarcha, Filmer's major work and the main target of Locke's attack,
was published for the first time in the 1680 collection (Laslett, 1949:
pp. 33–48). The occasion of their republication was the Exclusion Crisis
(1679–81), engendered by the Whigs' attempt to exclude James, Duke of
York, from accession to the throne. The Whigs saw his proposed accession
as threatening their attempt 'to establish effective control over the
monarch's conduct of policy' and establishing an arbitrary and quite
possibly Catholic monarchy (Dunn, 1969: p. 44). Filmer's writings were
pressed into ideological service by the Tories to neutralise the Whigs'
evaluation of arbitrary government as a threat and to legitimate passive
obedience to hereditary succession.[2]

Locke began to move against Filmer in this context, in 1679, on reading
the 1679 edition of Filmer's tracts. On this point, if on no other, there
seems to be agreement amongst the contributors to the seemingly inter-
minable debate on the dating of the composition of the *Two Treatises*.[3]
At this period Locke was working in close association with Tyrrell, whose
refutation of Filmer, *The Patriarch un-monarched*, was published in
1681. 'When Locke and Tyrrell began writing, their target was a collected
edition, published in 1679, of some of Filmer's minor works, but when
early in 1680 this was followed by his major work, *Patriarcha*, they
realized that they must modify their plans' (Gough, 1976: p. 584). Thus,

insofar as the Tories described and so legitimated court action in terms of Filmer's writings, it is the case that Locke was attacking their position in refuting Filmer and legitimating Whig resistance in writing his resistance theory.

Locke's ideological task is discharged in the language of natural law and rights, in the face of the prevailing 'Whig' convention of appealing to the prescriptive force of history. This move is completely understandable in light of Locke's reconstruction of the epistemological superiority of natural law theory and his complementary dismissal of any theoretical appeal to history. It is thus a revolutionary and distinctively rationalist contribution to the Exclusion Crisis without being, as Dunn has noted, an 'Exclusion tract' (1969: pp. 51–2). The implications of Locke's epistemological investigations are identical to Dunn's conclusion that the *Two Treatises* 'is not a piece of political prudence, advice on what to do, the status of which depends upon matter of fact, but a statement of the limits of political right, the status of which depends upon the knowledge of the law of nature' (1969: p. 50).

In addition to refuting Filmer and writing his own theory, Locke had the additional task of answering Filmer's criticisms of natural law. The conclusion of Filmer's *Observations concerning the Original of Government, upon Mr. Hobs Leviathan, Mr. Milton against Salmasius, H. Grotius The Laws of War* (1652), is that natural law is an inescapably confused and logically inconsistent foundation for political theory. In the chapter on Grotius' *The Laws of War and Peace*, Filmer begins by ridiculing the inconsistent classifications of natural law, civil laws and the law of nations by civilians, canonists, politicians and divines (p. 261). He then asserts that the 'principal ground of these diversities and contrarities of divisions, was an error which the heathens taught, that all things at first were common, and that all men were equal' (p. 262). Having located the source of confusion in 'a community of all things, or an equality of all persons', he proceeds to show that Grotius' account is contradictory because it is based upon this 'dream'. Filmer's final attack centres on the logical inconsistencies which result from explaining property in this manner (p. 274):

Grotius saith, that by the law of nature all things were at first common, and yet teacheth, that after propriety was brought in, it was against the law of nature to use community. He doth thereby not only make the law of nature changeable, which he saith God cannot do, but he also makes the law of nature contrary to itself.

If Locke's project was to appear at all plausible to his immediate audience, he had to show that property, and equality, could be explained in a way consistent with natural law. Without this underlabouring, Locke's primary ideological task, 'of justifying resistance to arbitrary government and legitimising its dissolution' (Kelly, 1977: p. 84), executed in terms of natural law and rights, would appear ridiculous to anyone who had read Filmer. Therefore the presence and widespread awareness of Filmer's critique renders a consistent, natural law theory of property a necessary precondition for Locke's major goal; a convincing resistance theory.

Locke is also confronted with another set of problems. Both Grotius and Pufendorf use the normative vocabulary of natural law and rights to construct their rationalist theories of absolutism. They both develop a 'compact theory' of property as a constituent part of their absolutist theories. Grotius' compact theory is also ridiculed by Filmer (p. 273). Locke is, therefore, not only faced with the problems of refuting Filmer's theory of property and constructing his own in a way which overcomes Filmer's criticisms of natural law accounts of property. He must also use the shared vocabulary of natural law and natural rights, yet develop a theory which avoids both the absolutist implications of compact theories and Filmer's criticisms of Grotius' compact theory. Finally, he must win through to a theory which provides a foundation for his resistance theory. This complex intellectual context provides the matrix in which Locke works and in the light of which we can understand his theory of property. Locke brings the workmanship model into play to attack Filmer's account of property and to reestablish natural law as a basis for his rights theory. To understand Locke's refutation it is necessary to examine what he describes on the title page of the *Two Treatises* as 'the false principles and foundation of Sir Robert Filmer'.

ii. The refutation of Filmer on property

1

Monarchy, family and government are the three key terms which Filmer employs in his analysis of property. The 'real as well as nominal definition of monarchy' is 'government of one alone' (p. 281). Filmer quotes with approval Jean Bodin's patriarchal definition of a family as 'all persons under the obedience of one and the same head of the family' (p. 75). It is therefore true by definition that a monarchy is a family and a family is a monarchy (p. 63). He buttresses the identity of family and monarchy with an etymological argument, pointing out that the Hebrew term for family is 'derived from a word that signifies a head a Prince or lord' (pp. 75–6). Since to 'be governed, is nothing else but to be obedient and subject to the will or command of another' (p. 205), it follows that government is identical to both monarchy and family. All three are patriarchies. The conclusion is that 'there is no form of government, but monarchy only', 'no monarchy, but paternal' and 'no paternal monarchy, but absolute, or arbitrary' (p. 229).

Due to the identity, not analogy, of government and family, as both in essence patriarchal and absolute monarchies, any necessary attributes of one will be present in the other (cf. Schochet, 1975: pp. 146–50). 'If we compare the natural duties [rights] of a Father with those of a King, we find them to be all one, without any difference at all but only in the latitude or extent of them' (p. 63). The absolute and arbitrary rights and duties which a monarch possesses will also be possessed by every father over his family: 'As the Father over one family, so the King, as Father over many families'. A family consists in the economic relations of master to servants, slaves and possessions, and of father and husband to children and wife. Filmer castigates Aristotle for differentiating these relations and analysing them in terms of their various rights and duties. The head is one and the same person in each case, and his rights and duties are the same in each relation (p. 76). Locke's express aim to show that these relations are different in kind (2.2) is obviously directed at Filmer, and it bears a close resemblance to the passage in Aristotle's *Politics* (1252a 7–10) referred to by Filmer (cf. McKeon, 1937: pp. 303–4).

Filmer strengthens his case and specifies the nature of the monarch's right and duty with an 'Adamite' argument (p. 188):

Adam was the Father, King and Lord over his family: a son, a subject and a servant or a slave, were one and the same thing at first; the Father had power to dispose, or sell his children or servants; whence we find, that at the first reckoning up of goods in scripture, the manservant, and the maidservant are numbered among the possessions and substance of the owner, as other goods were.

Adam's undifferentiated and unlimited power, termed interchangeably property and dominion, is the foundation of all types of government: 'it is not possible for the wit of man to search out the first grounds or principles of government (which necessarily depend upon the original of property) except he know that at the creation one man alone was made, to whom the dominion of all things was given, and from whom all men derive their title' (pp. 203–4). Adam's *natural and private dominion* (p. 71) was over all things and so 'none of his posterity had any right to possess anything, but by his grant or permission, or by succession from him' (p. 188). This is said to prove that all present title to dominion of any type 'comes from the fatherhood'. Every present father and ruler is an essentially indistinguishable present descendant of one original archetype: Adam's monarchy. Any right of authority, whether over things or people, is construed as a private property right of use, abuse and alienation. Thus, every present, legitimate proprietor holds a divinely sanctioned and absolute property right over his 'family'; whereas the sovereign has an absolute right over all subjects who, in turn, constitute his family (p. 63).[4]

Locke is of course intent on demonstrating that the authority of a governor, master and proprietor is different in each case. Also, he is equally adamant in overthrowing the argument that political authority is absolute and arbitrary. In addition, however, it is essential to see that one of his aims in writing on property is to refute Filmer's claim that any father holds a natural, unlimited and arbitrary right of private property. In his preliminary description of Filmer's right of private dominion or of fatherhood, Locke notes that it is possessed by all fathers, as well as rulers: 'this *Fatherly Authority*, this Power of Fathers, and of Kings, for he makes them both the same' (1.7). When Locke sets up Filmer's right as a target he emphasises the absolutist and wholly irresponsible concept of individual proprietorship it necessarily embodies (1.9):

This *Fatherly Authority* then, or *Right of Fatherhood*, in our A————'s sence is a Divine unalterable Right of Sovereignty, whereby a Father or a Prince hath an Absolute, Arbitrary, Unlimited, and Unlimitable Power, over the Lifes, Liberties, and Estates of his Children and Subjects; so that he may take or alienate their Estates, sell, castrate, or use their Persons as he pleases, they being all his Slaves, and he Lord or Proprietor of every Thing, and his unbounded Will their Law.

Locke feared, as we have seen, that if the dependency relation of man to God did not exist, obligation to natural law would disappear and a kind of egoism would prevail. If man were independent he would be under no law but his own will and this implies that he would consider no end but himself (above, pp. 36–42). 'He would be a god to himself and the satisfaction of his own will the sole measure and end of all his actions' (Ethica B MS. Locke, c.28, fo. 141). This matches Locke's description of Filmer's position. Locke points out that every father in Filmer's theory is an absolute monarch, exercising his right of sovereignty over his undifferentiated possessions in accordance with nothing but his 'unbounded will'. In redescribing and so stigmatising Filmer's theory in this way, Locke simply transposes Filmer's description of the consequences of any form of differentiated sovereignty (p. 224). Locke's fundamental step in dismantling Filmer's 'wonderful System' is thus to overthrow its theological premiss. He then reestablishes natural law and man's obligation to it, thereby undercutting the 'unlimited and unlimitable' right of private dominion.

2

Locke begins his refutation by quoting Filmer's statement that his right of fatherhood is based on the art of begetting. '[E]*very Man that is born is so far from being free, that by his very Birth he becomes a Subject of him that begets him*' (1.50). Although Filmer offers no explanation of why begetting confers a right, Locke says that he has 'heard others make use of' the argument that *'Fathers have a Power over the Lives of their Children, because they give them Life and Being'* (1.52). This is the only possible proof, 'since there can be no reason, why naturally one Man should have any claim or pretence of Right over that in another, which was never his, which he bestowed not, but was received from the bounty of another' (1.52). If there is a natural right, it must be a maker's right. The father must put life and being in his child. If it were true, the dependency relation between man and God would disappear and the foundation of Locke's political philosophy would be destroyed. If a Filmerian appeals to history or convention for justification, the right would not be natural and would fall under the criticisms directed at Bodin by Vico (1974: 1009–19).

The justification of a right of fatherhood which Locke says is used by others is called traductionism. Locke's belief that the being or essence of a child comes from God is called creationism. Aristotle is standardly taken to be the father of traductionism (*EN*: 1158b 22–3). In *Struggle for Synthesis*, Loemker discusses a lively theological debate in the sixteenth century over the two theories. He suggests that traductionism offers a better explanation of the transmission of original sin and justification of patriarchal obedience, whereas creationism highlights the creative powers of God and, by analogy, of man. Creationism also has the result of dissolving the mediating hierarchies between man and God and of tying man much more immediately and intimately to God (1972: pp. 76, 100). In addition to Locke, Hooker, Suarez, Baxter and Newton embrace creationism. Shortly after Locke's death, William Wollaston (1660–1724), in *The Religion of Nature Delineated* (1724), presents an extended critique of traductionism (pp. 87–93).

Locke immediately stresses the connection between traductionism and political theory and presents biblical support for his theological premiss (1.52):

They who say the *Father* gives Life to his Children, are so dazzled with the thoughts of Monarchy, that they do not, as they ought, remember God, who is *the Author and Giver of Life: 'Tis in him alone we live, move, and have our Being* [*Acts* 17.28].

Locke asks how 'can he be thought to give Life to another, that knows not wherein his own Life consists?'. The sole point of this and the following section is to show that man does not know what life is, nor could he 'frame and make a living Creature, fashion the parts, and mould and suit them to their uses' (1.53). Nor can man 'put into them a living Soul'. If he could, he 'might indeed have some pretence to destroy his own

Workmanship'. A traductionist might reply that he cannot do this but he nonetheless passes life and being along in the act of procreation. But this would be unsatisfactory. Locke's implicit assumption is that the being of any ordered and purposive object is the constitution of its parts in accordance with its essential idea. In turn, this presupposes a knowing maker. Since man manifestly lacks the requisite knowledge, and since the child is an ordered and purposive creation, this is 'sufficient to convince us of an All-wise Contriver, and he has so visible a claim to us as his Workmanship'. Therefore, God is '*King* because he is indeed Maker of us all, which no Parents can pretend to be of their Children'.

Parents are merely causal factors in the process; the 'occasions of their [children's] being' (1.54). God is the maker because he knows the description under which the child is produced and because 'He alone can breathe in the Breath of Life' (1.53; cf. Hintikka, 1975: pp. 90–1). As a result, man is born subject to God, not to man, and thus is born 'equal one amongst the other without Subordination or Subjection' (2.4). The argument overthrows Filmer's right of fatherhood and reestablishes the basis of man's obligation to natural law. In addition, it situates equality as the natural condition of man to man, thus making it a basic principle of political theory.

The truth that 'all men are naturally equal', Locke writes in *The Conduct of the Understanding*, when 'well settled in the understanding, and carried in the mind through the various debates concerning the various rights of men in society, will go a great way in putting an end to them, and showing on which side the truth is' (1823: III, p. 283). The argument undercuts Filmer's natural property right and presents the basis for one of Locke's. As Locke foreshadows (1.52), if man is to have an analogous maker's right in, and authority over, the things which he makes he will have to work in a God-like fashion.

3

Having shown the 'Book, which was to provide Chains for all Mankind' to be founded on 'nothing but a Rope of Sand' (1.1), Locke proceeds to develop his natural rights in a step-by-step contrast with Filmer's right of private dominion. The proof offered is twofold: by scripture and by natural law. Locke shares the Thomist assumption that scripture and reason are complementary. Natural law and the propositions in scripture comprise the two complementary and partially overlapping parts of Divine Law. In the *Essay* Locke writes that '*the same Truths may be discovered, and conveyed down from Revelation, which are discoverable to us by Reason*' (4.18.4). Scripture, which reveals God's purposes in making man and the world, can function as a check or affirmation of

reason, which discovers natural laws and derivative rights (4.18.7, 10).
The dual method is employed in the First Treatise and the conclusions are
laid down as premises in the Second Treatise, with the remark that they
are confirmed by reason and scripture (2.25).

Genesis 1.29 is the point of departure (1.23):

*And God Blessed them, and God said unto them, be Fruitful and Multiply and
Replenish the Earth and subdue it, and have Dominion over the Fish of the Sea,
and over the Fowl of the Air, and over every living thing that moveth upon the
Earth.*

Filmer, according to Locke, interprets this as granting to Adam '*Private
Dominion* over the Earth, and all inferior or irrational creatures'. Filmer
calls private dominion 'property'. Locke agrees that there is 'nothing to
be granted to *Adam* here but Property'. However, property is not
private dominion. By 'this Grant God gave him not *Private Dominion*
over the Inferior Creatures, but right in common with all Mankind' in
'the account of the Property here given him' (1.24). The first description
of property is thus right in common with all mankind, or, as Barbeyrac
glosses in his notes on *The law of Nature and Nations*, 'a right common
to all' (4.4.3.n). Property is characterised four sections later as 'the
Dominion of the whole Species of Mankind, over the Inferior Species of
Creatures'. He then supplies a slightly more extensive *passus*. The grant
was not given to Adam 'exclusive of all other Men', not a '*Private
Dominion*, but a Dominion in common' (1.29). Thus, property is right in
common, this is equivalent to dominion in common, and it is contrasted
to Filmer's 'exclusive' private dominion (1.36, 39, 45–7).

The word 'right' has two senses. It is used objectively in phrases asserting that such and such is right, and subjectively when a person is said to
have or to possess a right or moral power to something. Locke's property
or right in common with all of mankind is a subjective use right. After
agreeing with Filmer that God's grant includes the earth as well as
animals (1.39), he then gives his definitive formulation of the property of
mankind: 'a Right, to make use of the Food and Rayment, and other
Conveniences of Life, the Materials whereof he had so plentifully provided
for them' (1.41). The distinction between materials provided by God and
the things made out of them and useful to man, to which man's property
primarily refers, is left unexplained until the Second Treatise. The
property which mankind is granted, expressed by this natural use right, is
common property. Genesis 'is so far from proving *Adam* Sole proprietor,
that on the contrary, it is a Confirmation of the Original Community of
all things amongst the Sons of men' (1.40). Whatever the validity of
Locke's biblical exegesis may be, his meaning is clearly that all men
possess a use right in common and that the right is not tensed. This

property belongs to 'the Sons of Men', to 'all Mankind', to 'them all' and so on.

Locke's untensed and therefore natural property is different from Filmer's in five important respects. It is a right possessed by all men, not just Adam. It is a right of use only, not of use, abuse and alienation. Third, the right expresses common property, not private property. Macpherson has developed a terminology which can be used to illuminate this third contrast. Private property can be called an exclusive right because it is a right of the proprietor to exclude others from that to which the right refers, in addition to whatever other specified moral or legal powers over the referent the rightholders may enjoy. Common property can be re-described as an inclusive right because it is a right 'not to be excluded from', or to be included in, the use of that to which the right refers, in addition to whatever other moral or legal powers over the referent that the rightholders may possess. In each case the assertion of the right justifies a claim: either to exclude others or to be included (1975: pp. 123–5). Both Filmer's and Locke's right are claim rights in Hohfeld's sense that others have a duty to let the rightholder exercise his right. Others have a duty to stay off the property to which Filmer's right of private dominion (or a modern right of private property) refers. Others have a duty to move over and include the holder of Locke's right in the use of the common property. Fourth, Filmer's property is a right to own possessions. Locke's property is a right to something which belongs to all; a right to one's *due* rather than to one's *own*. Finally, Locke's property has a specified end, while Filmer's has no end but the proprietor's un-bounded will. It is a right to use things for the sake of 'conveniences of Life' or 'support'; 'a Right to make use of a part of the Earth for the support of themselves and Families' (1.37).

As these quotations illustrate, Locke uses the term 'property' for both a right and the referent of the right. In addition he sometimes uses the term 'right' for the referent of a right (2.28). He is clearly aware of the equivocity and it seems to be simply a continuation of the equivocity of similar Latin terms such as *ius* and *dominium*. Equivocity is normally a linguistic signal that two items are related in some way; a relation which might go unnoticed if two different terms were used. In this respect, equivocity is different from ambiguity, where two items bear the same name but do not stand in any relation one to another. 'Bank', referring to the sides of rivers and to institutions which safeguard and lend money, is ambiguous. 'Politics' referring to a range of activity and to the body of knowledge of that range of activity, is equivocal.

4

The next move is to show that scriptural community, redescribed as an inclusive right held by all men, is consistent with reason. There are two arguments, the first of which is based on the workmanship model. Since God made the world and the animals, He is their proprietor. Therefore, man's property can only be the right to use them as He allows: 'in respect of God the Maker of Heaven and Earth, who is sole Lord and Proprietor of the whole World, Man's Propriety in the Creatures is nothing but that *Liberty to use them,* which God has permitted' (1.39). In a similar manner, man's life is God's property and thus it is man's property to use only; not to destroy by suicide (2.23). The definitive proof of property as a right to use God's world, however, is Locke's argument that it is an implicate of natural law. He derives three natural rights from natural law, the third of which is the right or property which expresses scriptural community.

A normative proposition, asserting an action that we *ought* to perform, presupposes a proposition that informs us what *is* to be done and which, in so doing, establishes the normative proposition (Cavell, 1976: pp. 23–31). Locke manipulates a natural law and its presupposition to derive his first two natural rights. The fundamental Law of nature 'being *the preservation of Mankind*' (2.135), it enjoins the preservation of mankind and, employing Locke's distributive principles, of men. The end is the continued existence or subsistence of men. Since preservation is one of God's goals for man, and hence his natural duty is to bring it about, it follows that he has a natural right to it: 'Men, being once born, have a right to their Preservation' (2.25). It is an inclusive right not to be denied continued existence. Secondly, the fundamental law of nature is that man's being *is,* and therefore *ought* to be, preserved (2.16). This is redescribed as a natural duty of each man to preserve himself and, *ceteris paribus,* others (2.6).[5] This is a natural duty to engage in the end-directed activity of preserving man, whereas the first is a duty to ensure the end; the preservation of man. Therefore, there is a natural right to this activity: 'they [men] will always have a right to preserve what they have not a Power to part with [their lives, which belong to God and are theirs only to use]' (2.149). This 'original' right (2.220) is '*the Right he* [man] *has of Preserving all Mankind*' (2.11).

These two natural rights serve two purposes. Their primary role is to justify resistance to arbitrary and absolute rule. If a ruler arbitrarily violates my right or another's right to preservation he has violated natural law. My right to preserve my life and others comes into play and I can punish him (2.13, 135). I do not have a right to do so only in the sense of it being morally permissible. Since this right results from the duty to preserve myself and others, I have a positive and natural duty to exercise my right (2.149; cf. Dunn, 1969: pp. 180–6; Skinner, 1978: II, pp. 338–9; Franklin, 1978: p. 194). Secondly, they serve as the foundation for the natural right of common property. If men have a right to preservation and to preserve themselves and others, they have a right 'consequently to Meat and Drink, and such other things, as Nature affords for their Subsistence' (2.25). That is, each man has a natural right to the *means* necessary to preserve himself (Steiner, 1977: pp. 41–9). 'He that is Master of himself, and his own Life, has a right too to the means of preserving it' (2.172).

This property or inclusive right, *derived from natural law*, is identical to the concept of property interpreted from scripture (1.86–7). The derivation confirms his scriptural interpretation and adds one further specification. Since it, and the two other natural rights, results from the natural law to preserve oneself and others, man is not at liberty to exercise or not to exercise the right. He is under a positive, natural duty to do so. The three rights are entailed by, and are justifications of, claims to perform duties to God. The exercise of these rights *is* the duty to preserve oneself and others. It is therefore misleading to suggest, as Strauss does in *Natural Right and History*, that Locke is a theorist of natural rights and not of natural law (1953: p. 248). It is also a mistake to say that 'the right of nature is more fundamental than the law of nature and is the foundation of the law of nature' (p. 227). The law of nature is rather the foundation of Locke's three natural rights. To paraphrase Copleston, men have natural rights *because* they have natural duties (1964: V.1, p. 139); Dunn stresses that what 'defines human life [for Locke] is a set of duties and a right to promote happiness in any way compatible with these duties' (1969: p. 218).[6]

5

Having established original community property Locke is faced with the two standard types of problem. Common rights to use some thing do not, in themselves, specify how the commoners are to use that thing which belongs to them all in common. A principle specifying how the common is to be used is required if the common right is to be exercised. This is, as Marx points out in *The German Ideology*, an analytic feature of any form of communism (1976: V, pp. 228–30). Locke handles the problem by introducing a second kind of property rights, marked by the locution 'property in'. He simply notes this feature in the First Treatise, and points to his further analysis of it with 'a clear cross-reference to the fifth chapter of the *Second Treatise*' (Laslett, 1970: p. 224n). After repeating that 'men had a right in common', he adds that, 'nor can any one have a

Property in them [common things], otherwise then in other things common by Nature, of which I shall speak in its due place' (1.90). In an earlier passage, he notes the same conceptual connection between having a common right to use and rights specifying how the common property is to be used and then states that, 'how he, or any one else, could do [come to have 'a Property in a particular thing'], shall be shewn in another place' (1.87; cf. 1.86). We saw at the outset that this is precisely the problem with which chapter five of the Second Treatise begins and deals (above, p. 1).

In these passages in the First Treatise Locke speaks of the problem of individuation in the past tense and states that it refers to the state of nature. This foreshadows his argument in the Second Treatise that property is handled differently in a political society. The second problem is how the products of man's use of the common are to be used. We know they are to be used for preservation, since this is the purpose for the sake of which God granted the world to mankind. However, Locke hints that they can be also used for convenience (1.41) and for something more than simply preservation: 'God *gives us all things richly to enjoy* [1 Tim. vi. 17]' (1.40). Again, this is addressed in the fifth chapter of the Second Treatise (2.31).

It is essential to be aware of this framework of natural rights, expressing both common property and the right and duty of each man to use it, and natural law, defining the end of use, in order to understand what Locke does in the chapter 'of Property'. Since the framework constitutes the problem Locke addresses, it is scarcely possible to understand what Locke took himself to be doing unless we view it in light of the same description (cf. MacIntyre, 1962: pp. 48–70 for this general point). In setting out his natural rights, Locke's point is not only to refute and to provide an alternative to Filmer. It is also to rework natural law and natural rights in order to answer Filmer's criticism of Grotius' treatment of property. We are now in a position to see this aspect of Locke's theory and so to situate his initial conditions in the seventeenth-century natural law context.

iii. Natural rights in other seventeenth-century theories

1

There are three ways in which the analysis of property developed by Saint Thomas Aquinas (1225–74) in the *Summary of Theology* serves to illuminate seventeenth-century natural law writing. Aquinas provides a form of analysis which becomes conventional and in which what is common to all precedes discussion of what is rightfully one's own (*ST*: II. II. 66.1). Second, the revival of natural law by a school of Spanish neo-

Thomists in the late sixteenth and early seventeenth centuries is founded on Aquinas' theory. This neo-Thomist political philosophy is, in turn, important for understanding Locke. Third, Locke not only was familiar with Aquinas' writing, but also parallels Aquinas in his account of common property.

The three natural laws are, according to Aquinas, the preservation of mankind and society and the worship of God (*ST*: II. II.94.2). His interpretation of Genesis 1.26 in the *Summary Against the Gentiles* is the same as Locke's: man is capable of dominion because he has an intellectual nature (III, 81; cf. 1.30, 40). Similarly, Genesis 1.28 is said to grant man dominion over the earth and inferior creatures (*ST*: II. II.66.2). The world is properly God's property, so man has no power over its substance. Man's dominion, therefore, is 'the use of such things'. Man has natural property of use, 'for he can, in virtue of his reason and will, make use of things for his own benefit' (*ST*: II. II.66.1). This distinction is underpinned, as in Locke, with the belief that God made the world and therefore it is His (*ST*: I. 44–6).

When Aquinas speaks of the world as man's common property for use he uses *dominium* and *possessio*. When he speaks of some form of individual and exclusive possession he uses *proprietas* and contrasts it with common property (*communitas rerum, possidere communiter*) (*ST:* II. II.66.2). That is, he sets out man's natural and common property and proceeds to discuss 'the limits of individual property'. He develops this contrast in the course of his reply to Ambrose. Ambrose states that *dominium* means exclusive control over an object. Therefore, because bringing something into being is the criterion for possessing natural dominion over it, it follows that only God can be said to have natural dominion over substances. As a consequence, dominion or property is not natural to man. Aquinas agrees that *dominium* over natural things in this sense is natural to God alone but he states that *dominium* over natural things in the sense of use is natural and common to man (*ST*: II. II.66.1). Use is also for the sake of preservation and convenience (*ST:* II. II.62.5). Aquinas' innovative response creates an inclusive as well as an exclusive concept of property, and this distinction, as we have seen, is unequivocally reasserted by Locke.

2

Aquinas does not appear to use the terminology of subjective rights. Tuck suggests that rights theories emerged with the new science of Roman law in the twelfth century at Bologna, spreading from there to William of Ockham (*c*.1285–1347) and Jean Gerson (1363–1429) (Tuck, 1979). The great revival of Thomism in the sixteenth century involved placing political philosophy on a more objective foundation, and granting to subjective rights a more limited purchase, by grounding both in Aquinas' concept of natural law. This neo-Thomism begins with a Dominican theologian, Francisco de Vitoria (c.1485–1546). He began lecturing at the University of Paris on *The Summary of Theology* and then returned to his native Spain, to hold the Chair of Theology at Salamanca from 1526 to his death. Domingo de Soto (1494–1560), Vitoria's pupil and fellow Dominican, wrote *Ten Books of Law and Justice* (1553–7), which was republished twenty-seven times in the sixteenth century. Their ideas were adopted and carried forward in the latter half of the sixteenth century by the Jesuits, especially Luis de Molina (1535–1600) and Francisco Suarez (1548–1617) in Spain. Suarez's lectures on law at Coimbra were published in 1612 as *The Laws and God the Lawgiver*. He also wrote *The Defence of Catholic and Apostolic Faith* (1612) in response to the defence of the English oath of Allegiance by King James I. 'These two works', Skinner writes, 'not only represent his own major contribution to legal and political thought, but also provide the clearest summary of the remarkably homogeneous outlook which had been developed by the whole school of Thomist political philosophers in the course of the sixteenth century' (1978: II, p. 138). The work of this school constitutes the major ideology of the Catholic Counter-Reformation.[7]

Suarez was read by a large audience throughout the century and Loemker has suggested that he is the teacher of Early Modern Europe (1972: p. 119). Filmer found it necessary to take him to task for his views on natural law, natural equality and property (pp. 74–8). Although we have no definitive proof that Locke read Suarez, several historians have stressed the similarities between their political philosophies (von Leyden, 1970: pp. 36–7; Copleston, 1963: III, ii, pp. 168–9, 245–6; and Skinner, 1978: II, pp. 158–9, 163, 165, 174). Therefore, Suarez's work can be used as an object of comparison to illuminate innovations and continuities in seventeenth-century natural law theories.

In *The Laws and God the Lawgiver*, Suarez develops his concept of subjective rights by first noting that right (*ius*) 'has the same meaning as that which is just (*iustum*) and that which is equitable (*aequum*)' (1.2.4). These are the two objects of justice (*iustitia*). But justice also has two meanings. In its generic meaning it stands for every moral virtue, 'since every virtue in some way is directed towards and brings about equity'. In its more specific meaning justice 'may signify a special virtue which renders to another that which is his due'. Accordingly, right conforms to each of these two meanings. Right in the generic sense 'may refer to whatever is fair and in harmony with reason, this being, as it were, the general objective of virtue in the abstract'. Second, right in its more specific meaning 'may refer to the equity which is due to each individual as a matter of justice'. Having defined right as the two objects of the two Aristotelian meanings of justice, he refers to Aquinas to substantiate that the specific meanings of right and justice are their 'primary' and 'strict' significations.

Objective right in the specific and primary sense, that which is due to a person as a matter of justice, is redescribed, in two elegant steps, in terms of two subjective rights. According to the 'strict acceptation of right (*ius*), this name is properly bestowed on a certain moral power which every man has, either over that which is rightfully his own or with respect to that which is due to him' (1.2.5). Here the strict and traditional meaning of justice is shown to be the rendering of two objects (signified by the strict sense of right): that which is rightfully one's own (*rem suam*) and that which is rightfully due to a person (*ad rem sibi debitam*). The reason why 'right' can be predicated of the moral power to these two objects, which are right, is because the moral power cannot but be right in the objective sense. It is a power to what is right: one's own and one's due. The next step is to specify the moral power in each case:

For it is thus that the owner of a thing is said to have a right in that thing (*ius in re*) and the worker is said to have a right to his stipend (*ius ad stipendum*) by reason of which he is declared worthy of hire.

He adds that this terminology is frequent in law and scripture, 'for the law distinguishes in this way between a right already established in a thing (*ius in re*) and a right to a thing (*ius ad rem*)'. Both these rights express a 'right to claim, or moral power, which every man possesses with respect to his own property or with respect to a thing which in some way pertains to him'. The right to a thing (*ius ad rem*) is a claim to that which belongs to a person in the sense of being his due, but which he does not yet possess. A right in a thing (*ius in re*) is a claim to that which is already one's own and is possessed. These two types of rights are equivalent to Locke's property in the sense of a right to use and in the sense of 'a property in' something. Indeed, Locke's locutions, 'right to' and 'property in' seem to be a translation of *ius ad rem* and *ius in re*. The two rights are conceptually connected in the following manner. In fulfilling some criterion, a person who holds a right to something, a stipend for example, 'comes to have', to use Locke's locution, a right in that thing (stipend) and so possesses it. A modern example serves to illustrate the connection. Suppose it is considered that public transportation should be available to each citizen as a matter of civil justice. This is a citizen's due and he can be said to have a claim right *to* it, correlative with a positive duty of the community to provide it. The right in this case, is a right not to be excluded from or denied the use of public transportation when a citizen chooses to exercise it. When the right is exercised, the citizen comes to have a right *in* the use of the seat or floor space he occupies. This *ius in re* is a right to exclude others from using the same seat at the same time. The example shows that a right *to* requires a right *in* in order to be exercised. The way in which they are linked can be various. Conventionally, the criterion for the application of a right *in* on public transportation is first arrival, but this can be overridden by the rights of elderly, handicapped, overburdened or pregnant persons. However, the conceptual connection between the two types of rights still holds. Even if we hold common rights to use a factory, for example, and this is understood further as rights of common use, it is still the case that each person has a right in the use of, say, one tool for a specified time and not another person at the same time.

Suarez employs his concept of a right to one's due in his discussion of the initial conditions of property. He follows Aquinas in stating that according to natural law there is common ownership of all things, and in restricting *proprietas* to exclusive possession (2.14.14). An Adamite argument like Filmer's is attacked, and private dominion, as a donation from God or as a precept of natural law, is denied (3.2.3). Genesis 1.28 means that God gave the world to mankind. The same result is said to follow from natural law: 'Nature has conferred upon all men in common dominion over all things, and consequently has given every man a power to use those things; but nature has not so conferred private dominion' (2.14.16). He then introduces his *ius ad rem* to redescribe Aquinas' common dominion. 'For we have said that right (*ius*) is sometimes law (*lex*); while at times it means property (*dominium*) or quasi-property over a thing; that is, a claim to its use' (2.14.16). He adds that it is an inclusive right in the sense that all have a duty to make room for each to exercise his right. There was 'a positive precept of natural law to the effect that no one should be prevented from making the necessary use of the common property' (2.14.17). At this point, the Thomist concept of natural, common property can be said to be effectively translated into the language of subjective rights. Seventy years later Locke reasserts this neo-Thomist concept of common property in opposition to Filmer's Adamite theory, which, in turn, was enunciated in opposition to Suarez's anti-Adamite theory.

3

Grotius entered the University of Leyden in 1594 at the age of eleven and received his doctorate in 1598 from the University of Orleans, having travelled there in a diplomatic mission (Knight, 1925: pp. 27–32). In 1604 he was retained as a lawyer by the directors of the Amsterdam chamber of the East India Company to justify the practice of capturing enemy goods. The particular occasion was the capture of a richly laden Portuguese carack, the *Catharina*, by Jacob van Heemskerck in 1603. Grotius responded by writing the *Commentary on the law of Prize and Booty*, but it was not published. The manuscript came to light in 1864 and was published for the first time in 1868 (Fruin, 1925: pp. 3–74). The central argument is a justification of the right of the Dutch to trade with the Indies and, therefore, to make war on the Portuguese, who claimed a monopoly. The East India Company was therefore entitled to its booty from the captured *Catharina* (Daumbauld, 1969: pp. 27–8). In 1607 the Dutch East India Company was threatened again, by the King of Spain, and a defence of its right to trade with the Indies was required. Grotius vouchsafed chapter twelve of the *Commentary on the Law of Prize and Booty*, which was published as *The Freedom of the Seas, or the right which belongs to the Dutch to take part in the East India Trade (1609)* (De Pauw, 1965: pp. 18–21).

To perform his ideological task, Grotius seeks to prove that the sea is not a fit object for rights of private property and therefore cannot be monopolised. He does this in chapter five by reconstituting the vocabulary of property in such a way that it becomes impossible to express the Thomist concept of common property. The terms 'property' (*dominium*) and common ownership (*communio*) are said to have had, in 'the earliest stages of human existence', meanings different from their present ones (p. 22). In ancient times, '"common" (*communio*) meant simply the opposite of "particular" (*proprio*); and "dominion" meant the faculty of rightfully using common property (*dominium autem facultas non iniusta utendi re communi*)' (p. 23). However, this is no longer the case. Now, 'we call a thing "common" when its ownership or possession (*proprietas*) is held by several persons jointly according to a kind of partnership or mutual agreement from which all other persons are excluded' (pp. 21–3). 'Property' (*dominium*) now 'means a particular kind of proprietorship (*proprium*), such in fact that it absolutely excludes like possession by any one else' (p. 22). In addition, '"use" (*usus*), is a particular right' (p. 23). Therefore, property, as well as use, is, by definition, private. Common ownership means that each owner has a right over his share.

The old 'property' meant that 'a number of persons...were not debarred from being substantially sovereign or owners (*domini*) of something' (p. 24). But, Grotius immediately stresses, this 'is quite contradictory to our modern meaning of property (*dominium*)...[which] now implies particular or private ownership (*proprietas*)'. This great conceptual change came when men began to occupy and appropriate things and so to assert their proprietorship. Property therefore presupposes actual possession: 'it was decided that things were the property of individuals. This is called "occupation"' (p. 25). He then proceeds to draw two conclusions. The first is that that which cannot be occupied, 'or which never has been occupied, cannot be the property of anyone, because all property (*pro-*

prietas) has arisen from occupation' (p. 27). Property (*dominium*) is identified with exclusive possession (*proprietas*). The Thomist and Lockeian belief that the world belongs to mankind in common, logically prior to occupation, is elided because property is now said to result from occupation. The second rule is 'that all that which has been so constituted by nature that, although serving some one person, it still suffices for the common use of all other persons, is today, and ought in perpetuity to remain in the same condition as when it was first created by nature' (p. 27). The seas, not surprisingly, are said to fall in this category and so ought to remain open for the use of all. The seas are not the common property of all, with each possessing a claim right to use them. Rather, since property follows occupation, the seas belong to no one and may be used, but not occupied, by all: 'the sea is common to all, because it is so limitless that it cannot become a possession of all' (p. 28). The seas are common to all and the (private) property of none (*communia omnia, propria nullius*) (p. 28).[8] In executing his ideological aim, Grotius thus brings about a major simplification of the concept of property. Property is now confined to private property, in the sense of an exclusive right, and it presupposes actual possession.

In 1617 Grotius became involved in the constitutional conflict between the local and central governments. He was arrested in 1619 and sentenced to life imprisonment, but he managed to escape to France in 1621 and to receive a pension from King Louis XIII (Daumbauld, 1969: pp. 11–14; Knight, 1925: pp. 151–86). While in exile in Paris, he wrote his great work, *The Laws of War and Peace* (1625), and dedicated it to King Louis XIII. His radical break with Thomist theory is continued and clarified in the sections on rights and property.

He defines right (*ius*) in three ways. Right in the objective sense means that which is just (*iustum*) (1.1.3.1). The first subjective sense of right is 'a *moral Quality* annexed to the Person, *enabling him to have or to do, something justly*' (1.1.4). He then restricts the concept of a right to a right in that which one possesses, an exclusive right, thus eliding the concept of a right to one's due. 'Civilians call a *Faculty* that Right which a Man has to his *own*; but we shall hereafter call it a *Right properly, and strictly taken*' (1.1.5). The power over oneself (termed 'Liberty'), over others (such as a father over his son or master over his slave), property (*dominium*) and the 'Faculty of demanding what is due' are all subsumed under, or can be described by, this univocal concept of a right. He explains that what he means by 'demanding what is due' is simply the 'Restitution of my Goods, which are in the possession of another' (1.1.7). Grotius' property is therefore the same kind of right as Filmer's right of private dominion.

Therefore, when he discusses the origin of property, he begins by using *dominium* interchangeably with *proprietas*, since they both denote the same exclusive right. Let 'us examine into the Original of Property (*proprietas*), which our Lawyers do generally call dominion (*dominium*)' (2.2.1). These terms are accordingly translated into English as either property or dominion. The world was originally common according to Grotius' purely historical account, but in a way radically different from the description given by Suarez and Locke. The world belongs originally to no one and is open to all. It does not belong to everyone in the same manner, nor can it, because Grotius has divested himself of the terminology in which he could express common property. The kind of historical right a man is said to possess is an exclusive right in the things which he comes to acquire by first taking. 'God conferred upon the human race a general right in things (*ius in res*) of a lower nature' (2.2.2.1). The English translation (1738) further codifies Grotius' radical linguistic revision by rendering this exclusive right as 'a Dominion over things'. He achieves a further simplification in the range of uses appropriate for 'property' by stating that this right did 'at that Time supply the Place of Property' but was not property since it is only a use right (2.2.2.1).

The way in which Grotius' original position works is then illustrated with Cicero's famous simile of the theatre: 'Tho' the Theatre is common for any Body that comes, yet the Place that everyone sits in is properly his own.' The people who first take seats have an exclusive right in their use, and this correlates with a negative duty on the part of others not to occupy it at the same time. But, if the theatre fills to capacity, those excluded have no right to demand a seat (a point soon made by Pufendorf). In contrast, everyone in the theories of Suarez and Locke has a claim right not to be excluded and to demand that others make room for them, correlative with their positive duty to do so. By dispensing with common rights to one's due, Grotius evades this crucial step and so moves immediately to exclusive possession. He holds his concept of private property in the wings to solve the anarchic state of affairs which rapidly develops from his premises.

Pufendorf was born in 1632 in rural Saxony. After gaining his education at the Universities of Leipzig and Jena (1650–8), he took a position as tutor to the family of the Swedish minister in Copenhagen. When Sweden reopened the war with Denmark, Pufendorf was arrested and imprisoned. During imprisonment he composed his first major work, the *Elements of Universal Jurisprudence* (1660), after meditating on Grotius and Hobbes (Barbeyrac, 1729: p. 81). In 1661 he received, from Karl Ludwig, the Elector Palatine, an associate professorship in international law and philology at the University of Heidelberg. According to Barbeyrac, he was appointed by Karl Ludwig to lecture on Grotius (1738: p. x). He was granted a professorship in international law at the University of Lund, by Charles XI of Sweden, in 1667. Promotion to a Chair followed in 1670

and his voluminous work, *The Law of Nature and Nations*, dedicated to
Charles XI, was published in 1672. An epitome, *On the Duty of Man and
the Citizen according to Natural Law*, appeared in the following year
(Krieger, 1965: pp. 15–23).

4

In *The Law of Nature and Nations* (1672) Pufendorf continues and refines
Grotius' restriction of the term property to private property. He equates
dominium with *proprietas*: 'we take Dominion (*dominium*) and Property
(*proprietas*) to be the very same' (4.4.2). Property is defined in the following manner:

*Property or Dominion, is a Right, by which the very Substance, as it were, of a
Thing, so belongs to one Person, that it doth not* in whole belong, after the same
manner, to any other.

There are two central features of this modern concept of property as
exclusively private property. First, property is taken to be a right in the
substance of a thing. For Aquinas and Locke, with respect to natural
things such a right is held by God alone. Pufendorf is aware that he
departs from the Thomist belief and argues against the view that man's
dominion is confined to the use of the natural world (4.3.1–2). The different and opposed definitions of Pufendorf and Locke embody two radically
dissimilar views of the relation of man to the world. For Pufendorf,
property expresses man's right to dominate the world (4.3.2); for Locke,
it expresses man's privilege to use a world which is not essentially his own
and which is to be used, and not abused, for purposes not his own, of
preservation and enjoyment. Locke's attitude is best captured, perhaps, in
his discussion of travel in his journal (*Patriae Amor*). Man should treat the
world as a foreign country, using and enjoying what it offers yet leaving
everything as it is – with his thoughts on his true home which awaits him
at the end of the journey (1830: II, pp. 92–4).
    Secondly, Pufendorf makes explicit the result entailed by Grotius'
innovation. To say that property cannot belong in the same manner and
in whole to more than one person is to deny that common ownership is a
form of property. A possession may belong to several persons in different
ways, each having a different degree or kind of control over it: the rights
of commonwealth, landlord and tenant for example (4.4.2). Property may
be held in several, each with his distinct portion, but it can not be held
in common: 'many Persons may, even in the same way, hold the same
thing, yet not in whole, but each according to his Determinate Share'.
With this consummate definition the conceptual change initiated by
Grotius is firmly and unequivocally endorsed. The notion that property

is, *ipso facto*, private property passes from here into eighteenth-century Europe through the widespread use and republication of the writings of Grotius and Pufendorf. In his magisterial *Commentaries on the Laws of England*, Blackstone, in the mid-eighteenth century, reiterates that 'the right of property' is 'that sole and despotic dominion which one man claims and exercises over the external things of the world, in the total exclusion of the right of any other individual in the universe' (II.I.I). Barbeyrac's notes on Pufendorf refer the reader to Locke's repudiation of this conceptual collapse of property into private property and reassertion of the concept of common property (4.4.2–3n). He declares that 'Our Author Pufendorf gives us a Notion of a particular kind of property, rather than a general one, consider'd in opposition to an universal Community of Goods.'

Although Pufendorf and Locke disagree radically on the concept of property, they share many of the conventional assumptions concerning natural law. The preservation of mankind is the fundamental law of nature (2.3.14). Pufendorf denies, as does Locke, that the preservation of oneself *and* others is unnatural and that self-preservation is natural (2.3.16). This argument, and many others, is directed against Hobbes. Hobbes' premiss is that self-preservation is natural to man and the preservation of mankind 'artificial'. Therefore, political society, established for the preservation of mankind, is against nature (1651: 2.2.5; 1642: 2.17). Pufendorf continues the traditional natural law belief that political society is, in a sense, natural to man and is not radically discontinuous with the pre-political state of nature (2.3.6, 16). In order to substantiate this assumption Pufendorf seeks to disprove Hobbes' description of the pre-political state of man as one in which '*every Man hath naturally a Right to everything*' and, 'from the exercise of this *Right* there must needs arise a War of every Man against every Man, a state very unfit for the Preservation of Mankind' (3.5.2).

Pufendorf begins his riposte by considering two points: how obligations that are not natural arise in virtue of some act, and how other persons come to have rights (3.5.1). Whenever 'there is produced an *Obligation* in one Man, there immediately springs up a correspondent *Right* in another ...who can either fairly require it, or at least fairly receive it of me', but the contrary is not true. A magistrate, for example, has a right to punish criminals, but the criminal is not under an obligation to undergo it. The asymmetry of rights and obligations can be explained by distinguishing two types of rights. A right in the strict sense is 'a Power or Aptitude to *have* any thing' and it is always correlative with an obligation. However, there is not always or necessarily an obligation correlative with a right 'of *doing* any thing'. A right to have something thus correlates with either a negative service duty to abstain or a positive service duty to provide. It follows that Hobbes' right of every man to everything is not a right at all. 'For 'tis ridiculous Trifling to call that power a *Right*, which should we attempt to exercise, all other Men have an equal *Right* to obstruct or prevent us' (3.5.3).

This fails to answer Hobbes' argument. Barbeyrac notes that two ship-wrecked men could be washed upon a plank which could not save them both. Each has a right to it, and 'to thrust off his Companion', and there is 'no Obligation to answer each other' (3.5.1n). The same sort of case would arise if we all attempted, say, to exercise our right to a public park at the same time. However, Pufendorf proceeds to use his correlativity thesis to describe man's situation 'antecedent to any Human Deed' (3.5.3). Men have a power of using things, just as any animal has. This 'turns into a proper Right, when it creates this moral Effect in other Persons, that they shall not hinder him in the free Use of these Conveniences, and shall themselves forbear to use them without his Consent' (3.5.3). For such a right and obligation to be created, 'their Consent, either express or pre-sumptive' is required. Therefore, it is an analytic feature of a right to have something that it both correlates with an obligation and is created by an agreement. Pufendorf is quick to block the radical consequence, which his reply to Hobbes seems to imply, that rights of property have no higher sanction than the laws which men consent to in entering political society. To give conventional rights of property a natural foundation, he stresses that there is a natural right, with correlative obligations, which applies to whatever conventional rights of property are introduced (3.5.3):

a Right to all Things, antecedent to any Human Deed, is not to be understood *exclusively*, but *indefinitely* only; that is, we must not imagine one may engross all to himself, and *exclude* the rest of Mankind; but only that Nature has not *defined*, or determined, what portion of things shall belong to one, what to another, till they shall agree to divide her stores amongst 'em, by such allotments and divisions.

Before the introduction of private property by agreement, men are in a 'negative community' (4.4.2).

things are said to be negatively common, as consider'd before any human Act or Agreement had declared them to belong to one rather than to another. In the same sense, things thus consider'd are said to be *No Body's*, rather negatively, than privatively, *i.e.* that they are not yet assigned to any particular Person, not that they are incapable of being so assign'd. They are likewise term'd Things that lie free for any taker.

Pufendorf agrees with Grotius that the world belongs originally to no one and is open to all. This crucial starting-point, which differentiates Pufen-dorf's theory from the theories of Suarez and Locke, is the consequence of Pufendorf's acceptance of Grotius' definition of property. Pufendorf differs from Grotius in arguing that any right in things must be conventional, not natural. His statement that private property is not yet established, but can be established, is a reply to Filmer's criticism of Grotius. Filmer points out that it is contradictory to say that natural law prescribes community at one time and private property at another (p. 274). Pufendorf's reply is that natural law prescribes neither. He says that Filmer is mistaken in supposing that God granted Adam a right of private dominion. Because 'Property denotes an Exclusion of the Right of others to the thing enjoyed' it cannot 'be understood, 'till the World was furnished with more than one Inhabitant' (4.4.3).[9] Rather, God gave man 'an indefinite Dominion, not formally possess'd, but absolutely allowed; not actual, but potential'. This indefinite and natural right is the one which he first introduces in his discussion of Hobbes' right. It is indefinite in the sense that it applies to and underpins whatever form of property is agreed upon. Prior to this there is no property; only negative community, which is permitted, but not prescribed, by natural law. Since the only kind of property Pufendorf's terminology is capable of expressing is private property, he cannot but be sure that the agreement to institute property will serve to justify and to provide divine sanction for prevailing private property relations.

Pufendorf's reply to Filmer is thus that, although God did not *give* Adam private dominion, God sanctions conventional private dominion (4.4.4):

the Grant of Almighty God, by which he gave Mankind the use of earthly Provisions, was not the immediate Cause of Dominion, as this is directed towards other men, and with relation to them takes Effect to abstain. . .but that Dominion necessarily presupposeth some human Act, and some Covenant, either tacit or express.

Barbeyrac comments that this is to end up with a result similar to Filmer's and to miss the crucial point, which Locke makes, that God gave all men an inclusive right to use earthly provisions. 'But Mr. *Lock*, who has confuted that Book *Patriarcha* in an *English Work*, . . .answers judiciously. . . That he [God] gave him [Adam] no property over these living Creatures to possess them as his own, but as in a common Right with all Mankind' (4.4.4n).

Pufendorf is not unaware of the radical break that he and Grotius effect from the Scholastic concepts of common and private dominion. In 1674 Johann Strauch published his *Dissertation on the Sovereignty of the Seas*, in which he comments on Grotius' justification of the right of the Dutch to engage in East India trade, *The Freedom of the Seas*. Strauch revives the distinction which Grotius collapses. God gave to mankind a potential property or moral power to take and use, which he calls property in the first instance (*in actu primo*). This is analytically connected to property in the second instance (*in actu secundo*) which a person has as the result of coming to possess a thing, thus actualising his potential property.

Strauch illustrates the way in which these two kinds of rights are linked together with an analogy to inheritance (1.8). A man who stands to inherit something can be said to have a right to it and thus possess potential dominion over it as his due. Once he inherits it he actualises his potential dominion and it comes to be his own. Of course there are important dis-analogies between mankind's common dominion and the right to inherit as well. Pufendorf's consideration of this account brings out a termin-ological confusion which is prone to arise when these two competing concepts of property are discussed.

He denies that potential dominion is property or a right, as indeed he must if he is to be consistent with his definition of property. On the death of a testator, his goods are said to pass immediately to his heir and so are his property. Prior to that they are the property of the testator and the heir cannot be said to possess a right to them because he may, and often does, change his will at any time (4.4.10). The presence of a will prior to the testator's death creates a 'fiction' of dominion in the heir, but not true dominion. Thus, the heir's claim right to his due is reduced to either an actual right to his own (on the death of the testator), or a fiction of a right to what is, in fact and in law, the property of the testator. The conclusion is roundly drawn that property entails actual possession, or has purchase over only one's own:

And hence too, amongst Persons who live only under the Law of Nature, which is for the most part unacquainted with these *Fictions* introduced by civil Consti-tutions, there will be no admittance to any *potestative Possession* as opposed to actual; nor will the bare Right and power of acquiring Possession obtain the name of Possession it self.

Pufendorf appears to think that the notion of private property as the necessary actualisation of common property rests on a confusion of three distinct cases: a power to acquire an exclusive right, the possession and use of an exclusive right, and holding an exclusive right 'without Opera-tion or Exercise' (4.4.10). Holding an exclusive right is conflated with, according to Pufendorf, the power to possess a right and therefore this power is mistakenly called a right. This is like confusing the *capacity* to become musical with being actually musical but not exercising that *ability*. Pufendorf is wrong, and a bit disingenuous, in imputing this confusion to his adversaries. Nonetheless, the locutions which signal these distinctions are potentially confusing and it is therefore necessary that they be clarified.

In Suarez's and Locke's theories, since all men have a right to possess something, all men can be said to have a right *to* something. Also, in addition to saying a proprietor has a right *in* his possessions, one com-monly says that he has a right to his possessions. What is standardly meant is that he has a claim to his possessions and to exclude others from them, even if he is not using them. 'A right to', in these two cases, refers to the two quite distinct states of affair that Pufendorf says are conflated. One could define property as 'a right to any thing', as Locke does in the *Essay* (4.3.18), and by that mean to refer to both cases, as Leibniz insists Locke does in this passage (1916: 4.3.18). To prise apart the double reference, yet univocal sense (a moral power), one would have to ask for the referent of the right. The private proprietor's right *to* refers to what is his own; the common proprietor's to what is his due. One marks actual possession, the other potential. The conceptual simplification of Grotius and Pufendorf dissolves the distinction by proscribing a right to one's due. Locke exhibits the distinction with his locutions 'right to', signifying one's due, and 'property in', signifying one's own, but he also accedes to the conventional practice of using 'right to' to refer to one's own. The sense of 'a right' as a moral power is the same in 'a right to', in both sorts of reference, as well as in 'a right in'.

5

In 1609, England, under James I (1603–25), began to move against the powerful Dutch herring fisheries. A Privy Council proclamation was issued demanding that all foreigners obtain licences to fish in the adjacent seas (Fulton, 1911: pp. 755–6). A series of sea skirmishes ensued, followed by diplomatic missions to England. Grotius came to England as a Dutch Envoy in 1613 (Knight, 1925: pp. 137–49). Grotius' *The Freedom of the Seas* was seen as the basis of the Dutch case and thus was attacked by English pamphleteers. The first retort was fired by William Welwood (1578–1622) in Title XVII of his book, *An Abridgement of all Sea Laws* (1613). But, far the most famous reply to Grotius in England was *Of the Dominion or Ownership of the Seas in Two Books* (1636), by John Selden (1584–1654). Selden composed the work in 1618, but it remained unpublished until Charles I urged him, in 1635, to prepare it for publication in order to justify reactivation of the 1609 proclamation in the light of growing Dutch protest (De Pauw, 1965: pp. 12–13; Fulton, 1911: pp. 365–74). The purpose of the book is twofold. In the first book, Selden tries to show that the sea is not common to all men, but is susceptible of private dominion or property. It is maintained in the second book that the Crown of Great Britain enjoys lordship of the circumfluent and surrounding ocean (Fletcher, 1969: p. 10).

Chapter four of Book One contains Selden's account of the origin of property. He presents a definition of property (*dominium*) which compromises both common and private ownership (1652: p. 16).

Dominion, which is the right of using, enjoying, alienating and free disposing, is either common to all men as possessors without distinction, or Private and peculiar onely to some; that is to say, distributed and set apart by any particular states, Princes, or persons whatsoever, in such a manner that others are excluded, or at least in some sort, barred from a libertie of use and enjoyment.

It is a clear repudiation, for obvious reasons, of Grotius' restriction of *dominium* to private property. The title of the chapter is, 'Of Dominion, both Common to all and Private'. This account of common property, as belonging to all in the same manner, (as well as Grotius' account of community as belonging to no one) is rejected by Filmer (pp. 63–6), but endorsed by Locke and termed 'property' (1.23). Resistance to Grotius' conceptual delimitation is no less firmly supported by Richard Cumberland.

6

Cumberland wrote *A Treatise on the Laws of Nature* (1672) as 'A Confutation of the Elements of Mr. Hobbes's Philosophy' (p. 39). His methodology is similar to Locke's in many respects. We have already seen that God has divine dominion from his right of creation (above, p. 41). This is said to be a refutation of Hobbes' claim that God has a right to do anything in virtue of his irresistible power (1727: p. 321). As with Locke, God's dominion is consistent with man's '*Subordinate Right* to the use of many Things, and of human Aid' (p. 319). Cumberland's natural rights are, like Locke's, deduced from natural law. Once natural law is discovered, the actions necessary to achieve the end it prescribes can be inferred, and then the rights to use the things necessary to perform these actions can be inferred (pp. 313–15). This practical syllogistical method is employed throughout the treatise. Natural law prescribes preservation and so it prescribes 'a right to the life of this day' and 'a right to its necessary preserving Causes, *viz.* A limited and divided use of things and human labour' (p. 66–7). Or, he suggests, more briefly (p. 315):

There being a natural Law to procure the Common Happiness of All, there is given a natural Law, to establish and preserve, to particular Persons, Properties in those Things, which are evidently necessary to the Happiness of Individuals, as well as in Persons and their Actions necessary to mutual Assistance, as in other things.

The last step in the analysis, and thus the first step in the performance, is therefore a right over things, and this Cumberland calls 'property (*proprietas*) and dominion (*dominium*)' (p. 313). The reason for two terms is that Cumberland does not wish to be misunderstood as an advocate of private property only (p. 315):

I chose to use those indefinite Words *some kind of Property or Dominion*, because I readily *acknowledge*, That Nature does not always discover it to be necessary, that such kind of Property as consists in an *intire* Division of Things should be established; all that is *essential* to true Property or Dominion, is That any one should have a right secured by law, to possess or dispose of certain Advantages in a thing, for *Example*, an undivided Field, which we use and enjoy in Common with others, and from which others have no Right to exclude us.

This is a classic restatement of common property, consisting in an inclusive right to possess. Cumberland is nonetheless clearly aware that the concept of property has lost its fixed meaning in common use. 'If any one will contend, that this word *Property*, or *Dominion*, is *improperly* us'd in this Case, I will not dispute with him about *words*, being solicitous about the *Thing* only' (p. 315). He immediately adds that Grotius would not say that this is property *(dominium)*. He goes on to stress that he means a claim right not to be denied things necessary for preservation, and that this is a natural right (pp. 315–16). Therefore, the '*Dominion of men*' refers to 'those Things which are ours, either by a common Right of All, or our own particular Right' (p. 316).

7

The discourse in which Locke writes contains two concepts of property. One is restricted to private property as it is adopted by Grotius, Filmer and Pufendorf. The other is wider, comprising common and private property, as in Selden, or two related kinds, as in Suarez's and Locke's right *to* and right *in*. This serves to substantiate and to make specific Macpherson's claim that the restriction of the concept of property to private property 'goes back no further than the seventeenth century' (1975: p. 124). The simplification occurs in Grotius. The reason why he constructed it was to win through to the conclusion that the sea belongs to no one and is open to all, thus vindicating Dutch sea trade. Macpherson offers another form of explanation for this conceptual change, different from the teleological one I have presented. He suggests that 'it can be seen to be the product of the new relations of emergent capitalist society' (p. 124). If this were true, then there would seem to be a tension in Macpherson's analysis of the seventeenth century at this point. The authors who adopt the private concept, Grotius, Filmer and Pufendorf, integrate it into their absolutist theories. The author who adheres to the common concept most emphatically is Locke. The implication of Macpherson's explanation is that emergent capitalist society found the clearest reflection of its central concept, and so its ideology, in Sir Robert Filmer's *Patriarcha*.

The background to chapter five of the Second Treatise

1

When Suarez comes to consider how mankind's dominion in common might be individuated in pre-political society, he does not see any problem. He simply assumes that, 'without prejudice to the rectitude of their conduct, men could, in that state of innocence, take possession of, and divide amongst themselves, certain things, especially those which are moveable and necessary for ordinary use' (2.14.13). *In The Defence of Catholic and Apostolic Faith,* he calls this natural and exclusive use right 'peculiar property' (*dominium peculiare*), and says that it is the sort of right a man naturally comes to have in the fruit he gathers (3.2.14; cf. *Works,* III, 1.v.8.18). The right correlates with the natural law duty to abstain from that which belongs to another (2.14.14). Peculiar property is distinguished both from mankind's common property, which it completes, and from private property (*dominium* modified by *proprietas*), which is introduced by agreement in the transition to political society (2.14.16).

2

In contrast to Suarez's insouciance, Grotius explains in detail how his natural common which belongs to no one, but is open to all, is used. Man's historical use right in things attaches to whatever a person first lays hold of (*arripere*) (2.2.2.1; cf. Olivecrona, 1974a: p. 215). The right correlates with a negative duty on the part of others to abstain: 'no man could justly take from another, what he had first taken to himself'. It is derived from Grotius' irreducible concept of that which belongs to a person (*suum*) (1.17.2.1):

A Man's life is his own by Nature (not indeed to destroy it, but to preserve it) and so is his Body, his Limbs, his Reputation, his Honour, and his Actions.

It follows from the fact that man's life belongs to him to preserve that he has a right, 'to certain Acts whereby those Things may be procured, without which he cannot conveniently subsist' (2.2.18). This includes the right to defend with force what one has taken (1.1.10.7). Thus, taking and possessing things, and agreements or acts of the will, are just and natural in so far as they are necessary to preservation. What is acquired in this manner becomes part of the *suum*. The *suum* defines what is naturally one's own and this is protected by the natural principle of justice; 'the Abstaining from that which is anothers' (prol. 8). This negative and individualistic concept is the basis of society. Political society differs only in the replacement of man's use right by private property (1.2.1.5):

the Design of Society is, that every one Should quietly enjoy his own, with the Help, and by the united Force of the whole Community. It may be easily conceived, that the Necessity of having Recourse to violent Means for Self-Defence, might have taken Place, even tho' what we call Property (*dominium*) had never been introduced. For our Lives, Limbs and Liberties, had still been properly our own, and could not have been, (without manifest Injustice) invaded. So also, to have made use of Things that were then in common, and to have consumed them, as far as Nature required, had been the Right of the first possessor: And if any one had attempted to hinder him from so doing, he had been guilty of a real injury. But since *Property* has been regulated, either by Law or Custom, this is more easily understood.

The progression from this pre-political state to political society is historical, as we have seen (above, p. 31). If men had been content to live in simplicity and mutual affection there would be no reason for entering into a polity (2.2.2.1). However, men soon increased their knowledge and this could be put to either good or evil uses. Agriculture and grazing developed, men became crafty rather than just, and the age of giants, given over to murder, rivalry and violence, followed. The Flood ended the age of giants and ushered in an age of pleasure, incest and adultery (2.2.2.2). Ambition, 'a less ignoble vice', emerged and it became the major cause of disharmony in the next age (2.2.2.3). For Grotius, as for Locke, vice is a product of history. To avoid disharmony, division of things took place. Men divided into separate countries and private property was introduced, first of moveables, and then of immoveable things (2.2.2.4).

There are two reasons why ambition and the desire to avoid disharmony motivated man to introduce private property. First, due to ambition, men wished to live 'in a more commodious and more agreeable manner' (2.2.2.4). 'Labour and industry' were necessary to achieve this end, and some employed it on one thing, others on another. This inclines towards, but does not necessitate, abandonment of use rights. The most important reason was, 'the Defect of Equity and Love, whereby a just Equality would not have been observed, either in their Labour, or in the Consumption of their fruits and Revenues'. The lack of justice and equity is a direct result of Grotius' use right and concept of justice. If a man makes something and does not use it immediately, it belongs to no one and so is open to acquisition by others. Since there is no natural principle of justice other than to abstain from that which belongs to another, there is no way to avoid disharmony, short of introducing private property. Grotius' assertion that there is injustice with respect to labour and consumption presupposes that men have some sort of claim to the products of their labour. However, he cannot articulate a satisfactory natural principle within his framework of a use right and a duty to abstain. The disharmony which arises, and motivates man to institute private property, results from the way in which Grotius defines man's natural condition. Already, the problem which Locke sets himself to solve in chapter five of the Second Treatise is present.

Grotius explains the agreement to institute property in two steps. First, he maintains that the institution could not have come about naturally, merely by an act of the mind of any particular individual. One 'could not possibly guess what others designed to appropriate to themselves, that he might abstain from it; and besides, several might have had a Mind to the same thing, at the same Time' (2.2.2.5). These problems did not arise in the application of a use right because actual possession was the criterion for the right and for abstinence on the part of others. Private property, on the other hand, entails the right to exclude others when one is not using the thing. Therefore, the institution of private property 'resulted from a certain Compact and Agreement, either expressly, as by a Division, or else tacitly, as by Seizure'. Again, seizure does not now create conditions for the application of a use right. The compact included the proviso that what was not divided should become the property (*proprietas*) of the first possessor. Thus, private property is based on agreement, is a fixed property in land, is ownership independent of use, and it includes the right to rent and sell (1.1.5). It is, therefore, the same, full exclusive right discussed in the last chapter that one has over one's liberty (entailing the right to sell oneself into slavery), as well as his goods.

Since private property does not arise immediately from an individual act, it appears to fall outside the natural *suum*, and therefore to have no higher status than other conventional legal and promissory practices. Grotius blocks the potentially radical implication of this with a distinction originally made by Suarez (2.14.14; cf. Skinner, 1978: II, pp. 153–4). Things are said to fall under natural law either 'properly' or 'reductively'. Things which are either directly prescribed or proscribed by natural law relate to it in the proper sense. Other things fall under it permissibly, or by reduction, 'as some Things, we have now said, are called Just, because they have no Injustice in them; and sometimes by the wrong use of the Word, those things which our reason declares to be honest, or comparatively good, tho' they are not enjoined on us, are said to belong to this

Natural Law' (1.1.10.3). Thus, some arrangements that are permitted, but not enjoined by natural law, come to be backed by natural law once they are introduced. Private property is a member of this class (1.1.10.4):

> We must further observe, that this Natural Law does not only respect such things as depend not upon Human Will, but also many Things which are consequent to some Act of that Will. Thus, Property [*dominium*] for Instance, as now in use, was introduced by Man's Will, and being once admitted, this law of Nature informs us, that it is a wicked Thing to take away from any Man, against his Will, what is properly his own.

The distinction enables Grotius to explain how community and private property are consistent with natural law. Natural law enjoins abstinence from that which belongs to another, but it does not define what is another's. In the state of nature, therefore, men have a historical use right, and what one lays hold of is one's own to use. Once private property is introduced, there is a new definition of what is one's own, and one's rights over it. Natural law permits either, but, once one is instituted, the natural duty to abstain applies to it. Filmer ridicules this distinction, imputing to Grotius that natural law enjoins both community and private property (p. 266), and thus concludes that he has made, as we have seen, natural law self-contradictory (p. 283). Therefore, what man comes to acquire, by acts of the will, in political society, becomes part of the *suum* and this is what society is established to protect.

The constriction of rights to exclusive rights over one's own entails a similar restriction of justice to respecting and protecting the rights of others: 'the Abstaining from that which is another's, and the Restitution of what we have of another's, or of the Profit we have made by it, the Obligation of fulfilling Promises, the Reparation of a Damage done through our own Default, and the Merit of Punishment among men' (prol. 8). Grotius is aware that he has collapsed the concept of justice, 'to render to every man his due' (*suum cuique tribuere*), into solely the protection of one's own. To explain why one's due is not a part of justice, he divides rights into 'perfect' and 'imperfect' kinds. A perfect right is a 'faculty' over one's own, whereas an imperfect right refers to one's due and, as such, is not a right, but an 'aptitude' (1.1.4). A perfect right is said to be a moral faculty because to possess a right means that one can exercise sovereignty or control over the referent of the right. This element of sovereignty is the defining characteristic of a right. An aptitude or imperfect right lacks this element of sovereignty. It signifies that the agent requests, or should be permitted, that to which the imperfect right refers; but he does not control or exercise sovereignty over it (1.1.5–7). A perfect right is, in modern terminology, an 'active' right, whereas an imperfect right is a 'passive' right (Lyons, 1970: pp. 45–70).

To have a passive right is to have a right to be given or permitted something by someone else, while to have an active right is to have the right to do something oneself. If all rights are construed as passive, then to have a right is simply the recognition that one is in a position to be the recipient of positive or negative duties of others. Active rights theorists deny that all there is to an assertion of a right is the occasion for the activation of a duty, or set of duties, of others. This seems to diminish, if not to extinguish, the sovereignty and element of moral choice which it is the point of the assertion of a right to convey. To have a right, according to an active theory, is more than to be a recipient of certain duties, it is to exercise one's sovereignty and so to impose those duties, in some way, on others. A passive right expresses that a person is in a position where certain duties of others obtain. An active right expresses that a person is sovereign over a certain part of his moral world.

Grotius' distinction between faculties and aptitudes renders all rights as active. Locke and Suarez would agree with this, at least with respect to rights which are termed 'properties'. The crucial difference is that Grotius denies, and Locke and Suarez claim, that a right can have purchase over something that is not one's own. Both Suarez and Locke insist that each man has a claim right to his due, and not simply to his own; an active right to use the things necessary for preservation. Armed with his distinction between rights and aptitudes, Grotius criticises Aristotle's classification of justice and replaces it with his own. Expletive justice is true justice, corresponding to perfect rights, and consists in the protection of private property, contracts and the restitution of goods. Distributive justice, since it corresponds to one's due and imperfect rights, is not a part of justice (1.1.8). On this basis, Grotius denounces the theory which Suarez and Locke put forward (2.17.3):

But from a mere Aptitude or Fitness, which is improperly called a Right, and belongs to distributive Justice, arises no true Property, and consequently no obligation to make Restitution; because a man cannot call that his own, which he is only capable of, or fit for.

Grotius' account of rights and justice leads to a revision of the nature of charity. One exception to abstaining from that which belongs to another is incorporated into the original agreement to institute private property. If a person is in dire need, he may be said to have the original use right and, therefore, use another's property (2.2.6.2). The reason is not, and cannot be, that the needy have a claim to their due. Indeed, he remonstrates against theologians who describe charity as a positive duty. 'That sentiment is not founded on what some allege, that the Proprietor is obliged by the Rules of Charity to give of his Substance to those that want it' (2.2.6.4). Rather, 'the Property of Goods is supposed to have been established with this favorable Exception, that in such cases one might enter again upon the Rights of the Primitive Community'. Charity is thus a negative duty and need only be observed once the needy have proven that they are in a state of absolute necessity. It is necessary to dig common land down to the chalk line before one can use another's well (2.2.7).

Grotius introduces one final distinction in his rights theory which establishes an unlimited sovereign. Rights of individuals, either natural or acquired, are 'private' and 'inferior', and they tend 'to the particular Advantage of each individual' (1.1.6). The right of the sovereign is 'eminent' and 'superior' and it is exercised 'over the Persons and Estates of all its Members for the common benefit, and therefore it excells the former'. The sovereign's right is greater than that of a master or father and, therefore, 'a King has a greater Right in the Goods of his Subjects for the public advantage, than the Proprietors themselves'. A society in which there is such a sovereign is a perfect society (2.5.23). In his chapter on resistance, 'Of a War made by Subjects against their Superiors' (1.4), Grotius discusses the status, in a commonwealth, of the natural right men had in the state of nature to protect themselves from attack. Men retain this right with respect to other private individuals, but not with respect to the sovereign: 'those who are invested with the sovereign Power, cannot lawfully be resisted' (1.4.7).

There are two ways in which Grotius' theory of rights and justice serves to confirm the sovereign's absolute and unlimited nature. Devoid of any claim rights to one's due, either natural or acquired, the subjects have no rights on the basis of which they could resist an unjust ruler. Second, because property is conventional, the subjects have no natural principle of justice in terms of which they could judge and criticise the prevailing distribution of property. The distribution of property which is the unintended consequence of the concatenation of individual acts of will is just because it is based on the *suum*. Thus, whatever is the extant pattern of property is just and sanctioned by natural law. The sovereign has a duty to protect this only, by enforcing expletive justice, even though he has a superior right to override it. Without a natural principle of one's due and a claim right to impose the duty on the sovereign to enforce it, the *status quo* is validated and placed beyond question. Like Nozick in *Anarchy, State and Utopia*, Grotius leaves the subjects, with only their exclusive rights and negative duties, to cultivate their private interests: 'It is not then against the Nature of Human Society, for every one to provide for, and take care of himself, so [long as] it be not to the Prejudice of another's Right' (1.2.1; cf. Olivecrona, 1974a: p. 214).

3

Pufendorf develops his theory with point-by-point reference to Grotius. Like Grotius, he grounds his rights in the natural concept of what is one's own (*suum*). It comprises one's life, limbs, body, liberty, virtue, reputation and, 'so it must be supposed to spread itself thru' all those Compacts or Institutions, by which the Property of anything is made over to us' (3.1.1; cf. Olivecrona, 1974a: pp. 215–16; 1974b: pp. 223–4). He continues the convention that the natural law to abstain from that which belongs to another attaches to and protects the *suum*. He puts particular emphasis on this commonplace assumption, shared by Locke, in order to highlight the uniqueness of Hobbes' position. Hobbes tells us, 'that by a natural State is understood that Condition by which we are conceiv'd to live singly, or out of Society; and that this is a state of War' (2.2.5). 'But', he stresses, 'now here's a great Impropriety committed, the opposing a state of Nature to a Social Life; for those who live in a State of Nature both may and ought, and frequently do, consent to live socially.' However, it is not quite the same as Locke's unequivocal assertion that men, to be men, cannot but live in society, nor is it Locke's notion of a society as a state in which positive duties to oneself and to others obtain. Sociableness, for Pufendorf, as for Grotius, is characterised essentially by the negative duty of respecting what belongs to others (2.3.15).

Although there is a natural precept to abstain from others' things, there is no natural definition of what is one's own or another's, except for the items comprising the natural *suum*. The state of nature is a negative community, belonging to no one and open to all, but it lacks Grotius' 'first taking' criterion for calling something naturally one's own. Pufendorf departs from Grotius here in supposing that any concept of one's own, with respect to external things, is conventional. It follows that, if men are not to starve in the state of nature, there must be some sort of agreement about what can be legitimately one's goods. This innovation is, of course, entailed by Pufendorf's anti-Hobbes thesis that rights to have something correlate with duties and are necessarily founded on agreements. Therefore, at this point in his explanation of the origin of property, he introduces 'the first agreement'; 'what any person had seiz'd out of the common store of things, or out of the Fruits of them, with design to apply to his private Occasions, none else should rob him of' (4.4.5). Pufendorf agrees with Grotius that first taking entitles a man to a use right over the possession, not full property.

Pufendorf expostulates against Grotius' conviction that first taking is a natural criterion of what is one's own and so does not require an agreement (4.4.5). To do so, he borrows three arguments from *The Principles of Justice and Decorum* (1651), a brilliant and partially sympathetic consideration of Hobbes by Lambert Velthuysen (1622–85). First, all men are by nature equal and so must have an equal right to earthly provisions. Since there is no natural principle of distribution, any division must be based on a pact. This neatly begs the question and demonstrates only that a pact is one method of assignment. The second argument is ingenious and it helps to explain why Locke chose to reject 'first taking', whether natural or conventional. If first taking is the condition for the application of a right to exclude others, it follows that a person in dire need could conceivably be barred from things necessary for his preservation. But, according to Grotius, the right to use another's provisions, in the case of absolute necessity, is an exception built into the agreement to institute private property. Thus, prior to this agreement, it is possible that a man could perish as a consequence of the operation of natural rights. This contradicts natural law, which enjoins preservation, and so first taking cannot be a natural criterion. First taking, therefore, must be based on a pact which includes an exception in the case of dire need. A framework of natural positive duties to preserve oneself and others, enforced with natural claim rights, Barbeyrac protests, renders this problem superfluous (4.4.5n.5). Velthuysen's third reproof is that first taking is arbitrary: Why not first sighting an object? First possession turns possession into a race in which the slower are disadvantaged. Pufendorf stigmatises Grotius' account in these terms: 'in a state where everything is seized upon by the man who can get hold of it, it is staying much too late to wait until precisely the right moment' (4.6.2). Pufendorf's summation is that any criterion seems to prejudice man's natural equality, so consent is required to legitimate the use of first taking:

we can not apprehend how a bare corporal Act, such as Seizure is, should be able to prejudice the Right and Power of others, unless their consent be added to confirm it; that is, unless a Covenant intervene.

He also adds the qualification that it must be first taking with the clear intent to use.

Pufendorf now takes his natural men through a historical series of difficulties and quarrels, requiring complementary compacts, to the eventual establishment of private property. First, 'there could not but arise almost infinite Clashings, from the desire of many Persons to the same Thing, which was not able to satisfy them all at once; it being the Nature of the greatest part of what the world affords, to be incapable of serving more than one Man at the same time' (4.4.6). Further, most things require labour and cultivation to be of use for nourishment and clothing. With only a use right, labour-created goods which are not immediately used became common and open to all. This led to 'quarrels and Hostilities' and to the same injustice that Grotius pinpointed:

But here it was very inconvenient that a Person, who had taken no pains about a thing, should have an equal Right to it with another, by whose Industry it was either first rais'd, or exactly wrought and fram'd, to render it of farther service.

To solve these difficulties Pufendorf introduces a second 'tacit compact' conferring exclusive rights over moveables and necessary immoveables, such as houses. The compact instituted either private property or 'positive community'. Positive community is like private property in being exclusive, but it signifies that the goods belong to 'many persons together', rather than to one. He immediately explains that the positive commoners do not have common rights over the common. 'Now since none of these Commoners has a Right extending itself to the whole thing, but only to a part of it, though suppos'd to remain undivided; it is manifest that no one person can, by his own Right, dispose of the thing entirely, but only according to his fix'd Proportion' (4.4.2). This restriction of communism to property in several, omitting property in common, is, as we have seen, a consequence of his rights theory. The quotation also embodies the presupposition that property entails the right to alienate. This is an analytic feature of the concept of property for Grotius and Pufendorf: 'The Power and Privileges then of alienating our own Possessions, or of conveying them to others, ariseth from the nature of *full Property*' (4.9.1). For this reason a use right is not called 'property' by Grotius and Pufendorf. Alienation is not an analytic feature of the concept of property for Locke and Suarez since men cannot alienate the world which is their property in common. It follows that any resolution concerning the whole of the positive common, held in several, requires 'the Consent and Act of each Commoner' (4.4.2). Selden is then reprimanded for confounding negative and positive community in his commentary on Grotius when, in fact, he uses a different kind of positive common (property in common).

For some time land remained negatively common, with only a use right invoked to exclude others during periods of occupation. Eventually, a third agreement was made to bring land under the rubric of property. There was an 'express Agreement' that the land of 'Manurers and Improvers' should become their private property, and 'that what remain'd should pass into the Property of those who would afterwards fix upon it' (4.4.6; cf. 4.6.1–2). Pufendorf invokes Aristotle's argument against Plato's positive communism to corroborate his conclusion. The part of Aristotle's analysis which he emphasises is the injustice which is said to follow from the inequality between one man's labour to produce a good and another man's right to use the product (4.4.6; cf. 4.4.8): 'If they do not share equally in enjoyments and toils, those who labour much and get little will necessarily complain of those who labour little and receive or consume much' (*Pol*: 1263a12–15). The difficulty which gives rise to the need to introduce private property is, as with Grotius, the absence of a right tied to labour. Following Grotius, he says that this constitutes an injustice and the only solution which his rights theory proffers is private property. However, he demurs to Grotius' belief that it was 'possible for all Mankind to meet in one place' to consent to the division (4.6.2). Rather, it is to be understood that, 'when Mankind first began to separate into many families, distinct *dominions* were settled by Division; After this Division, he is said originally to acquire a thing, lying void and without a Possessor, who happens to be the most early *Occupant* of it' (4.6.2).

Pufendorf takes himself to have shown that private property is the solution to quarrels and wars which necessarily break out in a state of community. He is thus in a position to make his ideological point, against Sir Thomas More and Campanella, that, contrary to the 'vulgar Saying', that 'Mine and Thine are the Cause of all Wars and Quarrels in the World', the 'Distinction of *Mine* and *Thine* was rather introduc'd to prevent all Contention' (4.4.7). Hostilities and strife today have no other cause than 'the Advance of Men...aiming to break through those bounds of Mine and Thine'. Such an important institution is not to be left with no higher authority than positive law. Once men have decided to introduce private property, Pufendorf's rights theory leaving them no alternative, their natural, indefinite right is said to be made determinate in this form and to give divine sanction to private property (4.4.3). Also, the distinction between the 'proper' and 'reductive' dimensions of natural law is invoked and the natural precept to abstain from that which belongs to another now ratifies the institution of private property. 'Nor is it any absurdity to affirm, that the Obligation we lie under, not to invade the Goods of others, is coeval with [the] human Race', Pufendorf admonishes, 'And yet that Distinction of *mine* and *thine* was afterwards ordained' (4.4.14).

I therefore dissent from the assumption, generally held, but applied by Cabet, in *The Voyage of Icarus, a Philosophical and Social Novel* (1842), specifically to Pufendorf, that there is something inherently radical in construing property as conventional (p. 485). It is precisely because property is conventional for Grotius and Pufendorf that the *status quo* is validated. It is only with a natural standard of property to appeal to, that a radical can criticise and justify opposition to prevailing forms of property. The point is perhaps obvious but it should be borne in mind when considering Locke. The only way for a natural concept of property to be conservative would be for it to mirror the existing property relations. We have yet to see how Locke's theory of natural property unfolds, but his rejection of the rights theory in terms of which contemporary private property was conventionally legitimated signals his radical intention.

Although Pufendorf, like Grotius, goes on to establish a sovereign unhampered by subjects with natural rights to their due, he censures Grotius for his restrictive theory of justice. He accepts Grotius' distinction between 'perfect' and 'imperfect' rights, and notes that the standard way of asserting a perfect right is to say that a thing is claimed 'by his own right' (*suo jure*) (1.4.7). The difference between the two rights is really of degree and not of kind. Respect for perfect rights conduces 'to the very being' of society; imperfect rights to its 'well-being'. Therefore, imperfect rights, which refer to one's due, and not to one's own, correlate with duties in which 'there's less necessity of performing' and 'are left to every man's Conscience and modesty'. It is incorrect, therefore, to say they are not rights since they indicate but do not necessitate the performance of a duty.

Grotius failed to take into account Aristotle's distinction between universal and particular justice. Imperfect rights are rights appropriate to the realm of universal justice and this concerns the well-being of a commonwealth (1.78):

> When, then, we exhibit to another either Actions or Things due to him only by *imperfect* Right, or when we exercise towards another, Actions not coming under the head of strict Commerce, we are said to have Observed *general* or *Universal Justice*. As when a man supplies another with his Counsel, Goods, or Help, as he hath Need; or when he performs the offices of Piety, Reverence, Gratitude, Humanity or Beneficence towards those to whom he is in Duty bound to pay them.

When the subject is one's own, justice is particular and rights are perfect. Thus, both Grotius and Hobbes were mistaken in identifying all justice with particular or expletive justice; the 'keeping of faith and fulfilling of covenants' (1.7.13). Grotius' notion of rendering a person his due is not to give the person something new, but solely to return or to protect what is already his own. 'For example, a Man who hath borrowed a Book out of my Study, when he restores it, doth not properly increase my Study, but only fills up a Place made empty on his Account' (1.7.11). Universal justice, the sphere of imperfect rights, is properly called distributive justice, and this is a part of any society concerned with well-being. Distributive justice encompasses the apportioning of public rewards, titles, honours, offices, and public property, imperfectly due to subjects in accordance with their merit or need (1.7.11–12).

Both Grotius and Pufendorf concur in the judgment that exclusive rights are primary and that their distribution in a given society is just because it is the result of each individual's exercise of his liberty, either by physical acts or acts of the will in the form of contracts and agreements. The property thus acquired becomes part of one's own (*suum*) and it is the function of government to protect this through expletive justice. Grotius takes this to exhaust the justice required of the sovereign (which, of course, he may waive); whereas Pufendorf advances the further, non-necessary role of distributing certain goods in accordance with merit or need. These two theories of justice seem to exemplify the individualist and collectivist liberal theories of justice. What is significant in Pufendorf's theory, as in its liberal analogue, is the introduction of distributive justice on to a base of exclusive rights protected by expletive justice. The result is that distributive justice is, in most cases, as Nozick puts it, '*re*distributive' justice (1974: p. 168). A full blown distributive theory, on the other hand, begins with a principle of what is due to each, as Locke's does; property is distributed accordingly, and then this distribution is protected by expletive justice. The difference is that 'belonging to' in the inclusive sense of one's due, is primary; whereas the concepts of one's own and of exclusive rights are secondary and serve to put the distributive principle into effect. The principle of distribution thus determines the pattern of property; it does not simply exercise imperfect claims over a preexisting arrangement, as with Pufendorf.

Having reintroduced the classical view that justice is concerned with living well, in addition to living, Pufendorf shows how this leads to a different theory of charity. Private property was introduced, not only to extirpate the cause of war, but also to enable the 'dispensing more largely in the works of humanity and Beneficence' (2.6.5). Men are now able to exercise the virtue of liberality, whereas, in the state of nature, this would have been impossible with only a use right. Men thus have an imperfect and universal, positive duty to assist the needy; and the needy have an imperfect right to request aid. They have the right to ask an owner to hand over the necessary goods (2.6.6). Because there is a difference in degree, and not in kind, between an imperfect and perfect right, if help is not forthcoming, the needy may take the case to court and their imperfect right 'hardens' into a perfect one. If this is too lengthy, they may simply demand or take what is necessary.

4

There is a conspicuous absence of quarrels and hostilities in the state of nature posited by Selden. Working within the extended concept of property, as either inclusive or exclusive, Selden gives an historical account of the transition to private property. Private dominion was unknown in the 'golden days' and seems to have first appeared after the Flood with Noah and his sons (p. 19). After this, 'exchanges, buying and selling came into fashion' and Cain is said to 'first set bounds to fields'. At length 'came in private dominions (*dominia privata*)' by 'a consent of the whole body or universalities of mankind (by the mediation of something like a compact, which might bind their posterity)' (p. 21). He therefore disagrees with Grotius about the nature of the original community, but he does agree that natural law permitted either common (property) or private

dominion (p. 20). The resulting range of property available in a commonwealth is wider than that recognised by Grotius and Pufendorf. The agreement to introduce the institution of property includes three types: property
possessed individually, 'possessed in several' and 'expressly held in common' (p. 21). This third type, property in common, is inclusive and so
cannot be expressed with the terminology of Grotius' and Pufendorf's
rights theories. Selden does not explain how the commoners used their
common property, but apparently there was no contention, and the point
of introducing the three types of property was to facilitate a more refined
way of life (p. 22).

5

Cumberland, as we saw earlier (p. 79), employs the vocabulary of common
property. Unlike Selden, he shares with Locke the belief that the world is
mankind's natural property to use and, therefore, that each man has a
claim right to use it. Selden's concept of common property is that something belongs to more than one person, in the same manner, and, therefore, each has a liberty right to use it. That is, each commoner is permitted
to use it and cannot be excluded if he chooses to exercise his right, but he
is not under a duty to exercise it. He has a right in the sense of not being
under a duty not to use the common. Rights to public parks are inclusive
liberty rights of this sort. Locke and Cumberland both derive their natural
rights from natural law and so conclude that each man is under a duty to
exercise his inclusive right. A similar inclusive duty right is the legal right
to education in most Western countries.

Cumberland reduces all natural laws to one paramount duty (said to be
a utilitarian principle by Sidgwick (1906: p. 174)) (p. 16):

The Endeavour, to the utmost of our Power, of promoting the common Good of
the whole System of rational Agents, conduces, as far as in us lies, to the good of
every Part, in which our own Happiness, as that of a Part, is contained.

From this he infers that each man has an inclusive duty right to use the
world. The first step in individuation arises from the assumption, shared
by Grotius and Pufendorf, that the use of things is necessarily limited to
certain persons, times and places. 'Therefore, if right *Reason* enjoins,
That the use of things, or the *Services of men*, should be *Useful* to *all*
Men, it necessarily *enjoins*, That for a certain Time and Place, that use of
Things and of human Services should be limited to certain Persons' (p. 64).
It is said to follow that, 'a *Division* of Things, and of human Services, at
least for the time it may be of use to others, is necessary for the advantage
of all'. The exercise of an inclusive duty right entails an exclusive right in
the use of things necessary to preservation. This is an exclusive use right
and the land reverts to the common when use terminates. Such a natural

mode of individuation does not lead to contention because the agent has a natural maker's right in the product of his labour, analogous to God's right in the world (p. 320; above p. 41). Since the common good cannot be promoted unless one's life, health and strength is preserved, this particularisation of the common property is justified in virtue of being 'a means plainly necessary to that end'. Unlike Grotius, property is understood as a means to an end, and not as an end. In this manner the whole is preserved by preserving the parts, and the parts, 'particular Men', by the 'divided use of things and human Labour' (p. 65). Human labour is included on the understanding that one person cannot render a service to different persons, and in different places, at the same time. In this sense, it is like things. Another way in which 'property' (*proprietas*) is used differently by Cumberland, than by Grotius and Pufendorf, is that he calls this limited use right 'property'. As a result, he dissents from the view that property and community are mutually exclusive. Property, in the sense of a use right, is the means of distributing common property: 'Such *Division*, which is a kind of *Property*, after things are occupied and applied to uses truly necessary, is truly consistent with some Community.'

Cumberland concedes that this mode of use became inconvenient as population and industry increased. Men then decided 'to introduce a more *complete Dominion* or *Property*...that might be in some respects perpetual' (p. 65). Although inconvenience provides the motivation to introduce private property, the justification is that the common good may be more easily brought about. Therefore, it is a function and a duty of civil government to ensure that each man has enough property to enable him to promote the common good (pp. 67–8):

Since the Right to the making such a Division can only be deduc'd from a Care of the Common Good, it manifestly follows that the *Dominion of God over all things* is preserv'd unviolated; and that, from this Principle, no *Right of Dominion* can accrue to any man over others, which will license him to take from the *Innocent* their necessaries; but on the contrary, that the Right of *Empire* is therefore given to them, that the *Rights of all* may be protected from the evils of contention, and may be encreased, as far as the nature of Things, assisted by human industry, will permit.

With this move Cumberland completely reverses the roles of expletive and distributive justice. The government's duty is to distribute property in such a way that the common good can be realised, and then protect it. Private property is seen as the conventional means of individuating man's natural right to his due, and thus may be altered accordingly (p. 68):

Having already briefly *deduced*...the *Property* of particular rational Beings, at least in things necessary, some *Right* is granted, which every one may justly call *his own*, and, by the *same law*, all others will be obliged *to yield that to him*, which is usually included in the Definition of *Justice*.

He roundly states that what he means by justice is not particular justice, but universal justice (p. 316). Civil laws are established to distribute and to preserve property in accordance with the common good, thus reflecting natural law. The 'Law of Nature, which distributes Property, and... Justice (or the Will to preserve Property so distributed to each)', both constitute the duties of government (p. 324). Therefore, 'the Measure of our Property...[is] fix'd and determined by its respect to the Common Good'.

Pufendorf and Cumberland, writing in the same genre, against the same author, at the same time in history, evince two radically different conclusions with respect to the relation between law and property. For Pufendorf, the law must, except in cases of dire need, protect the existing distribution of exclusive rights. Cumberland concludes that it is the primary function of law to ensure that the distribution of exclusive rights is in accordance with each man's due (cf. pp. 326–7, 346–7).

Exclusive rights

i. Locke's apostrophe

1

Chapter five of the Second Treatise opens with a summation of the matrix of natural and inclusive rights, and this now functions as a set of premisses for the continuation of the study.[1] In the first eight lines Locke sets out the two initial conditions which partially define man's natural state. Scripture reveals that the world is a gift, given by God to mankind in common. Natural reason teaches that each man has a right to the things which nature affords for his subsistence. We have seen that these two propositions are derived from biblical exegesis and from natural law. The two derivations are complementary and, consequently, the two conclusions describe the same state of affairs. Kendall suggests that there is an illogical transition from the natural right which 'men' have to the world as the common property of 'mankind' (1965: p. 69; Laslett, 1970: p. 303). To say, however, that *each* man has an inclusive claim right, entailed by a natural duty, is logically equivalent to saying that the world belongs to *all* men in the same manner. Locke's right is designed, as we have seen, to perform this function. He immediately continues with the assertion that, if common property in this sense is supposed, then 'it seems to some a very great difficulty, how any one should ever come to have a *Property* in any thing' (2.25). That is, it seems difficult to some for anyone to have an exclusive right in (a property in) a part of that which belongs to all in common. Locke then states that this is the problem which he intends to solve in chapter five: 'I shall endeavour to shew, how Men might come to have a *property* in several parts of that which God gave to Mankind in common' (2.25; cf. Olivecrona, 1975: pp. 63–4). This is the same description of the problem that he presents in his prolepses in the First Treatise (above, p. 63).

Who are the 'some' who find difficulties with this particular problem of individuating common property? The reference is not to Suarez, Selden and Cumberland, since they have no difficulty in solving it; nor do they see it as a problem. One member of the 'some' is clearly Pufendorf, for as soon as Locke enunciates the problem he makes the following aside (2.25):

I will not content my self to answer, That if it be difficult to make out *Property*, upon a supposition, that God gave the World to *Adam* and his Posterity in common; it is impossible that any Man, but one universal Monarch, should have any *Property*, upon a supposition, that God gave the World to *Adam*, and his Heirs in Succession, exclusive of all the rest of his Posterity.

This is precisely the tack which Pufendorf takes. He argues that the Adamite theory is impossible and then asserts that use of a positive community involves insuperable difficulties (above, pp. 75, 88). Not only does he translate positive community into property in several, as his rights theory demands, but he says that any bargain made with respect to the whole necessarily requires the act and consent of each commoner. Content with these arguments, he posits instead a negative community (4.4.3). Locke replies that he will solve these difficulties 'without any express Compact of all the Commoners'.

The second person to whom Locke refers is Filmer (Laslett, 1970: p. 304n; Kelly, 1977). The analysis of property in the First Treatise is incomplete, as he himself notes in his cross-references. Having established an alternative natural condition of mankind, he is left with the vexing question of how it might work in practice. The way in which the issue is set out in chapter five is a restatement of the conclusions of the First Treatise. This sets the stage to continue the explanation of property from where he left it in the First Treatise, and so to achieve what he promises in his cross-references.[2] In the general sense of showing that his alternative to Filmer's Adamite theory is practicable, chapter five is directed against Filmer. Locke makes this explicit halfway through the exposition (2.39). This conclusion is substantiated by Dunn's more general judgment: 'it is *this* structure, Filmer's explicit doctrines, to which Locke addressed himself in the *Two Treatises* and which set him the particular set of dialectical problems which his most important notions were intended to resolve' (1969: p. 64).

The description of what Locke is doing in writing chapter five, in terms of his intention to continue his refutation of Filmer, is often overlooked (Day, 1966; Nozick, 1974: pp. 174–82; Becker, 1977: pp. 33–43). One reason for this is the unwarranted assumption that Locke was addressing a separate topic in chapter five; 'the origin of property' (Olivecrona, 1976: p. 87). We have seen that the origin of property in the sense of common property is God and natural law. The origin of 'property in' is, in turn, man's common property: 'Property, whose Original is from the Right a Man has to use any of the Inferior Creatures, for the Subsistence and Comfort of his life' (1.92; cf. 1.86). Both of these origins are explicated in the First Treatise. When Locke begins chapter five, he has shown that man has a claim to exclusive property, why he has it, and for what purposes he is to use it. How man comes to have his due within this framework is the outstanding question. In chapter five he explains one natural way in which this could be achieved. The successful execution of this task would neutralise Filmer's allegation that his subversion of Grotius counts as a confutation of all theories that postulate original community (p. 262).

Chapter five is directed at Filmer in a more specific sense as well. Filmer redescribes Grotius' original right as 'a right to the common use of all things in the world' (p. 273). This claim right is a misdescription of Grotius' general right in things (*ius in res*); it turns Grotius' negative community into a kind of positive community. Filmer is not alone in the seventeenth century in making this error. Pufendorf points out that Selden, Johann Heinrich Boecler (1610–72), in his *Commentary on Hugo Grotius* (1633), and Caspar Ziegler (1621–90), in his *Commentary on Hugo Grotius* (1662), all make the same mistake (4.42, 4.4.9).[3] On the basis of his misinterpretation Filmer concludes that there is an insoluble difficulty in Grotius: 'to have given a propriety of any one thing to any other, had been to have robbed him [another man] of his right to the common use of all things'. Applied to Grotius, the argument is infelicitous because the concept of belonging to, presupposed by the concept of robbery, does not appear until exclusive rights are present. It is appropriate to the kind of common property expressed by a right to the common use of all things. Locke's common property is different in two respects. It is the common right to use, not the right to the common use; and not all things, but things necessary to preservation. Nonetheless, it is incumbent on Locke to illustrate that the use of his common property does not lead to robbery. Locke responds expressly to this issue in chapter five (2.28). But in replying to this objection, Locke is, and *eo ipso*, replying to the same censure of positive community advanced by Pufendorf (4.4.11).

The third author who finds difficulty with common property is Locke's friend, Tyrrell. In *The Patriarch un-monarched*, he, like Socrates, takes positive community to mean that each commoner has a right in every item. That is, it is property in several with the added specification that each man's exclusive right refers to every object. If this were true, then 'no man could have eat any thing which another might not have pulled out of his mouth, pretending he could not eat it without his leave because he had a share in it' (p. 109, 2nd set of pages; cf. Kelly, 1977: p. 83). (Aristotle made explicit the impracticability of this condition and Hobbes drew out the unsavoury consequences with unstinting relish.) Tyrrell adopts a negative community which, as he retrospectively explains in *The Library of Politics or an Enquiry into the Ancient Constitution of the English Government* (1694), men are permitted to use 'if they please';

but they are under no duty to do so (p. 135). Thus, Locke equally could have had Tyrrell expressly in mind. After Locke explains how a man comes to have an exclusive right on the common, he makes a direct reply to Tyrrell's type of complaint, stressing that the inclusive rights of other commoners are not transgressed: 'Nor will it invalidate his right to say, Every body else has an equal Title to it' (2.32). Pufendorf, Filmer and Tyrrell all fit the description of those who find great difficulty in individuating common property.

2

One further point is necessary to clarify Locke's task in chapter five. Filmer's central criticism of Grotius is directed at his transition from the common to the institution of private property (p. 273):

> Certainly it was a rare felicity, that all the men in the world at one instant of time should agree together in one mind to change the natural community of all things into private dominion: for without such a unanimous consent it was not possible for community to be altered.

We have seen that Pufendorf avoids this sort of censure by revising Grotius' obviously implausible doctrine of universal and instantaneous consent to institute private property. He advances the amendment that men agreed to institute private property in several temporal stages, and different places, as they came together in suprafamilial groupings. Locke replies to Filmer's reproof by carrying Pufendorf's amendment one radical step further.

At this point Locke makes two extremely important moves: first, he subscribes to the view of Grotius and Pufendorf, as well as of Suarez, Selden and Cumberland, that property in political society is conventional and based on consent. Second, he dissents from the tenet that this conventional property predates the institution of government. Instead, he expounds the belief that the agreement to institute conventional property succeeds the establishment of political society (2.38):

> it was commonly *without any fixed property in the ground* they made use of, till they incorporated, settled themselves together, and built Cities, and then, by consent, they came in time, to set out the *bounds of their distinct Territories*, and agree on limits between them and their Neighbours, and by Laws within themselves, settled the *Properties* of those of the same Society.

Locke repeats his remarkable conclusion that property in political society is a creation of that society: 'by *positive agreement*, [they] *settled a Property* amongst themselves, in distinct Parts and parcels of the Earth' (2.45).

Three issues are involved in this part of Locke's explication of property. The first concerns the nature of the property which he says is conventional. To make this point I will use the two-part definition of private property enunciated by Macpherson: 'it is a right to dispose of, or alienate, as well as to use; and it is a right which is not conditional on the owner's performance of any social function' (1975: p. 126). This right necessarily refers to land: 'The right to alienate one's property in land' (p. 126n). In the above passages Locke denies that fixed property in land, alienable property, is natural, and endorses the standard natural law opinion that it is conventional. But it does not follow from this that the kind of property which is conventional is private property. This is so because he holds the belief that any kind of property is not only conditional on the owner's performance of a social function, but is held specifically for the sake of the performance of a social function: to preserve mankind. It is never the case that, for Locke, property is independent of a social function. Locke attributes to Filmer the theory that property in land is independent of social functions and admonishes that it is the 'most specious thing' (1.41). Therefore, the kind of property introduced in political society, since it fails to meet this condition, is not private property. *A fortiori*, the kind of property which is natural and succeeded by political property, since it is neither alienable property in land, nor independent of social functions, is not private property.

Locke not only denies Filmer's argument that private property is natural, he also controverts Grotius' and Pufendorf's assumption that the kind of property established by consent is private property. His express statement that property under government is conventional contradicts the standard, but not exclusive, interpretation of Locke's analysis of property. Locke is normally taken to have attempted to justify private property by showing that it is natural (Macpherson, 1978: p. 12). This interpretation is held in the face of his repeated assertion that whatever property men have in political society is conventional. He writes, 'those who are counted the Civiliz'd part of Mankind, ...have made and multiplied positive Laws to determine Property' (2.30). 'For in Governments the Laws regulate the right of property, and the possession of land is determined by positive constitutions' (2.50). That is, 'Locke clearly distinguishes between the natural property rights that he sees as holding in a state of nature antecedent to [positive] law or social convention and the systems of property that arise later with the introduction of money and the creation of government' (Scanlon, 1976: p. 23).

The second issue is the placing of the agreement to introduce political property posterior to the formation of a polity. This serves to undermine the primary ideological conclusion of Grotius and Pufendorf. In situating the agreement to private property prior to government, they conclude that 'governments were established to protect those prior agreements; the contracts instituting governments bind them to respect the property of the individual' (Schlatter, 1951: p. 148). This avenue is now closed to Locke and, in chapter five, he gives only a hint of what his point might be (see below, pp. 170–4).

3

The third and consequential issue is to determine the horizon of the project Locke sets himself. He does not show how common property can be individuated naturally in order to bypass grounding prevailing systems of property on consent. His explication is, therefore, not set up to answer Filmer's confutation of Grotius' consent theory by providing a natural alternative.[4] Locke accepts that contemporary property relations are founded on consent and he answers Filmer by modifying the theories of Grotius and Pufendorf. Equally, natural individuation is not set up to provide a natural alternative to Pufendorf's consent theory of private property.[5] Since Locke bifurcates natural property in the state of nature and conventional property in a civil state, the assumption that one serves to underpin the other shared by both these interpretations is contradicted by his own statements. The explicit rejection of this ideological manoeuvre by Locke proves that, as Hundert has argued against Macpherson, Locke 'certainly did not provide a rationale for existing social relations' (1972: p. 17). We are thus left with the conclusion, enunciated by Yolton and Dunn, that Locke's intention is to show that particularisation of the natural common is *possible*. (See above, p. 3.)

This is, of course, essential to his theory as a whole and to his polemic against Filmer. More specifically, it is directed at Filmer's assertion that it is logically impossible: 'where there is community there is neither *mine* nor *thine*' (p. 264). It is nonetheless important, in the light of the difficulties experienced by Grotius and Pufendorf. Grotius' individuation of negative community with a right in things leads him to difficulties and contentions, especially with respect to labour. In addition, Pufendorf presents a three-fold refutation of Grotius' right and proceeds to experience similar quarrels and strife with his conventional treatment of the use of natural community. If Locke's overall rights theory was to appear at all plausible, and the natural right to revolution vindicated, he had to demonstrate that he could avoid all these pitfalls. In his concluding paragraph Locke roundly states that he has done precisely this (2.51):

And thus, I think, it is very easie to conceive without any difficulty, *how Labour could at first begin a Title of Property* in the common things of Nature, and how the spending it upon our uses bounded it. So that there could then be no reason of quarrelling about Title, nor any doubt about the largeness of Possession it gave. This left no room for Controversie about the Title, nor for Incroachment on the Right of others. . .

ii. The place of exclusive rights in the *Essays on the Law of Nature*

Locke's first theoretical discussion of exclusive rights is in chapter eight of the *Essays on the Law of Nature*, entitled, 'Is every man's own interest the basis of the law of nature?'. He defends natural law as the foundation of morals against the view that morality is based on self-interest or utility. Locke accepts the convention that there is an analytic relationship between willing something and the agent regarding that thing as good.[6] That which is willed is called the 'formal object' of the will, or, in more modern terms, the 'description under which' a thing is picked out as an object of volition. What an agent does will is the apparent good; what he should will is the moral good. The status of the apparent good is descriptive; whereas the moral good is normative (cf. Hooker: 1.1.8; Pufendorf: 1.1.4).[7]

The view which Locke wishes to refute is the identification of moral with apparent good. What the agent takes to be to his utility, advantageous, or expedient in the given circumstances (apparent good) is said to be the moral good and, as such, the basis of morality (p. 207). He denies this for three reasons and seeks to establish natural law as an objective criterion for moral good, independent of man's subjective will. The moral good furnished by natural law is then shown to be useful or advantageous to the agent. However, it is not morally good because it is advantageous. Rather, it is morally good because it is in accordance with natural law and the result of it so being is that it is advantageous: 'the rightness of an action does not depend on its utility; on the contrary, its utility is a result of its rightness' (p. 215). But the sense in which the moral good results in being useful is not the sense in which the apparent good is immediately so. Indeed, the immediate result may be, and quite often is, disadvantageous: 'for example, the restitution of a trust that diminishes our possessions' (p. 215): Therefore, even on the opponents' own grounds, utility cannot be the basis of morality.[8]

Locke employs the premiss, common to most radical as well as conservative moral theories, that the preconditions of a moral life are security and the possession of more than enough goods to ensure subsistence. Moral agents must have goods which furnish the means of enjoyment in addition to use: 'Happynesse cannot consist without plenty and security' (MS. Locke, c.28, fo. 139). This commitment leads to a conservative theory if the inference is made that only some can, or do, have the requisite plenty. A radical, on the other hand, infers that this condition should be available to all. We have seen that Locke takes this radical turn in constructing his natural law and rights to bring about God's wish that all things He gave richly are to be enjoyed by mankind. In this early work Locke gives his first analysis of the moral conditions necessary to achieve this result.

If a set of principles is to be the basis of morality, it must be the locus of the binding force of all derivative precepts (p. 205). Thus, the first reason for rejecting utility or self-interest is that, as a matter of fact, the dutiful actions of life are not binding because they are immediately advantageous to the agent (pp. 207–11). 'In fact a great number of virtues, and the best of them, consist only in this: that we do good to others at our own loss' (p. 207). The accumulation of private wealth and concern with one's private interests are the antithesis of moral principles: 'if it were the principal law of nature that each man should be mindful of himself and his own affairs, those noble examples of virtues which the records of history have hallowed would have to be assigned to oblivion' (p. 209). Self-interest and acquisitiveness are the basis of immorality: 'Besides (since there is nothing so sacred that avarice has not at one time or other treated it with violence), if the ground of duty were made to rest on gain and if expediency were acknowledged as the standard of rightness, what else would this be than to open the door to every kind of villainy?' (p. 209).

The second argument explains why natural law morality must be primarily a set of positive duties to others. Locke overthrows Grotius' belief that natural law consists in a matrix of negative duties which protect a life of self-interest. The resulting concatenation of private interest could not but be immoral because private interests inevitably conflict. 'Yet, if the private interest of each person is the basis of that Law [natural law], the law will inevitably be broken, because it is impossible to have regard for the interests of all at one and the same time' (p. 211). The assumption which clearly underlies this argument, as well as his later rights theory, is that the interests of all are of primary importance. The reason why an individual's interest conflicts with the interests of all, and so cannot provide a moral foundation for social life, is that the resources necessary for an adequate moral life for everyone are finite:

the inheritance of the whole of mankind is always one and the same, and it does not grow in proportion to the number of people born. Nature has provided a certain profusion of goods for the use and convenience of men, and the things provided have been bestowed in a definite way and in a predetermined quantity; they have not been fortuitously produced nor are they increasing in proportion with what men need or covet.

Therefore, accumulation by one person implies the injury of another: 'when any man snatches for himself as much as he can, he takes away from another's heap the amount he adds to his own, and it is impossible to for anyone grow rich at the expense of someone else'. It follows that if each man is to receive his due share all goods, both necessary and contingent, must be for the use of all; not private, but common:

Victuals, clothes, adornments, riches, and all other good things of this life are provided for common use.

Locke does not explain here how distributive principles of natural law solve the problem of one man's gain being another's loss; this is a problem which the *Two Treatises* addresses. Locke simply states that once it is accepted that all good things are for common use, then natural law dissolves conflict and ensures that social actions 'kindle and cherish one another' (p. 213). Thus, the fundamental argument of the *Two Treatises*, that God gave the world to man as common property, is continuous with his early thought.

In the third refutation, Locke discusses the criterion in accordance with which common goods could not be distributed. This negative proof clears the ground for his positive theory in the *Two Treatises*. He admits that goods must be distributed to each in some manner, but the justification for individual ownership cannot be self-interest: 'what personal property [is there] when a man is not only allowed to possess his own, but what he possesses is his own, merely because it is useful to him?' (p. 213). This would entail that men could never perform a social function with their property 'it would be unlawful for a man to renounce his own rights or to impart benefits to another without a definite hope of reward'. He finds a theory of property which is not conditional on the performance of social functions as 'absurdity' (p. 215).

The primary flaw in a morality of self-interest is that it is based 'in men's appetites and natural instincts rather than in the binding force of law, just as if that was morally best which most people desired' (p. 215). As a result it serves to legitimate unlimited accumulation of property which, in turn, denies others their fair share and makes impossible the performance of social duties. This commitment to debunk a theory of property which licenses acquisitiveness is continued and reinforced in his series of letters on education written between 1684 and 1689. These were collected together and published as *Some Thoughts Concerning Education* in 1693 (Axtell, 1968: pp. 3–13). Here, he stresses that two humours must be weeded out of children as early as possible, for they are the 'two Roots of almost all the Injustice and Contention, that so disturb Humane Life' (p. 207). The two humours are the power and right to do as one desires which underlie a system of property based on self-interest: 'they [children] would have *Propriety* and Possession, pleasing themselves with the Power which that seems to give, and the Right they thereby have, to dispose of them as they please'.

It seems, therefore, to be a persistent concern of Locke to probe the inadequacies of a system of morality based on self-interest. It is no less clearly the case that he is equally adamant in making explicit the immoral consequences of a system of private property built upon an ethic of self-interest. His insistence, in the *Two Treatises*, that the question of property must be answered within a context of positive duties to others, and equal claims to common goods, is his exposition of an alternative and morally superior system of property grounded in natural law.

iii. The person and his action

1

Section twenty-six opens with a reiteration of two principles: that the world is the common property of men; and that it is their property to use 'for the Support and Comfort of their being'. This brings God's purposes back into play and provides an end at which to aim. Reason is then introduced as the faculty appropriate 'to make use of' the common. Those driven by the desire to covet are excluded, since their activity is non-rational (2.34). The theme of man being capable of dominion in virtue of his God-like intellectual nature, left idle in the First Treatise, is thus re-activated. The kind of reason Locke has in mind is practical reasoning in accordance with natural law (2.31). A number of lines of argument are gathered together in this step. Man has a natural duty to use his reason and to act in accordance with natural law. In this case, making rational use of the common is the exercise of his natural claim right and thus, in turn, is the performance of his natural duty to preserve himself and others. As in the previous section, the whole lattice work of natural law and rights is presented to define and delimit the problem to be solved.

God's pronouncement that the world belongs to man for his enjoyment as well as for his necessary use is woven into the analysis by stating that convenience, in addition to support, is an end to be achieved. The distinction between necessities and conveniences is made in a journal entry on 8 February 1677: 'we are in an estate, the necessities whereof call for a constant supply of meat, drink, clothing, and defence from the weather; and our conveniences demand yet a great deal more' (MS. Locke, f.2, fos. 247–55; 1936: p. 84). If Locke can win through to an exclusive right which encompasses these two ends, a right of 'due use' (2.37), he will be able to avoid the difficulty, experienced by Grotius and Pufendorf, of goods not in immediate use falling back into the common. Once the constraints constituting the original condition are made explicit, the line which the analysis must take can be defined: earthly provisions, 'being given for the use of Men, there must of necessity be a means *to appropriate* them some way or other before they can be of any use, or at all beneficial to any particular Man' (2.26). Locke stresses that this individuation does not dissolve, but merely realises property in common by pointing out that the agent with an exclusive right still remains 'a Tenant in common'.[9]

Man as a practical agent, the individual and particular person, appears for the first time in the following section and is said to have the first, natural and exclusive right: 'Though the Earth, and all inferior Creatures be common to all Men, yet every Man has a *Property* in his own *Person*' (2.27). Locke signals that the right in one's person is exclusive by adding that this, 'no Body has any Right to but himself'. Up to this point in the *Two Treatises* Locke deals with man as such, as a rational being and as God's workmanship. The three natural rights which are predicated of all men in virtue of these two criteria are inclusive. Locke now turns to the particular moral agents who are duty bound to act in accordance with the laws and rights constituting their existential condition. It is individual persons who must make use of God's gift and so they must have within themselves as agents the foundation of exclusive property (2.44):

though the things of Nature are given in common, yet Man (by being Master of himself, and *Proprietor of his own Person*, and the Actions or *Labour* of it) had still in himself *the great Foundation of Property*...

The distinction between man and person is central to Locke's theory. God is the proprietor of man because, as we have seen, God makes man. Man, on the other hand, is said to be the proprietor of two items. He has a property in, or is the proprietor of his person and, he is also the proprietor of the actions of his person. These two exclusive rights provide the crucial link between man's theoretical inclusive rights and the exclusive rights men come to have in particular things as a result of their practical activity. Some account of their derivation is therefore required. A right, according to Locke, arises from an act. God's right in man and man's resulting inclusive rights arise from God's act of making. If this is so, then, Locke syllogises in *Morality* (1677–9), men cannot be born with any exclusive rights (MS. Locke, c.28, fo. 139; Sargentich, 1974: p. 27):

Man made not himself nor any other man.
Man made not the world which he found made at birth.
Therefore noe man at his birth can have noe right to any thing in the world more then an other.

This sort of argument is presented early in the Second Treatise (2.4) and we have seen Locke employ it against Filmer's right of fatherhood. Therefore, there should be a sense in which the person and his action come to be such that a man comes to have rights in them.

2

In book two of the *Essay* Locke explicates the concept of the person and his action as it is conventionally used in the seventeenth century (Yolton, 1970: p. 145).[10] '*Person*', Locke writes, 'is a Forensick Term appropriating Actions and their Merit; and so belongs only to intelligent Agents capable of a Law' (2.27.26). Since only agents who are free are capable of law (1.3.14), a necessary condition of being a person is being a free man. Locke explains in the *Two Treatises* that to be capable of law is to be able to use or to exercise one's own reason (2.57, 61); this is the condition of being free, or a free man (2.59, 60, 63). Children lack this ability and so are not free (2.57). A child 'has not *Understanding* of his own to direct his *Will*, he is not to have any Will of his own to follow' (2.58). Children are not, therefore, persons. Coming to have the ability to exercise one's reason makes the child free: 'If this *made* the Father *free*, it shall *make* the Son *free* too' (2.59). Thus, the free man is not there in the beginning but, rather, comes into being: 'when he comes to the Estate that made his *Father a Freeman*, the *Son is a Freeman* too' (2.58). Until he reaches this state, and is transformed into a free man, the child remains under the will of his father (2.59).

Once the state of freedom is attained, a man is capable of becoming a free agent by using his reason to discover natural law and to direct his will in acting (2.57). A free man is in the state of freedom in virtue of his ability to use his reason. A free agent is a free man who acts freely. In the *Essay* Locke examines the conditions necessary for free action. These conditions provide the groundwork for his concept of a person. The defining condition is to be under one's own will. The will is the power of the mind to consider, or to forebear considering any idea, or to prefer any motion of any part of the body to its rest, or *vice versa*, in any particular instance (2.21.5). Willing or volition is defined as the exercise of the will by directing any particular action of its forebearance. An action consequent upon such thought, will and volition is a voluntary action. A voluntary action is not necessarily a free action. For example, a man could be taken into a room while asleep, the door locked behind him, and then awake to find himself in the desirable company of a friend. He may prefer to stay and his staying would then be voluntary. However, it is not in his power to go so his action is not free (2.21.10). A free agent must have the power to do or forebear any particular action and must make the choice. Thus, a free action, in addition to being voluntary, must follow from a choice (2.21.8).

Thus, a free agent is a man who brings any action into existence as a result of volition or choice (2.21.27). Choice, in turn, consists in examination or deliberation. Deliberation is not only necessary to free agency; it is the duty and perfection of man's intellectual nature (2.21.47). A free agent is a deliberative agent: 'Examination is *consulting a guide*. The determination of the *will* upon enquiry is *following the direction of that Guide*: And he that has a power to act, or not to act, according as such determination directs, is a *free Agent*' (2.21.50). The free action which follows from deliberation is necessarily deliberate and intentional action: 'What follows after that [deliberation], follows in a chain of Consequences linked one to another, all depending on the last determination of the Judgment' (2.21.52). The guide which the free agent consults in deliberation permits the agent to judge if the proposed action conduces to a moral or evil end. This is precisely the function which divine law, comprising natural law and revelation, performs in deliberation (2.28.8). In the *Two Treatises* Locke repeats his commitment to natural law as the guide in practical reasoning (2.59). This explains the way in which man is to be the agent or vehicle of God's purposes in engaging in free and deliberate action, first canvassed in *The Essays on the Law of Nature*, thus defusing Filmer's objection that each man would be free to do as he lists (2.22, 57).

Since the term 'person' is predicated only of free agents, a person is an agent who performs intentional, deliberate action (cf. Yolton, 1970: p. 148). The identity of a person, as opposed to a man, is self-consciousness (2.27.9):

[a person] is a thinking intelligent Being, that has reason and reflection, and can consider it self as it self, the same thinking thing in different times and places; which it does only by that consciousness, which is inseparable from thinking, and as it seems to me essential to it...

This consciousness which always accompanies thinking, ''tis that, that makes every one to be, what he calls *self*...in this alone consists *personal Identity*'. Locke now shows how this definition implies a conceptual or non-contingent connection between a person and his action. In being consciousness of thinking, self-consciousness is also consciousness of action: 'as far as this consciousness can be extended backwards to any past Action or Thought, so far reaches the Identity of that *Person*; it is the same *self* now it was then; and 'tis by the same *self* with this present one that now reflects on it, that that Action was done'. Locke is not arguing here that a person is aware that he performed a certain action by observational knowledge. If this were the criterion, then difficulty would arise over whether the observed action was his or another's (2.27.13). Locke's point is that the person is necessarily aware of performing his actions through the consciousness accompanying his thinking. Actions are actions of a person in virtue of his non-observational knowledge of the idea or description under which the action is performed: 'as far as any intelligent Being can repeat the *Idea* of any past Action with the same consciousness it had of it at first, and with the same consciousness it has of any present Action; so far it is the same *personal self'* (2.27.10). Actions of a person are those which he is conscious of performing, or of having performed, in virtue of being conscious of the thought in accordance with which they are brought into being (2.27.20). This seems to be the only way in which the kind of consciousness constituting personal identity could extend to action.

That a person has non-observational or intentional knowledge of his actions is another way of saying that the actions of the person are necessarily intentional actions (Anscombe, 1972: pp. 82–3). This corroborates Locke's view that only free agents are persons. He does not go on to explore the topic of non-observational knowledge, but notes in another context its salient feature: 'Thus I see, whilst I write this, I can change the Appearance of the Paper; and by designing the Letters, tell beforehand what new *Idea* it shall exhibit the very next moment, barely by drawing my Pen over it' (4.11.7; cf. Yolton, 1970: p. 151n). In addition to restricting action of the person to intentional action, the criterion of identity highlights the crucial point that a person is the author of his actions (2.27.26). His knowledge of his actions is a species of maker's knowledge and his action a species of making;[11] the person is therefore said to 'own' his actions (2.27.26):[12]

This personality extends it *self* beyond present Existence to what is past, only by consciousness, whereby it becomes concerned and accountable, owns and imputes to it *self* past Actions, just upon the same ground, and for the same reason, that it does the present.

The criterion of ownership is consciousness of having performed those actions, of being their author (2.27.17; cf. Yolton, 1970: p. 152).

3

Locke's exposition of the relation between a person and his actions explains his statement in the *Two Treatises* that a man is proprietor of the actions or labour of his person. The relation between a person and his intentional action is a central feature of contemporary philosophy of action. 'The relation obtains in virtue of the agent's intentional action's [sic] being *his* action, the action of that *person*; as opposed to being merely the action or movements of that body which just happens to be his though it might as well have been someone else's body as far as his knowledge of what it is doing is concerned' (Olsen, 1969: p. 331). To own one's actions is equivalent to being the proprietor of them. Although man makes not himself nor the world, he makes the actions of his person and so has a natural and exclusive maker's right in them. In section twenty-seven he carefully writes that the '*Labour* of his Body, and the *Work* of his Hands, we may say, are properly his'. His body and his limbs are God's property: the actions he uses them to make are his own. Barbeyrac comments, 'everyone is the only master of his person and actions; the labour of his body and the work of his hands entirely and solely belong to him' (1729: 4.4.3n.4). This is equivalent to '*Labour* being the unquestionable Property of the Labourer' (2.27). Although man neither makes the world nor himself, and so has no exclusive rights at birth, he comes to have a natural and exclusive right in the actions he makes as a person.

In these passages Locke uses the term 'labour' interchangeably with 'actions'. This accords with his grouping of making and doing in the same category of practical activity (above, p. 11). His account of actions of the person also suggests that intentional doing can be seen as a species of making. The use of the term 'labour' to cover most sorts of action is conventional in seventeenth-century literature, especially Puritan literature (Walzer, 1974: pp. 199–232). Locke's letter to Dr Denis Grenville in 1677 provides the clearest account of the meaning of the term 'labour'. It is defined by a contrast with recreation: 'the doeing of some easy or at least delightfull thing to restore the minde or body tired with labour, to its former strength and vigor and thereby fit it for new labour' (1976: I, No. 328). Labour is coterminous with non-recreational actions and consists in doing 'our main duty which is in sincerity to doe our dutys in all our callings as far as the frailty of our bodys or mindes will allow us'. All labour or action in the analysis of property fits this description since it is the performance of the positive duty to God of preserving mankind. 'Labour', Dunn summarises, 'is an obligation which must be analyzed as a component of the calling' (1969: p. 219). In addition, then, to being a positive moral duty, labour is wider than the modern concept in comprising both making and doing. It is narrower in that it is restricted to free, intentional actions and thus, in this respect, is closer to Arendt's concept of work (1973: pp. 136–67).

Although ownership of one's intentional actions is a paradigmatic case of maker's rights, property in one's person is less clearly explicable in the same terms. A child becomes a free man on attaining the age and use of reason, and the free man becomes a free agent and a person in thinking and acting. The free man does not make his person in thinking and acting. The criterion of personhood is the consciousness which always accompanies thought and action. Consciousness is not made; it is something for which a man is obliquely responsible in virtue of thinking and acting. As agents, we have consciousness and this 'makes everyone to be what he calls *self*' (2.27.9). Nonetheless, since the identity of a person is consciousness *of* thought and action, and the thought and action are his workmanship, it is his consciousness, not another's, and so his property. Therefore, nobody has any right to it but he himself (2.27, 1.52).

Locke's introduction of the conceptual model of a person and his action as the foundation of property in things thus unfolds a further component of the major and constitutive theme of his philosophy. The theory of maker's knowledge, which both verifies the certainty of the moral sciences and underpins God's relation to man, is now shown to be embodied in man's relation to his action. God as maker has non-contingent knowledge of, and a natural maker's right in, His workmanship. The implication of this is that man has positive duties to God and resulting natural claim rights to perform those duties. Man as maker is now shown to have analogous maker's knowledge of, and a natural right in his intentional actions. This analogy is a logical feature of the workmanship model; it was first employed to explain the relation of God to man and the world. In introducing it here, Locke signals that man is to come to have property in his own workmanship by working in a God-like fashion: 'God makes him *in his own Image after his own Likeness*, makes him an intellectual Creature, and so capable of *Dominion* (1.30). This imitation thesis, that the best life for man is to act like God in bringing about modes of his own, is shared by all the creationists. 'Man in perfection of nature', Hooker writes, 'being made according to the likeness of his Maker, resembleth him also in the manner of working; so that whatsoever we work as men, the same we do wittingly work and freely' (1.1.7). Even the fact that man is under an obligation to engage in this activity for the sake of moral ends given by natural law does not, Locke points out, weaken the analogy: 'the Freedom of the Almighty hinders not his being determined by what is best' (2.21.49).

Labour, therefore, is a moral form of activity in two senses. Not only does it take place within a context of, and is the means of, performing moral duties, it is a moral form of activity itself. It is the form of activity characteristic of man, as we have seen, and so his duty (Hundert, 1972). The kind of person we are is a result of the kind of action we perform and, therefore, in 'this *personal Identity* is founded all the Right and Justice of Reward and Punishment' (2.27.18). The rewards and punishments which God administers on judgment day each man shall '*receive according to his doings*' [1 Cor. 14.25] (2.27.26). It is, therefore, a question of radical moral importance not only how men use their property, but also how they come to have it (McKeon, 1937: p. 344). 'For Locke', Hundert stresses, 'industriousness was indissolubly tied to personal morality' (1972: p. 6). With the transition from man as such to the human agent, the moral analogue of the person and his action is on stage to actualise the natural duties derived from the conceptual model of God and His workmanship.

4

Locke's account of free action shares many of the features common to similar discussions by other natural law writers. Pufendorf writes that moral actions so 'depend on human Will as a free Cause, that without its determination they would never have been perform'd' (1.5.1). The action and its moral effect are said to belong to and to be imputed to the agent because he is 'the Author of it' (1.5.3). In a discussion which is as long and as detailed as Locke's, concerning voluntary and involuntary, free and necessary action, Pufendorf draws on Aristotle's analysis in book three of the *Nicomachean Ethics*. Although he is not alone in this, it is one of the routes by which Aristotle's conceptual model of the human agent as author of his intentional actions was transmitted to the seventeenth century. Aristotle, like Locke, writes that a free agent 'owns' his actions (1114a 12). This form of action is the best form of living for man, εὐδαιμονία, but Aristotle contrasts it with property: 'εὐδαιμονία is an activity; and activity clearly comes into being and is not present at the start like a piece of property' (1169b 30). What Locke wishes to stress in calling one's actions 'property' is that they are created by the agent and he is responsible for them. Also, he wishes to deny Filmer's claim that individual property is 'present at the start', with Adam. Individual property comes into being both with and as a result of human activity. By calling human action property, and placing it at the root of his theory, Locke signals that his concept of individual property is to have the widest possible reference.

Locke's use of the term 'person' is also traditional. 'A person', writes Aquinas, 'is master of his action through his will' (*ST*:1. 11. 2.1). A person is a free man; 'a free man is one who is master of his own actions, but a slave owes all that he is to another' (*ST*:1. 11. 7.4; cf. Suarez: 2.14.16). Aquinas' account of practical knowledge is, as we have seen, based on the model of a person and his action.

5

An examination of Suarez's use of a similar proprietorship model will help to throw light on a linguistic difficulty facing Locke in writing in English. Man is said to be the natural proprietor or master (*dominus*) of his liberty and his action: 'nature itself confers upon man the true property [*dominium*] of his liberty, [and]...he is not the slave, but the master [*dominus*] of his actions' (2.14.16). When he writes of man's control over his life and limbs, however, he describes it in terms of a power, use, or a possession. 'By virtue of the very fact that he is created and has the use of reason, he possesses a moral power [*potestas*] over himself and over his faculties and members for their use.' Man has 'the use and possession of his life' (2.14.18). The term *dominium* here entails the right to alienate and Suarez wishes to convey the meaning that a man may freely and naturally alienate his liberty, thereby legitimating slavery: 'for the very reason that man is proprietor [*dominus*] of his own liberty, it is possible to sell or alienate the same'. The refusal to apply the term *dominium* to man's control of his life and body signifies that man is not at liberty to injure himself or to take his own life. We have seen that Grotius and Pufendorf discuss life, limb, liberty and action under the single term *suum*; that which is naturally one's own. The single feature common to all these items is that they are protected by the natural precept to abstain from that which belongs to another. To say they are naturally one's own does not in itself specify the degree of control the owner has over them. Grotius and Pufendorf agree with Suarez that a free man may alienate his liberty (2.5.27; 6.3.4), but not his life (2.1.6, 2.4.19). Man, therefore, has a different degree of control over his life than he has over his liberty, even though they are both described as belonging to him.

Locke uses the term 'property', as we have seen, to connote that something is one's own, either inclusively or exclusively. That is, anything which is in any sense one's own is one's property. This seems to be the conventional seventeenth-century use of the term. 'In seventeenth-century English usage the word 'propriety' [property] corresponded to the Latin *suum*' (Olivecrona, 1975: p. 113). The result of adopting this convention is that the degree of control one has over something is not specified merely by saying that it is property, just as it is not specified by saying it is *suum*. The Latin authors use various terms to distinguish degrees of control. Suarez restricts *dominium* in the above example, and in most contexts, to a right to alienate the thing denominated. Grotius and Pufendorf normally use the terms *proprietas* and *dominium* in this way. They say, however, that the right to alienate a thing is properly termed complete property or full property (1.1.5; 4.9.1). The reason for this modification is that they wish to say a use right over another's private property is a kind of property, even though the user cannot alienate the owner's property. With a use right 'a man secures only daily and necessary advantage from another's property without impairing the substance' (Pufendorf: 4.8.8). Grotius calls a use right 'incomplete property' (1.1.5); Pufendorf 'useful property' (4.4.2, 4.8.3). With these two terms they are able to distinguish when a proprietor may alienate an item (complete property) and when he may only use it (incomplete property). This is, to use Locke's example, 'the difference between *having Dominion*, which a Shepherd may have, and having full Property as an Owner' (1.39).

Since a use right entails neither possession, nor a right to alienate what one uses, an explanation is required of why it is a kind of property.

In providing an answer Pufendorf also discusses, and throws further light on, the concept of property adopted by Locke. If we distinguish between transferring a right and transferring an item to which a right refers, then we can consider property from two viewpoints (4.9.6):

either as it denotes a bare *moral Quality*, by virtue of which we understand that a thing belongs to some Person, and that it ought to be subject to his Disposal; or as it implies, farther, some degree of *natural Power*; by which we are enabled to put immediately in execution any Purpose that we may have concerning the said thing.

This is equivalent to distinguishing property abstracted from possession and property 'united to it', as the 'final completion of Property'. These two 'considerations' of property are parallel to Locke's common property as a claim right and its completion with a property in an individual possession. Although he finds the distinction contrary to his own rights theory, Pufendorf notes that it is made in canon law with the locutions 'a right to a thing' (*ius ad rem*) and 'a right in the thing' (*ius in re*) (4.9.8). A use right is similar to property abstracted from possession, since the user barely retains, but does not possess, the land he uses (4.9.7). But it also contains the attributes of possession and alienation appropriate to property in its proper meaning. The rightholder possesses his right, an incorporeal thing, and he may alienate his right, but not the land over which it obtains (4.9.7, 4.8.3).

Locke's use of 'property' to connote man's claim right to use earthly provisions is consistent with Pufendorf's use of *dominium* in the sense of a moral quality, as well as with the usage of Suarez, Selden and Cumberland. He is also consistent with Latin usage when he uses 'property' to describe cases where both the right and the referent are alienable and where only the right is alienable. This too is consistent with English usage. A commoner, for example, terms his right 'a property' and he has 'a property in' the game he catches (Nelson, 1717: pp. 82–99, 297). However, the Latin terms *proprietas* and *dominium* have a more restricted range of uses than the English term 'property', used to signify anything that is one's own, adopted by Locke (1968: p. 215), and so prevalent in the seventeenth century (Woodhouse, 1974: passim).

The reason for this difference consists in the twofold English assumption: to say that anything is in any way one's own is to say that it is one's property; and to say that it is one's property is to say that one has a right to it or in it. Property is a right to any thing, or, as Barbeyrac glosses, any sort of a right.[13] If this equivalence is assumed, then a person has a right to or in anything his own. Suarez, Grotius and Pufendorf agree that life and limb are one's own to use, but they deny that a person has rights to them, because this would entail that the rights were inalienable. It is an analytic feature of a right for them that it is alienable (Grotius, 1.1.5;

Pufendorf, 1.1.20). It is correct to say that a man has a right to his liberty precisely because the right is alienable. Locke and his English contemporaries, with their linguistic convention that anything 'one's own' is property and redescribable in terms of rights, are left, therefore, with a number of inalienable rights.[14]

Locke concurs with Suarez, Grotius and Pufendorf that man's life is his own only to use, but, because it is his own, it is his property and so he has a right to use it (2.23, 123). Here, both life and the right to it are inalienable (2.135, 149). Liberty, too, is property, and, contrary to Suarez, Grotius and Pufendorf, it and the right are inalienable (2.123, 135). Man's life is God's property in the full sense of having a right to end man's life (2.6). It follows that slavery cannot be based on consent (2.22). Slavery is a permissible option only for a man condemned to death for killing another; that is, for breaking the law of nature and so proving himself not to be a man at all, but a savage beast (2.11). These rights are inalienable because they result from positive duties to preserve oneself and others. Locke's inalienable rights are his three natural, inclusive rights. Locke is, therefore, not inconsistent in saying that man's life is both God's and man's property, as Day implies (1966: pp. 117–18). It belongs to both, but in different ways: man's property is the right to use and preserve what is essentially God's property, similar to a tenant's property. This shows the kind of misunderstanding which arises if it is assumed that there is a paradigmatic and atemporal concept of property logically tied to the concept of a right to alienate (Day, 1966: p. 119).

For Grotius and Pufendorf, one's own is defined in terms of the natural and negative duty to abstain from what belongs to others. Whatever is one's own and whatever sorts of right one has over these items, the negative duty always applies. The negative duty is a formal criterion because it does not dictate the content of one's own, nor the nature of the rights over it. This is why Pufendorf can say that the negative duty is natural and logically prior to the conventional determination of mine and thine. It also explains why private property is a part of the *suum*. The negative duty applies to whatever is one's private property as well as to one's life, limb and liberty, even though the rights over these items are of various kinds.

Locke wishes to retain a natural and purely formal criterion, but not this traditional and passive concept. Therefore, in one of the most significant moves in the history of rights, he redescribes the traditional rule in terms of the owner's moral power over his own, either exclusively or inclusively. This moral power or right is 'property': 'The nature whereof is, that *without a Man's own consent* it *cannot be taken from him*' (2.193). Locke emphasises that it is a natural definition by showing in this passage that it holds against government. The same formal function as the traditional natural precept to abstain is performed by this concept; it neither determines one's own, nor does it entail any additional rights over one's own. It also protects one's own, but it does this by focusing on the agent's moral power to exercise his consent, his natural right or property, rather than granting primacy to others to perform their negative duties. Any rights, of whatever kind and of whatever reference, contain this element and so are called 'properties' (Kendall, 1965: p. 64). 'Their *Persons* are *free* by a Native Right, and their *properties*, be they more or less, are *their own, and at their own dispose*, and not at his; or else it is no property' (2.194).

Locke's major point in defining property in this way is just to stress the degree of sovereignty any right confers over its object. Without this minimum authority it is not property at all. 'For I have truly no *Property* in that, which another can by right take from me, when he pleases, against my consent' (2.138). Thus, not to take that which is another's without his consent is the *'Fundamental Law of Property'* (2.140). It does not follow from this definition that the rightholder can consent to transfer something that is his own. His person, action, liberty and life are his property, yet these inalienables cannot be taken with consent. 'Property' defined in this way can be predicated of things, life, liberty and estate (2.123), since without consent they cannot be taken. Anything to which a right refers may thus be called the agent's right (2.38). The English Common is property precisely because no part of it can be taken by a non-commoner without the consent of all the commoners (2.35).

Since 'property' means 'right' in this sense, and not any particular right, it can be used in place of 'right' in the locution 'a right in' as well as in 'right in common' (1.24). Although these are different sorts of rights, inclusive and exclusive rights, they are both property because the rights and their objects cannot be taken without consent. Thus, the fact that life is property, even though it cannot be taken with consent, entails an inclusive right 'to preserve what they have not a Power to part with', against those who attempt to take it (2.149). Barbeyrac was correct to note that 'property' means 'any sort of right' because it is true of all rights that they cannot be taken without consent.

The definition in the *Essay* serves the same purpose (4.3.18). Property is 'a right to any thing' and injustice is 'the Invasion or Violation of that right'. Therefore, *'Where there is no Property, there is no Injustice'*. Inclusive and exclusive rights are both included in this definition. Leibniz brings out the universal character of Locke's definition and draws the inescapable conclusion (1916: p. 433):

Thus if there were no property, as if all things were common, there nevertheless might be injustice. By *thing* in the definition of property you must also further understand action; for otherwise, if there were therein no rights to things, it would be always an injustice to prevent men from acting where they find it needful. But according to this explanation it is impossible that there be no property.

A seemingly analytical truth yields a synthetic truth on the assumption that there are natural principles of justice.

'Without a man's consent it cannot be taken from him', is Locke's definition of property and what he means when he uses the term 'property'. 'By *Property* I must be understood here, as in other places, to mean that Property which Men have in their Persons as well as Goods' (2.173). Whatever the goods and whatever the rights over them, 'that property' or right, is that without consent they cannot be taken. This seems to be the solution to the long-standing debate over the meaning of Locke's term 'property'. Viner and Macpherson, two recent contributors, both assume that the meaning of the term is equivalent to its reference (1963: pp. 554-5, 559-60). This, in turn, has led to the 'two senses' doctrine: that Locke uses the term in a wide and a narrow sense, depending on its reference.[15] Yet, the meaning of 'property' is, for Locke, independent of reference. Locke means by 'property' what he says he means and what Barbeyrac says he means: any sort of right, the nature of which is that it cannot be taken without a man's consent (cf. Olivecrona, 1975: p. 111; Ryan, 1965: p. 226).

iv. Man as maker

1

Locke now extends this theory to the conclusion that objects constituted by a person's labour on the common material are his own, just as man and the world are God's own (2.27):

Whatsoever then he removes out of the State that Nature hath provided, and left in, he hath mixed his *Labour* with, and joyned to it something that is his own, and thereby makes it his *Property*. It being by him removed from the common state Nature placed it in, it hath by this *labour* something annexed to it, that excludes the common right of other Men.

It is held by Nozick that 'Locke views [exclusive] property rights in an unowned object as originating through someone's mixing his labour with it' (1974: p. 174). If this is true then the obvious question arises, 'Why should one's entitlement extend to the whole object rather than just to the *added value* one's labour has produced?' (p. 175). However, it does not seem to be Locke's view that a person mixes his labour with a preexisting object which persists through the activity of labouring. Rather, he sees the labourer as making an object out of the material provided by God and so having a property in this product, in a manner similar to the way in which God makes the world out of the prior material He created.

Labour transforms the earthly provisions provided *for* use into man-made objects *of* use; this is necessary 'before they can be of any use' (2.26). The argument is an application of the theory of making which he discusses in the *Essay* in terms of cause and effect. A cause, as we have seen, is that which makes any other thing begin to be; and an effect is that which had its beginning from some other thing (2.26.2). The intrinsic relation of cause and effect obtain: when 'a thing is made up of Particles, which did all of them before exist, but that very thing, so constituted of pre-existing Particles, which considered altogether make up such a Collection of simple *Ideas*, had not only *Existence* before'. The effect, considered as the constitution of particles, is brought into being by the cause. There are two ways in which a man can act as a cause in this authorship sense: in making, when he juxtaposes discernible parts; and in altering, when he introduces a simple idea or new sensible quality which was not in the subject before. The ability of man to constitute modes out of the materials provided by God is his dominion. 'The Dominion of Man. . .however managed by Art and Skill, reaches no farther, than to compound and divide the Materials, that are made to his Hand; but can do nothing towards the making the least Particle of new Matter' (2.2.2).

The crucial feature of this Baconian picture of man's creative and transformative powers is that there is not a thing which persists through making and altering and from which one would have to subtract the value added by the labourer.[16] The labourer constitutes a new object identifiable as that object under the idea of description which informs his making or altering (3.6.40):

the *Idea*, or Essence, of several sorts of *artificial* Things, consisting, for the most part, in nothing but the determinate Figure of sensible Parts; and sometimes Motion depending thereon, which the Artificer fashions in Matter, such as he finds for his Turn. . .

In modern terminology, the result (Locke's 'effect') of an act (made up of the person's actions) is the end state of the change by which the act is defined (Kenny, 1975: p. 54). Man's creative activity is like making words by the arrangement of letters (2.7.10). Thus, Vaughn is correct in labelling Locke's theory as a formation theory: 'bestowal of labour upon any product of nature, not already appropriated by another, suffices to give a man the ownership of that which he has shaped or formed' (1925: I, p. 174). In a passage which Barbeyrac incorporates into his commentary on Pufendorf (8.1.3), Wollaston enunciates the theory succinctly (1724: 6.2):[17]

Before all human laws, the effect or produce of the labour of B is not the effect of the labour of C: and this effect or produce is B's, not C's. Because what the labour of B causes or produces, B produces by his labour; or is the product of B by his labour: that is, it is B's product, not C's, nor any others.

Grotius criticises a similar theory presented by the Roman jurist Paulus in the *Digest* (XLI 2.3.21). He argues that the elements which are blended to make a new product are already owned or not owned. If owned, the effect belongs to the original owner; if unowned, then ownership is acquired by first taking (2.3.3.2). This begs the question by presupposing the validity of first taking as the natural criterion of acquisition. Pufendorf surveys the manifold distinctions invented by Roman lawyers commenting on Paulus, and finally assents to Grotius' position with the proviso that first taking must be based on consent (4.6.7).

2

Locke applies his theory to three types of case: spontaneous products of nature, animals and land. The transformative labour which constitutes spontaneous natural products into goods fit for use is gathering, 'if the first gathering made them not his, nothing else could' (2.28). Gathering God's gifts potentially for use 'added something to them more than Nature, the common Mother of all, had done' (2.28); and this brings into being useful goods which are the gatherer's under that description: 'He that *gathered* a Hundred Bushels of Acorns or Apples, had thereby a *Property* in them; they were his Goods as soon as gathered' (2.46). The same 'so constituted' theory of ownership applies to animals; 'this Law of reason makes the Deer, that *Indian's* who hath killed it; 'tis allowed to be his goods who hath bestowed his labour upon it, though before, it was the common right of every one' (2.30). Catching and domesticating also make the beasts one's own goods suitable for use (2.30, 38). This is the first explicit statement that ownership of the effect of which an agent is the cause is a law of reason, although it is a thread running through the whole fabric of Locke's thought. It is a first principle of justice: '*Justice* gives every Man a Title to the product of his honest Industry' (1.42).

The alteration and appropriation of animals from their natural state to a condition in which they are useful for man's subsistence creates a serious problem because killing constitutes the destruction of God's property. Locke returns to first principles to find a solution. 'Man's *Property* in the Creatures, was founded upon the right he had, to make use of those things, that were necessary or useful to his Being' (1.86). Killing animals, therefore, is only justified if it is a necessary and obliquely intended consequence of the intended act of making use of the animal for support: 'they had then given them the utmost Property Man is capable of, which is to have a right to destroy any thing by using it' (1.39). In opposition to Pufendorf, for whom it is true by definition that property is a right over the natural substance of any thing, Locke holds that this is true only in the case of animals, and only when it is an unavoidable consequence of use. He reiterates the unique and conditional nature of property in animals: 'he may even destroy the thing, that he has Property in by his use of it, where need requires' (1.92). A further condition is that the species of animals must be preserved (1.56).

Locke introduces the ascription of his theory of natural individuation to the earth by underscoring its importance. The *'chief matter of Property'* is now 'the *Earth it self*; as that which takes in and carries with it all the rest' (2.32). The singular significance of land does not, however, interfere with the applicability of the theory:

I think it is plain, that *Property* in that too is acquired as the former. *As much Land* as a Man Tills, Plants, Improves, Cultivates, and can use the Product of, so much is his *Property*. He by his labour does, as it were, inclose it from the Common.

Prior to cultivation the land is 'waste' provided by God for use (2.42). A person blends his labour with the earth and so comes to have a property in the effect: a tilled, planted, improved or cultivated field. The earth, as such, remains God's property. The labourer has a property in his improvement of it, what he makes it to be and which did not exist before. He that 'subdued, tilled and sowed any part of it, thereby annexed to it something that was his *Property*' (2.32). Locke calls this *'appropriation* of any parcel of *Land*, by improving it' (2.33). The amount of improved field which the agent can call his own is limited by the amount of products he can use, not by the amount of land he could conceivably reconstitute by his labour.

There are two effects of the labourer's action which he may eventually call his own: the reconstituted wasteland, and the products of that tilling, planting and cultivating (2.38). The argument of Grotius and Pufendorf, that first occupation confers a use right with a correlative negative duty, is turned by Locke on its head. For him, use for the sake of making useful goods ushers in ownership of those goods, and this activity necessarily entails the exclusion of others (2.35):

And hence subduing or cultivating the Earth, and having Dominion, we see are joyned together. The one gave Title to the other. So that God, by commanding to subdue, gave Authority so far to *appropriate*. And the Condition of Humane Life, which requires Labour and Materials to work on, necessarily introduces *private Possessions*.

Olivecrona rejects this interpretation of Locke's theory of appropriation on the following grounds: 'The meaning cannot be that a man becomes the owner of an object when it has been *created* by his work. That interpretation would be incompatible with Locke's words and examples'

(1974b: pp. 225–6). It is right to say that Locke does not use the word 'create'; this is confined to God's act (2.26.2). Yet, as I hope I have shown, he does use the word 'make' consistently and repeatedly to signify man's ability to change natural things into useful goods. The original item changes its identity by mixing one's labour with it and, as a result, comes to be one's own. Olivecrona endorses the interpretation that a thing becomes one's own through labour because 'something of the spiritual ego was infused into the object' (1974b: p. 226; cf. Euchner, 1969: p. 82). Hundert has shown that there is this variety of expressivist thought in Locke's writing and in Puritan literature. He writes, 'One's property was the extension of self by virtue of the injection of personality through work' (1972: p. 9). It does not seem, however, to carry the weight Olivecrona wishes to place on it. His Aristotelian conclusion that something is one's own *because* one's ego is fused with it is an inference Locke denies. If it were the explanation of property, then children would be the property of their parents (cf. 2.56). The point for Locke is that actions of joining and mixing with external material are present in the intentional acts of catching, killing, gathering, tilling, planting and cultivating. These change the material into useful goods and thereby make them one's own. The non-contingent cause and effect relation which ties man to God also links the product to the labourer. The commodities and instruments of production are the 'effect' of labour (2.43). This intrinsic relation of act to result explains why, as Wollaston puts it, 'the product of a man's labour is often still called his labour' (7.2).[18]

The natural right in the product of one's labour is distinguished from the three natural rights of all men in that an agent comes to have it as a result of rational activity, which Locke takes to be natural to and characteristic of man. The use of these two kinds of property, dominion in common and its completion in individual possession by rational action, originates with Aquinas. We have seen that he begins with the same inclusive framework as Locke, although not expressed in terms of subjective rights, and also denies that individual ownership is natural to man as such. He proceeds to say that there is a form of natural right (*ius naturale*) which applies to the individual agent (*ST:* II. II.57.2). Natural right is embodied in the logical relation between the reason of an agent and the non-contingent result of his application of reason, exemplified in the relation of cultivator and cultivated field:

Take the ownership of property (*proprietas possessionum*); considered in itself there is no reason why this field should belong to this man rather than to that man, but when you take into account its being put under cultivation and farmed without strife; then. . .it tallies with it being owned by this, not that, individual.

Aquinas' point, contrary to Locke's, is to justify existing property relations, and thus the theory extends to full ownership while Locke's does not. It nonetheless exhibits the same logical structure. The argument is also supported by the analogy of God's creative powers: 'man was an artist made to God's image and, though he cannot create in the strict sense of the word, he was called to make things grow through his own initiative... and here some anticipation may be detected of Locke's teaching' (Gilby, 1958: p. 155).

The themes of making, knowing and being one's own, which underpin Locke's natural concept of one's own, run not only through Locke's philosophy, but also through seventeenth-century philosophical thought generally (Hintikka, 1975; von Leyden, 1968: pp. 200–23). Locke's argument that the ascription of an intentional action to a person as *his* action is logically independent of, and presupposed by agreements defining, mine and thine, is surely correct. For a person could not give *his* consent to the agreement unless he already understood that that speech act was his own. 'Contract', Green concludes, 'presupposes property' (1927: p. 214). Pufendorf's claim that mine and thine presuppose an agreement is thereby refuted. Locke's use of this model to include results of acts when these are mixed with earthly provisions does not seem to be an illogical extension. Rather, the contemporary movement to draw a categorical distinction between making and doing seems to cut us loose from what Locke and his contemporaries were seeking to emphasise: man's creative accomplishments and their connection with the concept of the person as a moral and responsible agent (Hintikka, 1975: p. 102).[19]

3

Appropriation is the first step in the series of means and ends which lead to the preservation of mankind. As Locke put the general point in his journal of 1677: 'Nature furnishes us only with the material, for the most part rough and unfitted to our use; it requires labour, art and thought, to suit them to our occasions' (MS. Locke, f.2, fos. 247–55; 1936: p. 84). The next step is to determine the rights which an owner has over his product, in addition to the right not to have it taken without his consent. Contrary to most labour theories of property, labour confers no additional rights over the product (2.27). To determine what type of exclusive right it is, Locke returns to the natural law framework of which it is an implicate. 'The same Law of Nature, that does by this means give us Property, does also *bound* that *Property* too' (2.31). Locke's purpose here is to neutralise Pufendorf's objection to Grotius' natural use right that 'any one may *ingross* as much as he will'. He replies, as 'much as any one can make use of to any advantage of life before it spoils; so much he may by his labour fix a Property in'; or 'within the *bounds*, set by reason of what might serve for his use'. Locke understands this limit in two ways: as limiting the amount to what a person can use; and limiting a person's utilisation of any of that amount to use only, not abuse: 'he had *no Right, farther than his Use* called for any of them, and they might serve to afford him Conveniences of Life' (2.37).

A property in something is more extensive than a traditional use right. Because God gave us all things richly to enjoy (2.31), the right permits use for the sake of conveniences as well as for subsistence. This condition, along with God's proprietorship of the material out of which man fashions his products, makes Locke's exclusive right similar to usufruct: 'the right to use and to enjoy the things of another without impairing the substance' (Pufendorf: 4.8.7). There is one crucial difference, however. Usufruct is the right to use and to enjoy another's property for one's own purposes. Locke's 'property in' by contrast, is the right to use and to enjoy God's property for God's purposes. The kind of exclusive right which Locke develops is the uniquely English concept of the *use* which a trustee is said to have in another's property. The central aspect of this is 'the recognition of the duty of a person to whom property has been conveyed for certain purposes to carry out these purposes' (Holdsworth, 1926: IV, p. 410). The trustee is also said to have a property in the use. The condition of the trustee corresponds to man's existential condition in using his property because he is God's servant 'sent into the World by his order and about his business' (2.6). Describing man's property in terms of use serves to underline the major point that proprietorship exists for, and is conditional on, the performance of positive duties to God.

A property in something is the completion of man's natural right to the means necessary to preserve and comfort himself and others. It is a paramount and remarkable feature of the initial claim right that it is not to the earth itself, but to the manmade products useful to man's life: food, raiment, conveniences of life, meat and drink (1.41; 2.25). The teaching of the *Essays on the Law of Nature* is that this must be the case. The exclusive right individuates the background claim right in the same way as a right in the use of a seat on public transportation particularises a prior right to use public transportation. That the exclusive right is a use right in the products of one's labour follows immediately from its being the actualisation, in possession, of the prior right to use these manmade products. This unique construction serves to establish Locke's main ideological conclusion: that fixed property in land does not have a natural foundation. This is necessarily the case because the complementary and natural inclusive and exclusive rights respectively refer to and inhere in products of labour. The result is that the common remains common and the persons remain tenants in common. In order to have property in the fruit of his labour, an agent requires some land on which to work and therefore, a right to exclude others while he is using it. This leads Locke to his reversal of Grotius and Pufendorf by making the exclusionary right to use land conditional upon, and entailed by, cultivation or other forms of making useful products (2.35).

Locke reconfirms and accentuates this point in his analysis of the limits governing the use of property. The boundary of the use right is set on the common by the tendency of most things to spoil: 'if they perished, in his Possession, without their due use; if the Fruits rotted, or the Venison putrified, before he could spend it, he offended against the common Law of Nature, and was liable to be punished' (2.37). Punishment is justified because 'he invaded his Neighbour's share'. His offence is to misuse the provisions he had made and so to invade the share his neighbour has in these provisions. The argument makes sense on the presupposition of a prior inclusive claim right to provisions, though not to raw materials, necessary for subsistence. That is, any product of the labour of a person which is more than he can make use of 'is more than his share, and belongs to others' (2.31). The proprietor is thus punished for taking more of the common goods than he can use, even though he made those goods. The neighbours exercise their right to enforce the law of nature in punishing him for invading the inclusive right of others (2.11).[20]

Locke then states that the 'same *measures* governed the *Possession of Land* too' (2.38):

Whatsoever he tilled and reaped, laid up and made use of, before it spoiled, that was his peculiar Right; whatsoever he enclosed, and could feed, and make use of, the Cattle and Product was also his. But if either the Grass of his In-closure rotted on the Ground, or the Fruit of his planting perished without gathering and laying up, this part of the Earth, notwithstanding his Inclosure, was still to be looked on as Waste, and might be the Possession of any other.

The first sentence underscores the point that property attaches primarily to, and is conditional on, the use of the second level of products: the products of the product of one's work on land. These are the direct means of support and comfort and that to which one's natural claim right refers. This requires and presupposes a prior right in the improved land so constituted by one's tilling and reaping. Section thirty-two grants this prior right on the same condition that it is to be governed by the due use of the second level products. It is also clear from his concept of making, that the prior right attaches to the improved land as a constituted mixed mode and not simply to the value added or improvements. If the products of the improved field are not used in the sense of being collected for the sake of use for support and comfort, then the cultivated land ceases to be one's own and reverts to the common. There is, therefore, no right in land as such, but only a use right in improved land conditional upon the use of its products. The right in land is twice removed from fixed property. It exists only in the land as long as it is being used, and only if the products are being utilised. The primary and determining criterion for any exclusive right is the due use of the direct means of production. Any abuse or disuse at this level entails the dissolution of the other conditional use rights, as well as the right in the product itself. Property is conditional upon its use to perform our positive duties to God. (cf. Barbeyrac, 1729: 4.4.3n). The cultivated field and its products are both property because they cannot be taken without the proprietor's consent; the definition obtains only because these are his property as objects of use. The moment they cease to be objects of use, they cease, by definition, to be his property and so the inclusive rights of others apply.

v. Property in community

1

One of the obstacles to understanding Locke's theory of natural individua-tion is the predisposition to read 'property' as a term comprising un-conditional rights over land and so to equate it with 'private property'. Macpherson is representative in this respect when he comments on section thirty-two: 'If Locke had stopped here he would have had a defence of limited individual ownership, though the argument would have had to be stretched pretty far even to cover the property right of the contemporary English yeoman' (1972: p. 202). The reason he gives for the inability of Locke's theory to justify the property rights of English yeomen is that they could not meet the proviso, laid down by Locke (2.27), that appropria-tion must leave enough and as good for others. Quite apart from this limit, however, the kind of property the yeoman enjoys is different from Locke's property in the just acquisitions of one's labour. What the yeoman has is fixed property in land, a right to exclude others independent of the use to which the land is put. Locke's tenant in common has a use right in his improved land, conditional on his continuing strict use and on his due use of the products. It could not be stretched, nor, was it intended to be stretched, to cover fixed property in land. The conflation of Locke's 'property in' with private property is a quite recent phenomenon. Early nineteenth-century radicals fixed on Locke's theory of a natural property in the product of one's labour and used it to legitimate revolt against the prevailing system of private property (Driver, 1928: p. 91).

Once this obstacle is removed the puzzle still remains of what system of property Locke might have been thinking of in solving the difficulty of individuation in precisely this form. Locke is quite explicit in saying that his model is the English Common. 'We see in *Commons*, which remain so by Compact, that 'tis the taking any part of what is common, and remov-ing it out of the state Nature leaves it in, which *begins the Property*; without which the Common is of no use' (2.28; cf. 2.35). All the exclusive rights which Locke's commoners possess were present on the English Common and called 'properties'. The combination of a conditional use right in land and an usufruct in the products of one's labour was the standard form of property (Gonner, 1912: pp. 7, 15–17, 78, 99, 101–2; Nelson, 1717: pp. 70–8).

The idea and practice of exclusive property within positive community, which Filmer finds incomprehensible, is thus available to Locke. Cumberland employs a similar model and even Pufendorf concedes that such an arrangement is possible. The concession occurs in the course of his discussion of Boecler's commentary on Grotius. Boecler makes the point, later repeated by Green (1927: pp. 214–15), that Grotius should not have withheld the term *proprietas* to designate his natural use right. What one had thus seized could not be taken from him without injury and this is the end and effect of property. Boecler concludes that there is therefore property in community (*proprietatem in communione*) (1633: 2.2.1). Pufendorf gives his qualified approval to Boecler: 'the Substances of things belong to none, but their Fruits become matter of *Property*, when gathered' (4.4.13). It illustrates his meaning with the example of gathering acorns, adding that 'This Notion of *Community*, tempered with such a degree of *Property* (*proprietas*), may, we think, be easily apprehended by Persons of no very nice or philosophical Heads.' By conceding that first gathering confers a natural right which may be termed 'property', Pufendorf contradicts his own theory. The excursus not only employs the language of property in community Locke was shortly to use, it also includes the same example Locke presents (2.28; cf. Olivecrona, 1974a: p. 225; Laslett, 1970: p. 306). The way in which Boecler and Pufendorf employ *proprietas* here is the same as the conventional English usage of 'property' adopted by Locke.

2

Locke situates the acorn-gathering example in the context of his positive community, similar to the English Common, and not in Pufendorf's context of negative community. This leads Locke to bring up two possible objections to this theory (2.28):

And will any one say he had no right to those Acorns or Apples he thus appropriated, because he had not the consent of all Mankind to make them his? Was it a Robbery thus to assume to himself what belonged to all in Common?

These are two of the objections Pufendorf borrowed from Velthuysen and deployed against Grotius' natural use right. Locke has already neutralised the major causes of strife in the state of nature according to Grotius and Pufendorf. A natural right in the just acquisition of one's labour and the extension of this right to use and enjoyment removes the two primary causes of contention: 'there could be then little room for Quarrels or Contentions about Property so establish'd' (2.31; cf. 2.34, 36, 51). Now Locke turns to the question of whether or not individuation constitutes a violation of the inclusive rights of other commoners.

Locke also may have had Filmer in mind at this juncture. Filmer points out that anything less than unanimous consent to individuation of positive community would constitute robbery; 'to have given a propriety of any one thing to any other, had been to have robbed him of his right to the common use of all things' (p. 273). The context of Filmer's argument is the transition to private property and the form of positive community he describes is different from Locke's. Nonetheless, it is still incumbent on Locke to show that his theory meets the objection (Kelly, 1977: pp. 82–3; Yolton, 1970: p. 195). Zeigler, as well as Tyrrell, makes a similar sort of objection in his commentary on Grotius. Indeed, Pufendorf quotes Ziegler's analysis and uses it as one reason for embracing the concept of negative community (4.4.11; Ziegler, 1662: 2.2.2).

For such is the Nature of things which lie in common, and which admit only of undivided Shares, that every single Atom of their Substance is no less undivided, than the whole; so that if any private Man apply it to himself alone, he is an injurious Robber of the community.

We have seen Pufendorf use this argument in his own consideration and rejection of positive community.

The problem Locke is faced with cannot arise in the theories of Grotius and Pufendorf. If the world belongs to no one, then the first concept of belonging to will be an individual and exclusive one. The first appropriator could not commit robbery because things belong to no one. Consequently, robbery will necessarily be defined in terms of the violation of exclusive property. This leads to the conclusion that any taking from another, taxation for example, is a form of robbery (Nozick, 1974: p. 169).

Locke's reassertion of the Scholastic theory which grants logical priority to 'belonging to all in common' gives rise to an opposite view of robbery. As all the opponents of positive community emphasise, robbery is defined in terms of invading the inclusive rights of the other positive commoners. Here exclusive property is the form robbery can take, not invasion of exclusive property. To take more than one's share of the common property constitutes robbery. Locke is thus faced with the problem of robbery as it arises in communism. Locke's first answer is, if a man takes more than necessary for his due he takes 'more than his share, and [it] belongs to others' (2.31); 'else he took more than his share, and robb'd others' (2.46). The man who accumulated more than he can use 'invaded his Neighbour's share' (2.37).

This answer presupposes a solution to the problem all adversaries of positive community say is insoluble. They all assume positive community means that everyone has a right to everything at one and the same time. If this is conceded, then the consequence is, as Hobbes puts it, 'a war of every man, against every man' (1651: 1.13). Mine and thine do not have a natural foundation; they are the artificial construction of the sovereign: '*Mine* and *Thine*, and *His*; that is to say, in one word *Propriety*; and [this] belongeth in all kinds of Common-wealth to the Soveraign Power' (II.24). Therefore, it cannot be an injustice for the sovereign to violate the subjects' Property: 'the Propriety which a subject hath in his lands, consisteth in a right to exclude all other subjects from the use of them; and not to exclude their Soveraign'. The undesirable conclusion Hobbes draws from this form of positive community furnishes the primary reason for Pufendorf's rejection of positive community. Negative community is then adopted to serve as the foundation for his development of a system of private property underpinned by natural law.

Locke's solution, like Cumberland's, is to redefine positive community. Although the common belongs to everyone in the same manner, it belongs to them to use for the duty of acquiring the means necessary for support and comfort. Their inclusive rights refer to these means which are due to each. Thus, each right does not refer to every item on the common. Indeed, it does not refer to any item on the common but, rather, to items made from the common. 'Things necessary for support and comfort' is a natural definition of the share which ought to belong to each. Since each man has a right to his due share and no more, acquisition of it cannot be robbery. Thus the logically prior inclusive right to one's due, limited in scope to things necessary for support and comfort, underlies Locke's answer to the question of robbery.

The restructuring of common rights so their reference does not conflict is the answer to all the critics of positive community. In neutralising the charge of robbery Locke also undercuts the objection that consent is required. Consent would be necessary only if the rights or liberty of others were infringed. The same restrictions which apply to man's natural rights apply to his natural liberty as well. Filmer bases his attack on positive community on the assumption that a man's 'natural right to community' and 'his natural liberty' entail that he may 'take what he please and do what he list' (p. 274). This kind of liberty is untrue even for Grotius, and it seems to show that Filmer's polemic is partially premissed on imputing Hobbes' state of nature to Grotius. Locke's reply is that liberty, like natural rights, must be defined in terms of law: 'a *Liberty* to dispose, and order, as he lists, his Person, Actions, Possessions, and his whole Property, within the Allowance of those Laws under which he is' (2.57). Therefore, in the natural condition men are in 'a *State of perfect Freedom* to order their

Actions, and dispose of their Possessions, and Persons, as they think fit, within the bounds of the Law of Nature, without asking leave, or depending upon the Will of any other Man' (2.4). The condition that man can act in the state of nature without the consent of others is an analytical feature of natural liberty. It is met, without developing into an Hobbesian state of war and without infringing the liberty of others, by deriving the range of liberty from natural law. Man's freedom to act with respect to earthly provisions is the '*Liberty to use them*, which God has permitted' (1.39). Liberty is thus equivalent to the exercise of the natural right to make use of things necessary for comfort and support. Acting within the bounds of the law of nature infringes neither the liberty nor the rights of others.

3

Locke effects an important conceptual clarification in his analysis of natural property and belonging to everyone in common. His adversaries call both a right and its object 'property', but, applied to the object of a common right, this seems to imply that the whole common is property. They conclude from this that every commoner must have a right to everything and this is taken to defeat any form of positive communism. Locke agrees that a right and its object are properly called property but, since this implies the rightholder's consent on any matter concerning property, he moves to a more careful analysis of the object of a common right. Although an inclusive right expresses common or joint property, it does not refer to the whole common. Rather, it refers to one's share of the common, *tout court*, and this may be called property. One's share of the common is defined by the end or purpose of the common right, but this is not a determinate thing or place on the common. For if this were true, the common would be property in several and not really common at all. Rather, one's share must be made from use of the common, so in fact the common remains common. To call the whole common 'property' would entail that consent is needed and this would be for each commoner to treat the common as 'one's own' in the exclusive sense. Consequently, one would speak of giving and taking; not of shares and sharing. Therefore, it is necessary not to call the common, 'property', but only the right to it, if there is to remain something that can be shared. (Of course, with respect to non-commoners, it is the commoners' property since their consent is required (2.35).) That which belongs to everyone in common, then, cannot be called property as that which belongs to a person can. To refrain from predicating 'property' of that which belongs to everyone in common saves this concept from reduction to property in several. Locke illustrates this point with an analogy which shows that the common remains common (2.29):

Though the Water running in the Fountain be every ones, yet who can doubt, but that in the Pitcher is his only who drew it out? His *labour* hath taken it out of the hands of Nature, where it was common, and belong'd equally to all her Children, and *hath* thereby *appropriated* it to himself.

We can see Locke's point by employing the example of public transportation. If we say that the seats are common property, in addition to our inclusive right to use them, then the consent of every potential commuter would be required before one person could ride on it. This would be like saying that the common is property and so consent would be required. As Locke remarks, 'If such a consent as that was necessary, Man had starved, notwithstanding the Plenty God had given him' (2.28). Thus, the seats belong to everyone in common but are not property. Without this distinction, the concepts of inclusion and of sharing are elided and common property is reduced to property in several (2.29):

By making an explicit consent of every Commoner, necessary to any ones appropriating to himself any part of what is given in common, Children or Servants could not cut the Meat which their Father or Master had provided for them in common, without assigning to every one his peculiar part.

Locke illustrates his positive theory by referring to the conventional practice of a commoner making use of the English Common without the express consent of all his fellow commoners (2.28; Gonner, 1912: p. 101).

4

We have seen that natural individuation does not quite skim over the surface of the common: a conditional use right in improved land is required for the production of supportive and enjoyable goods. This leads to the possibility that all accessible and utilisable land might be, at some time in history, under cultivation. When this occurs the situation is similar to one noticed and roundly criticised by Pufendorf in Grotius' theory. The important difference is that each commoner who is potentially excluded in Locke's theory has a claim right to be included. At this point consent would necessarily come into play because the exercise of any natural right would violate the right of another. Movement to a new form of individuation based on consent is then necessary. Therefore, Locke states at the outset that his theory of natural individuation only obtains prior to this situation; that is, 'where there is enough, and as good left in common for others' (2.27; cf. 2.33, 34, 36).

This quantitative (enough) and qualitative (as good) proviso is fulfilled in the early stages of man's history: 'Nor was this *appropriation* of any parcel of *Land*, by improving it, any prejudice to any other Man, since there was still enough, and as good left; and more than the yet unprovided

could use' (2.33). Once the proviso no longer obtains, natural individuation ceases to be justifiable and some form of conventional individuation
based on consent is required (2.36; Olivecrona, 1974a: p. 227; Mackie,
1977: p. 176).

We have seen that this second phase of Locke's theory occurs after the
establishment of government (2.38, 45). His solution consists in two
elements: an historical account of how 'the *Property* of *Labour* should be
able to over-ballance the Community of Land' (2.40); and a theoretical
account of how property must be conventionally distributed in accordance
with natural law and natural rights. I wish to leave these analyses to the
last section of the following chapter and the seventh chapter respectively.
In the intervening sections I discuss the remaining features of his analysis
in chapter five.

Locke has shown that particularisation of positive community is possible
and legitimate without consent as long as his proviso obtains. In so doing
he has answered all the critics of positive community and shown that it
occurs without strife. Why should Locke choose to do this in the face of
widespread opposition to positive community, rather than embrace negative community? There are several reasons which he brings out as he
develops the theory further. However, one reason which is readily apparent at this point is his need to show that man's natural right to the means
of preservation, which makes the common a positive community, is
operative through time. This is a consistency requirement of his theory of
revolution, because the right and duty in terms of which revolution against
arbitrary government is legitimated, is the natural right to the means of
preservation (2.149). In fulfilling this requirement of his primary objective
in the *Two Treatises*, Locke provides a justification, not of private
property, but, rather, of the English Common.

CHAPTER SIX

Property and obligation

i. Charity and inheritance

1

It is sometimes assumed that labour is the only natural title to and justification of individual ownership. Macpherson's interpretation is that 'the whole theory of property is a justification of the natural right...to unlimited individual appropriation' (1972: p. 221). He states that 'the root of that justification' is Locke's 'insistence that a man's labour is his own property'. Consequently, the 'traditional view that property and labour were social functions, and that ownership of property involved social obligations, is thereby undermined'. Aside from the fact that it is Locke's opponents, Grotius and Filmer, who present theories in which property is free of social obligations, Macpherson seems to place the wrong emphasis on labour. Labour justifies neither the accumulation of nor rights over one's goods; it provides, as I have attempted to show, a means of identifying something as naturally one's own (cf. Ryan, 1965: p. 225). Justification of accumulation and use is derived from the prior duty and right to support and comfort God's workmanship. The priority of natural law renders all rights as means to this end, and therefore Locke's account is a limited rights theory. An unlimited theory, like Grotius', grants priority to exclusive rights. Such a theory employs natural law to protect exclusive rights, through reducing it to the natural duty to abstain from another's property. Locke's theory is constructed in opposition to an unlimited rights theory; precisely the sort of theory which Marx took to be the typical justification of private property (1970: p. 6).

Certainly Locke wishes to emphasise that labour is the most suitable means for a rational animal to perform the first phase of his duty to preserve mankind. It is not, however, the sole means. In the same sentence in which he first announces that honest industry naturally entitles a person to his just products, he also proclaims two other natural titles: charity and inheritance (1.42). '*Charity* gives every Man a Title to so much out of another's Plenty, as will keep him from extream want, where he has no means to subsist otherwise.' Where no means are available for a man to provide for himself, the right to the means of subsistence applies directly to another person's goods. 'God the Lord and Father of all, has given no one of his Children such a Property, in his peculiar Portion of the things of this World, but that he has given his needy Brother a Right to the Surplusage of his Goods.' A proprietor who has more than enough to sustain himself is under a positive duty to sustain those who do not: "twould always be a Sin in any man of Estate, to let his Brother perish for want of affording him Relief out of his plenty'.

By making charity a natural and positive duty Locke answers Pufendorf's second objection to Grotius' theory. Pufendorf uses the possibility that a man might starve in Grotius' state of nature through exclusion to argue that individuation must be based on a pact incorporating the duty of charity. Locke replies that charity is a natural duty which follows from the nature of property in a manner strikingly similar to Aquinas' formulation of charity (*ST*: II. II.66.7). Since a person has a property for the sake of preserving himself and others, once his own preservation is secured, any further use for enjoyment is conditional on the preservation of others (2.6). Locke, rather than undermining the traditional obligations associated with property, gives them a particularly firm basis. Charity is a right on the part of the needy and a duty on the part of the wealthy (Dunn, 1968: pp. 81–2). 'The individualisation of the right is matched symmetrically by an individualisation of the duty' (Dunn, 1969: p. 217; cf. 1977: p. 92).

Locke's integration of charity into his theory, as a means of individuating man's natural claim right to his needs, where circumstances preclude an alternative, makes explicit another feature of his argument. Although the 'due use' limit on property is coincident with spoilage in the state of nature, it cannot be identified with it as Macpherson assumes (1972: p. 204). It should be noted as well that the positive duty of charity is not inconsistent with Locke's definition of property as that which cannot be taken without the proprietor's consent. The inclusive rights of each refer to the goods of a given society, and these are held individually because this serves the function of preserving mankind. If a case of need arises then, *ipso facto*, one man's individual right is overridden by another's claim, and the goods become his property. By failing to hand over the goods, the proprietor invades the share now belonging to the needy and is liable to punishment (2.37). The necessary goods 'cannot justly be denied him' (1.42). Individual ownership provides the means by which a moral agent may exercise his choice in performing his duties to others. However, in a manner similar to that of Pufendorf's analysis, if the duty is not discharged voluntarily, the claim right of the needy imposes the duty. As Lady Masham quotes Locke, the needy, like everyone else, have 'a right to live comfortably in the world' (cited in Cranston, 1957: p. 426).

2

The third natural criterion of identifying something as one's own is the title each man has to 'the fair Acquisitions of his Ancestors descended to him' (1.42). Locke's account of inheritance unfolds another dimension of the social nature of man. Men's duties to God and 'the Duties they owe one another' (2.5) constitute the community of mankind (2.128). Since man cannot exist without society, the performance of these duties is existentially necessary. In addition to this community man is also born into, and dependent upon, conjugal society, which is sustained by a set of familial duties (2.52–86). The individual commoner in the state of nature is twice removed from the isolated and presocial individual, who is often thought to underlie late eighteenth-century economic and political thought. Schochet has demonstrated how anachronistic it is to impose this individualist hypothesis on the *Two Treatises* (1969: pp. 81–98). Also, Laslett has brought to light the way in which the family formed a basic category in terms of which seventeenth-century men understood their place in the world (1964). Filmer's right of private dominion is tied to the family in the sense that it is exercised over the family members and belongs to only the patriarch. In discussing inheritance Locke comes to the conclusion that his use right is familial in the sense that it applies to the goods of the family, and it belongs to all the family members.

Locke acknowledges that there is almost universal consent to the institution of inheritance and infers, 'where the Practice is Universal, 'tis reasonable to think the Cause is Natural' (1.88). Parents have a natural and positive duty to provide support and comfort for their children, and the children have 'a Right in the Goods they [the Parents] are possessed of' (1.88). It follows that any family man's property is not his property at all; it is the common property of the whole family. 'Men are not Proprietors of what they have meerly for themselves, their Children have a Title to part of it, and have their Kind of Right joyn'd with their Parents.'

The standard form of a right of property is not an individual right for Locke; it is a common right enjoyed by all the family and, if necessary, by the whole kinship unit (1.90). The reason for this unique familialisation of property is to preserve mankind by preserving its basic unit: the family (1.88, 89). Locke destroys the very foundation of individual rights: the unquestioned assumption that a proprietor is the patriarchal head of a family (Grotius: 2.5.2; Hobbes, 1651: II.20; Filmer: p. 63; Pufendorf: 6.2.6). The family remains the basic sociological category but, instead of a hierarchy it becomes a communal organisation with common property, 'Community of Goods, and the Power over them, mutual Assistance, and Maintenance. . .[are] things belonging to *Conjugal Society*' (2.83). Just as

Filmer uses his patriarchal family as a model for society, so Locke uses his radically restructured communal family as a model for society (Schochet, 1975: pp. 247–67). A father has no more dominion over the property of his children than Adam and his descendants have over man's property (2.65, 74, 170). Children, like God's children, do not require their father's consent to individuate their common property (2.29).

Inheritance is not justified in terms of a father's right to dispose of his property as he pleases, since it is not wholly his property. Inheritance marks the fact that the parents have ceased to use that which belongs to the family in common. A possession 'comes to be wholly theirs [the children's], when death having put an end to their Parents use of it, hath taken them from their Possessions, and this we call Inheritance' (1.88; cf. 1.93). It now belongs to them for 'maintenance, support and comfort ...and nothing else' (1.93). The whole institution of primogeniture is unceremoniously dismembered, and all the children share in the inheritance (1.93). If there is no heir, the goods revert to the community; that is, they become common in the state of nature or pass into the hands of government in political society (1.90).

This aspect of Locke's theory is one of his most radical departures from convention. One need only contrast the account of the family by the Bishop of Ely, William Fleetwood (1656–1723), entitled *The Relative Duties of Parents and Children, Husbands and Wives, and Masters and Servants* (1705), to see how untoward Locke's conception must have appeared (cf. Schochet, 1975: pp. 83–4). He seems to have been driven to this position by what Dunn terms 'a polemical crux inflicted upon him by Filmer' (1969: p. 211). For it not only neatly decapitates the unlimited and unlimitable individual subject of Filmer's irresponsible natural right, replacing it with the entire family as the subject of a limited and responsible use right; it also provides a non-patriarchal model of the family, which he employs to conceptualise a human society of 'community of goods, mutual assistance and maintenance'. This seems to be Locke's point because he uses his reconstituted concept of the family as an analogy not only for natural society, but also for political society. In the analysis of the family in the First Treatise Locke gives his first analogous description of a commonwealth, 'each of whose parts and Members are taken care of, and directed in its peculiar Functions for the good of the whole, by the Laws of the Society' (1.93).

Locke's account of one's own and appropriation can be further illuminated by following Tribe's suggestion in *Land, Labour and Economic Discourse* to use the greek roots of seventeenth-century terms describing the household as a guide to their meaning.[1] The text most commonly referred to in discussions of the concept of one's own amongst natural law writers is a passage in Aristotle's *Rhetoric* (1361a 21–5). The term Aristotle uses for 'one's own' is οἰκεῖα, which means 'belonging to the household or family'. Similarly, the term for appropriation or making something one's own is οἰκειόω, which means 'to make a part of the family' (Liddell and Scott, 1845). With Locke's reply to Filmer, Greek etymons displace Hebraic ones as the linguistic foundation of the household.

ii. The social division of labour

1

One of Locke's illustrations of how labour creates a right in its product, without the consent of other commoners, consists in an example drawn from the English Common (2.28):

> Thus the Grass my Horse has bit; the Turfs my Servant has cut; and the Ore I have digg'd in any place where I have a right to them in common with others, become my *Property*, without the assignment or consent of any body. The *labour* that was mine, removing them out of that common state they were in, hath *fixed* my *Property* in them.

The purpose of this passage is to render, by an example familiar to his audience, the argument that consent is not required to appropriate on the natural common (see Gonnor, 1912: p. 16 for the right to dig ore on the English Common). In doing this, Locke seems to assume that his horse's biting of grass and his servant's cutting of turf, as well as his own ore-digging, are all his labour. The clause, 'the *labour* that was mine', which establishes his property in the grass, turfs and ore, seems to refer to all three cases. The conclusion sometimes drawn from this is that Locke withdraws his own explicit conclusion that the product of labour belongs to the labourer and accedes to the view that the labour and the labour-products of a servant belong to his master. This 'turfs' passage has launched a myriad of commentaries which fall into three major classifications.

One interpretation is that Locke's theory of labour-created property is a thoroughly modern conception; the classical belief being that labour and property are incompatible. Those who labour can own no property and those who own property do not labour. The 'turfs' passage is thus a mixture of the classical view that the master owns the labour and products of his servants, as in Filmer's theory, and of the modern view that labour creates a property in the product (Arendt: MS. 023475–8). The second type of interpretation is that Locke holds two modern and contradictory concepts of property. Ritchie comments that in chapter five, 'we seem to come upon the theoretic base of modern socialism – that to the labourer belongs the product of his toil' (1893: p. 179). The 'turfs' passage, on the other hand, implies that 'the capitalist employer of labour would, according to this clause, be fully entitled to the entire product created by his servants if he can manage to get it'.

Macpherson suggests an interpretation which is a refinement of the second wing of Ritchie's interpretation. He argues that the 'turfs' passage is consistent with the rest of Locke's theory if we assume that Locke was 'taking the wage relationship entirely for granted' (1972: p. 215). By 'the wage relationship', Macpherson means selling one's labour, or 'capacity to labour', to another for a wage (pp. 48, 54, 60, 214–15). Given this assumption, Locke's theory that the labourer has a property in his labour and products 'is not at all inconsistent with the assumption of a natural right to alienate one's labour in return for a wage' (p. 214). Thus, his comment on the 'turfs' passage is, 'it does not occur to Locke that one man's right can be established only by the labour of his own body; it is equally established by the labour he has purchased' (p. 215). Seen in the light of this assumption, Locke's phrase, 'the *labour* that was mine', refers to the servant's labour which Locke purchased for a wage (p. 215). Acceptance of this assumption leads to Macpherson's major interpretive conclusion. He claims that the right to alienate one's labour for a wage is an essential feature of capitalist or modern competitive market societies (p. 60). Therefore, in providing a natural foundation for this right (pp. 216–17), Locke is said to have 'erased the moral disability with which unlimited capitalist appropriation had hitherto been handicapped' (p. 221).

The third class of interpretation comprises commentaries which stress the contradictions either in the 'turfs' passage or in Macpherson's attempt to render it consistent (Laslett, 1964; Ryan, 1965; Mabbott, 1973: p. 148; Hundert, 1972, 1977; Tribe, 1978). The interpretations, in summary, span the views that Locke, in allegedly denying the servant a property in his product, is classical and modern, inconsistent and consistent. I will show what Locke is doing in the 'turfs' passage, support this with historical evidence, and then discuss Macpherson's interpretation.

2

All that Locke assumes in the 'turfs' passage is the master–servant relation. It is not only not the wage relationship of capitalism, it is a fetter to the development of capitalism which was not supplanted until the late eighteenth century. Locke describes the '*Master* and *Servant*' relation in the following manner (2.85):

a Free-man makes himself a Servant to another, by selling him for a certain time, the Service he undertakes to do, in exchange for Wages he is to receive: And though this commonly puts him into the Family of his Master, and under the ordinary Discipline thereof; yet it gives the Master but a Temporary Power over him, and no greater, than what is contained in the *Contract* between 'em.

He says that this form of contract is as old as history and history antedates civil society (2.101). It would be unusual, however, if Locke did not assume that this arrangement obtains in the state of nature, since many other instituted relations appear in the state of nature (2.14). Also, other natural law writers place masters and servants in the state of nature (Aquinas, *ST*: I.II.92.1; Suarez: 3.2.3; Grotius: 3.6.9). 'Natural' and 'existing in the state of nature', it should be noted, are not equivalent. Something is natural to man if a man possesses or may do it without consent, whereas something is conventional if it is based on consent. Man may consent to various sorts of (conventional) practices in the natural state; marriage for example (2.83). These distinctions are sometimes conflated (Macpherson, 1972: p. 216). The master–servant relation is a voluntary relation (2.28.3) in both the state of nature and civil society.

Since it is a freeman who makes himself a servant, the agreement must presuppose that the choice not to become a servant is available to him. This condition is fulfilled by the availability of spontaneous products of nature and utilisable land on the English Common in the 'turfs' passage. If, for some reason, there is no alternative, then the man is not free and the master–servant relation cannot arise. Locke is particularly emphatic on this point in his discussion of the right of the needy to support by charity (1.42):

Man can no more justly make use of another's necessity, to force him to become his Vassal, by with-holding that Relief, God requires him to afford to the wants of his Brother, than he that has more strength can seize upon a weaker, master him to his Obedience, and with a Dagger at his Throat offer him Death or Slavery.

This remarkable condition makes it impossible for the capitalist to appear in Locke's theory. If a man is driven by necessity to work for another, then the relation is based on force and is, *ipso facto*, a master and vassal arrangement. A person is not allowed to treat another in this way; he must feed him instead.

The precondition for the capitalist to emerge is the appropriation of all land such that a labourer is forced to work for another, and Locke explicitly denies that landholders can force a man to work under these conditions. Macpherson redescribes Locke's master–servant relation as a capitalist–worker relation on the basis of a mistaken inference. He writes that Locke posits 'the natural right of every man to get the means of subsistence by his labour' (1972: p. 213). The right is then said to be fulfilled either by labouring on land or by selling one's labour and working for another person where no unappropriated land is available (p. 214). The original right, however, is to the means of subsistence, and labour is only one means, not the means, to complete it. We have seen that need, without alternative means, naturally realises a man's right to subsistence in the surplus goods of another. A man may labour for himself or he may work for another, but only if an alternative is available. If it is not, he cannot labour for himself and he cannot be forced to work for another; he is simply given the necessary relief. The capitalist not only never appears in the *Two Treatises*; there is no place for him to appear.

Locke underscores this crucial point in section eighty-five. Servants are contrasted with slaves: men who have 'forfeited their Lives, and with it their Liberties, and lost their Estates; and being in the *State of Slavery*, not capable of any Property'. The person who is forced to work for another and is, therefore, a vassal, is *compared* to a slave in the earlier passage. Locke rebuffs this Filmerian economic relation which gives '*Despotical power to Lords*', rather than freely chosen power to masters (2.173–4). Macpherson, as Ryan and Hundert have noted, imputes to Locke an economic relation, based on force, which Locke stigmatises and eliminates from his theory (1965: p. 226; 1972: p. 15).

In the eighty-fifth section Locke describes the servant as a freeman who contracts to sell to another a service he undertakes to do, for a wage he is to receive. Since the labour of a person is defined as actions determined by the will of that person, it is logically impossible for an agent to alienate *his* labour. Therefore, what is sold by a freeman, and bought by another, is not his labour but, as Locke carefully writes, 'the Service he undertakes to do'. That is, a man agrees to sell a service or complete task which he himself does. A task or service may be spoken of as labour: the labour of writing a book or cutting turf, but this is not equivalent to the labour or activity which the person performs in order to do his task. Nor is it equivalent to Wollaston's second sense of 'labour': the achievement or result of one's labour-activity (Day, 1966: p. 110). Since, as Locke writes, the person does the service himself, he cannot sell his labour activity. The master tells the servant what to do, but he does not tell him how to do it, nor does he direct the servant in doing it. As a result, the labour, as activity, remains the labour of the person who is the servant. Locke emphasises that this is the case in a situation where there is a division of labour: 'the Labour of those who broke the Oxen, who digged and wrought the Iron and Stones, who felled and framed the Timber imployd about the Plough, Mill, Oven, or any other Utensils' (2.43). It seems safe to assume that at least some of these labourers work for another and, yet, it is their labour.

The term 'servant' had a wide range of uses in the seventeenth century (Thomas, 1972: pp. 70–8). Locke's account employs one of the two major conceptual models used to explain hiring for a service. William Perkins (1558–1602), in *Christian Oeconomie or a short survey of the right manner of erecting and ordering a family, according to Scripture* (1618) uses this same model: 'A free-servant is he, whom his master hireth for wages to do him service' (p. 692). Grotius explains the model in detail. 'Things which are ownerless', Grotius writes, 'become just as much the property of those who take them for themselves' (3.6.9). Consequently, 'free men, who in fishing, fowling, hunting or gathering pearls, have given their assistance to others, at once acquire what they have taken for those persons whom they serve'. The master has a conventional right in the product in virtue of his agreement. Although the arrangement is conventional, it precedes civil law: 'If, then, we disregard the civil law, the principle holds goods that one may do through another what he can do himself, and that the effect is the same whether any one acts for himself or through another.'

Grotius uses a quotation from the comments on the *Edicts* by Paulus, the Roman jurist, to explain the relation:[2]

'We acquire possession through an agent, a guardian, or an executor'; and he explains that this happens when they act with the intention of rendering us a service. The reason is that naturally one man by his own volition becomes the instrument of another's will.

The salient point for this concept of a servant is the sense in which a person is the instrument of another's will. If he is wholly under the will of another, he has neither a person nor action of his own, is thus incapable of property, and is a slave (2.5.27). This is the model Locke imputes to vassals and slaves dominated by despotical lords and 'stripp'd of all property' (2.173). Grotius' servant is under his own will when he acts; he is only directed to do a service by his master (1.5.3):

By Instruments, we mean not Arms, nor such like Things; but certain Persons who act by their own Will, but yet so as that their Will depends on another, that sets it in Motion: Such is. . .a Servant.

There are two descriptions of an act which a servant performs. As a person, he acts in accordance with his will; his actions and products are naturally his own. As a servant, the labour, or service, and product are the property of the master by convention or contract, just as the wage becomes the property of the servant. The servant has the intention *to* render a service to another; as the person who is the servant, he has the intention *with which* the service is performed. Thus, Locke is perfectly consistent in the 'turfs' passage when he says that the cutting of turfs by his servant is the '*labour* that was mine'. It is an analytical feature of the master and servant relation that the labour or service of the servant is the master's. The turf-cutter, who is Locke's servant, does not and cannot alienate his labour activity, and, as a result, has a natural property in the turf he cuts. As a servant he fixes Locke's conventional property in the cut turf because this is what he agrees to do.

3

The importance of Locke's description of masters and servants is that it embodies his view of the division of labour. A person who undertakes to do a service for another must know how, and be able, to do that task. He acts like a maker in his activity, just as he would if he were working for himself. He requires the skill to know how to do the task, and the instruments with which to do it. In his letter on *Some Considerations of the Lowering of Interest and Raising the Value of Money* (1691), Locke takes it to be an attribute of labourers, tradesmen and artificers that they own their own tools (1823: v, p. 24). The technical knowledge of how to do one's task is also understood to be possessed by labourers of various kinds in the *Two Treatises* (2.43, 44), the *Essay* (3.6.40, 4.12.11) and in *The Conduct of the Understanding* (1823: iii, p. 225). Indeed, technical knowledge should become the property of every man (1967: p. 319) and it is to be esteemed along with moral knowledge (1830: i, pp. 162–3). The servant, whether he be a ploughman, baker, workman or whatever, necessarily works in this analogous fashion to God his maker and, therefore, has a natural property in his achievement. If he did not, then no man would have property in anything, since all men are God's servants (2.6). This is also true of Grotius' theory, since every man is a servant of the sovereign: 'As a Servant is in a Family, the same is a Subject in a State, and is therefore the Instrument of the Sovereign' (1.5.3).

The organisation of work in which each man has a task to do, and in which he employs his own knowledge and instruments of production, is what Braverman calls, in *Labour and Monopoly Capital*, the '*social division of labour*' (1974: p. 72). Conception and execution remain in one and the same man, thus preserving the integrity of what for Locke is essential to the person as a human agent. Braverman, like Pufendorf, suggests that this form of work is characteristic of all pre-capitalist societies (p. 71; Pufendorf 5.2.9, 5.6.1; and *Digest* xix). Indeed, the notion that work consists in the conception and execution of a practical syllogism is the definition of 'making' bequeathed to the West by Aristotle (*Met*: 1032b 6–11). We have seen that in the seventeenth century it takes on the dimension of a religious duty, analogous to the way God works. 'My Father worketh, as yet, so I', Hooker enjoins in quoting Jesus (1.1.2; John 5.17).

A social division of labour, in which a labourer is hired to do a complete service, was the dominant and non-capitalist mode of production in England until at least the late eighteenth century (Dobb, 1947: pp. 266–7; Landes, 1969: pp. 58–9; Braverman, 1974: pp. 59–83; Tribe, 1978). Marx treats this as a distinct organisation of work which had to be dissolved before a capitalist mode of production could supplant it. In the *Grundrisse* he characterises it in terms of the worker's ownership of the instruments of production and their possession of a skill. 'Here labour itself [is] still half artistic, half end-in-itself etc. mastery' (1973: p. 497). Labour is the labourer's own: 'the relation to this one moment of the conditions of production constitutes the working subject as owner, makes him into a working owner, this [is] historic situation No. II' (p. 499). He identifies this situation with the master–servant relation, and states that it is dissolved by capitalism, or historic situation No. III (pp. 500–1). Locke's account of the social division of labour describes this historical situation. One person breaks the oxen, others work iron and stone, fell timber, construct ships, sow seeds, bake bread and so on (2.43). Each has a service which he himself does.

Braverman suggests that this social division of labour is different from the organisaton of work under capitalism. 'The division of labour in capitalist industry is not at all identical with the phenomenon of the distribution of tasks, crafts or specialities of production throughout society, for while all known societies have divided their work into productive specialities, no society before capitalism systematically subdivided the work of each productive specialty into limited operations' (p. 70). The distinguishing characteristic of capitalism is that the worker sells, and the capitalist buys, '*not an agreed amount of labour* [a service], *but the power to labour over an agreed period of time*' (p. 54). The capitalist directs the worker *in* his activity by breaking the labour process down into 'manifold operations performed by different workers' (p. 72). The degradation of tasks into separate operations assigned to several workers, and the creation of detail workers, did not begin, according to Braverman, until the labour process itself became an object of analysis in the late eighteenth century (pp. 75–7). The instrument of production eventually came to be removed from the worker. His activity is managed and controlled by a managerial class on one side, and an engineering class, which appropriates technical knowledge and divorces it from the agents who execute it, on the other (pp. 169–83; Unger, 1975).

In purchasing an agent's power to labour and in directing it, the capitalist destroys the autonomy of the person. For Locke, this would be to destroy his very humanity; that combination of concept and execution which makes a human agent like God. In this respect, the agent who is directed in his activity is like the slave or vassal, the very relation to which Locke's servant is contrasted. The apprentice is the other relation in the seventeenth century which approximates such a servile condition. He does so, however, not because he alienates his labour power, but because he does not possess the requisite knowledge and has to be directed by the master (Thomas, 1972: p. 76). The sovereignty which Locke's servant retains over his own labour activity came to be one of the major obstacles to the capitalist organisation and control of the labour process (Landes, 1969: pp. 58–9).

4

Therefore, in the light of Locke's concept of the master–servant relation, and in terms of our historical knowledge of the period, it is incorrect and anachronistic to impute the assumption of capitalist wage-labour to Locke. Macpherson's definition of the capacity to labour, which he claims is alienable in Locke's theory, is the same as Braverman's description of what the labourer sells under capitalism (p. 60). He describes it in the following manner (p. 48):

> If a single criterion of the possessive market society is wanted it is that man's labour is a commodity, i.e. that a man's energy and skill are his own, yet are regarded not as integral parts of his personality, but as possessions, the use and disposal of which he is free to hand over to others for a price.

According to Locke, this is precisely what cannot be placed at the use and disposal of another. Rather, the complete task or service which is executed with one's skill and energy, and its result, is conventionally exchanged. (If, on the other hand, this is what Macpherson really means here, then it is not the labour or the capacity to labour which is alienable and, therefore, he imputes to Locke a pre-capitalist mode of production.)

Macpherson supports his imputation of wage-labour on three grounds. First, he simply interprets 'the Service he undertakes to do' (2.85) as equivalent to labour (p. 215). This elision of service and labour activity is supported by the claim that 'the more emphatically labour is asserted to be property, the more it is to be understood to be alienable' (pp. 214–15). The reason is that 'property in the bourgeois sense is not only a right to enjoy or use; it is a right to dispose of, to exchange, to alienate' (p. 215). This may well be the 'bourgeois sense' of property but it is not Locke's nor the seventeenth-century English sense (cf. Ryan, 1965: pp. 225–6). 'Property', as we have seen, means only that something is one's own such that it cannot be taken without the owner's consent. The other rights which a person may exercise over his property are a separate matter. Life, liberty, person, the right to the means of support and comfort, are all property, yet they cannot be exchanged or alienated. Further, it is logically impossible, with Locke's concept of the person, to alienate one's labour. The third reason Macpherson evinces for his assumption is that 'any property right less than this would have been useless to Locke, for the free alienation of property, including the property in one's labour, by sale and purchase is an essential element of capitalist production' (p. 219). He clearly presupposes here as proved what the argument is supposed to prove: that Locke was out to justify capitalist production (cf. Ryan, 1965: p. 222).

If, as I have argued, the assumption of a right to alienate one's capacity to labour is infelicitous, it seems to follow that Macpherson's explanatory model is equally inappropriate. This is so because one is essential to the other: 'that each individual's capacity to labour is his own property and is alienable, is self-evidently required: without it, one of the essential features of modern competitive market societies would be impossible' (p. 60). Tribe draws the following conclusion in his theoretical survey of seventeenth- and eighteenth-century economic writing, *Land, Labour and Economic Discourse*: 'Thus it is not only wage labour which is absent from Locke's writings; the capitalist finds no space there either. The economic agents that are constructed in Locke's writings on property are not dependent on capitalist relations for their plausibility, as Macpherson argues, but the categories that are set to work there make such relations redundant' (p. 51).[3]

5

Although Locke's theory is, in hindsight, an obstacle to capitalism, nascent capitalism is not his target; the adversary at hand is Filmer. The servant, in Filmer's theory, is under the absolute will of his master and equivalent in status to a slave (above, p. 56). In undercutting primogeniture, which sustains Filmer's despotical Lords, Locke seems to clear the ground for his economic organisation of skilled workmen. To deny man the space to control his task with his own will, in whatever occupation God pleases to call him, is, for Locke, to endorse a society not of men, but of brutes (1823: III, p. 225):

Those who have particular callings ought to understand them; and it is no unreasonable proposal, nor impossible to be compassed, that they should think and reason right about what is their daily employment. This one cannot think them incapable of, without levelling them with the brutes; and charging them with a stupidity below the rank of rational creatures.

The horse of the 'turfs' passage is a brute in this sense. The labour of domesticating a horse, which makes the horse and what it brings about Locke's property, is 'the labour that was mine' (2.38). Since the horse has no will of his own, or at least lacks the power to abstract (2.11.11), it is functionally equivalent to a slave. All the slave acquires is naturally acquired for his master. Pufendorf explains, 'to whom any Person fully belongs, to him shall belong whatever that person can procure or produce' (6.3.7).

The practice which both Grotius and Locke seek to overturn is the assimilation of servants to the status of a slave. The way in which the assimilation is done is to elide the distinction between being under a master's will to do something and exercising one's own will in doing it (Pufendorf: 1.5.2). The conclusion, as Hobbes draws it in *Of the Political Body*, is that the servant has no property which does not belong to his master (1650: II.3.4). Only masters or fathers are proprietors according to this model. Locke acknowledges that slaves are called servants, but retorts that theirs is a 'far different condition': The slave, in contrast to the servant, has lost his life, liberty and capacity for property (2.85). Locke's servant has life and liberty and he both exercises and actualises his capacity for property in his work. Thus, a tenant farmer retains the products of his labour that are naturally his property and which he has not contracted to the landholder (2.194).

6

Locke's endorsement of creative labour, as the form of activity appropriate to one range of duties to God, is further enhanced by his treatment of value. Like many of the seventeenth-century English reformers, he holds a use theory of value: 'the intrinsick value of things. . .depends only on their usefulness to the Life of Man' (2.37). A similar view of value is expressed by Samuel Hartlib (d.1670?), in *A Description of the Famous Kingdom of Macaria* (1641), Peter Chamberlen (1601–83), in *A Poor Man's Advocate* (1649), and John Bellers (1654–1725), in *Proposals for Raising a College of Industry of all Useful Trade and Husbandry* (1696). Usefulness for the life of man is the criterion of natural value. Locke contrasts usefulness with various kinds of conventional value. Useless things, such as gold, silver and diamonds receive their value from 'Fancy or Agreement' (2.46), that is, 'from the consent of Men' (2.50). Land can become of value due to scarcity (2.45). Also, the desire for more than one needs puts non-use value on some things (2.37). This desire is unnatural, however, since it emerges with the conventional institution of money (2.50, 107).

Usefulness is not proven to be the criterion of value; it is simply posited as such. However, since man's fundamental duty is to preserve mankind, and since this requires useful products, such utilities are not only 'goods', but also things of inestimable value. The point of Locke's discussion is to discover the source of the usefulness of things. Although God gave the world to be used for the purpose of supporting and comforting the human race, He did not make it directly of use to man. Labour transforms nature into useful products, and so it is the source of value: '*labour makes the far greatest part of the value* of things, we enjoy in this World' (2.42; 2.40):

I think it will be but a very modest Computation to say, that of the *Products* of the Earth useful to the Life of Man 9/10 are the *effects of labour*: nay, if we will rightly estimate things as they come to our use, and cast up the several Expences about them, what in them is purely owing to *Nature*, and what to *labour*, we shall find, that in most of them 99/100 are wholly to be put on the account of *labour*.

Natural land furnishes only the material out of which useful products are made. It is of such minuscule usefulness in itself that it 'is called, as indeed it is, *wast*; and we shall find the benefit of it amount[s] to little more than nothing' (2.42).

Locke illustrates his argument with fairly complex examples drawn from a social division of labour (2.42, 43). At each stage, labourers receive a product useful to them from the workers at the prior stage. The product then becomes material to be reconstituted by their labour into a new product to be used by the workmen at the next stage as material out of which to make their product (2.43). The usefulness and, *ipso facto*, the worth of the product at each stage is created by labour. Since labour makes a product as an object of use, its usefulness and value is almost equivalent to the whole thing labour constitutes (2.42). If Locke were to justify the capitalist anywhere in the *Two Treatises*, one would think that he would say capital played at least some role in creating valuable and useful things. But the capitalist is absent here as elsewhere, along with the landowner and the master. The ploughman, reaper, thresher, baker, oven-breaker, planter, tiller, logger, miller, shipbuilder, clothmaker and tanner alone make things useful to the life of man and create value. The products are theirs, and any non-worker, except the needy, has no title to them (2.34).

Ritchie asks, to whom does the final product (bread) belong in Locke's example (1893: p. 183)? He has in mind the standard problem associated with theories in which the worker has a right to the product of his labour: because the workers cooperate it seems impossible to separate one man's product from another's (Miller, 1976: pp. 102–14). This is not an insurmountable difficulty for Locke, because although the workmen cooperate, they each have a distinct and readily identifiable task in which they achieve a discrete result. The answer is that the bread belongs naturally to the baker, the timber to the timberman, the leather to the tanner, and so on. The conventional arrangements for payment can thus be made in accordance with the natural principle of justice: every man has a title to the product of his honest industry.

iii. Passages from antiquity to polity

1

Locke's analysis has now reached a major turning point: particularisation within the community has been demonstrated, defusing Filmer's criticism of natural equality as the foundation for political theory. He forges his theory to liberate man from Filmer's right of private dominion, 'which was to provide Chains for all Mankind' (1.1). His argument works in two ways. First, it removes the ideological justification of the arbitrary and absolutist pretension of James II and his supporters during the Exclusion Crisis. Second, it demonstrates that there is no natural right of private dominion in land. The natural justification of landed estates, and the concomitant absolute and unlimited power of the landlord to reduce his servants to vassals, is undermined. Indeed, although landowners have natural property in their lives and liberties, as do all men, it is labourers who enjoy, in addition, natural property in the products of their labour. Locke also dissolves the major legal support of large, landed estates, primogeniture (Landes, 1969: p. 67). Therefore Locke's reply to Filmer exposes two types of slavery: despotical monarchs over their subjects and despotical lords 'over those who are stripp'd of all property' (2.173).

It is perhaps germane to note the social positions of Filmer and Locke. Filmer, being the eldest son of Sir Edward Filmer, inherited the whole of East Sutton, three Kentish manors and much other landed property. His relatives and friends were caught up in most of the commercial ventures of the day and Filmer wrote a justification of usury for them (Laslett, 1949: pp. 1–3). At the time he wrote the *Two Treatises*, Locke was a servant to the Earl of Shaftesbury, a small landlord through inheritance and a relatively unknown intellectual labourer, 'employed', as he described his position, 'as an Under-Labourer in clearing Ground a little, and removing some of the Rubbish, that lies in the way to Knowledge' (*Essay*, epistle, p. 10). His radical political beliefs and his involvement with Shaftesbury in the revolutionary activity for Exclusion led to his being spied upon by the King's informers at Oxford, and finally to underground existence as a revolutionary exile in Holland (Cranston, 1957: pp. 214–30).

Locke has also demonstrated that individuation on the natural common can occur without strife. Although this answers Grotius and Pufendorf, it also leaves Locke without the motive they employ to explain the instituting of private property and the transition to political society. For Grotius and Pufendorf, the desire to avoid strife and contention, consequent upon the absence of private property, serves as the crucial motivating factor for this transition. Locke is thus left with a problem of his own making (2.123):

If Man in the State of Nature be so free, as has been said; if he be absolute Lord of his own Person and Possessions, equal to the greatest, and subject to no Body, why will he part with his Freedom? Why will he give up this Empire, and subject himself to the Dominion and Controul of any other Power?

The penultimate objective of chapter five is to introduce a factor, the repercussions of which will motivate men to seek the protection and enjoyment of government. The institution which serves to create the requisite state of affairs is money.

Locke explains the introduction of money in the traditional, Aristotelian manner. Prior to its emergence, the commoners were permitted to do three things with the products of their labour: use these goods themselves for support and comfort, give them away, or barter with them. In so doing, a commoner 'did no injury; he wasted not the common Stock; destroyed no part of the portion of Goods that belonged to others, so long as nothing perished uselessly in his hands' (2.46). Out of barter grew the practice of coveting which Locke describes as heaping up and hoarding:

If he would give his Nuts for a piece of Metal, pleased with its colour; or exchange his Sheep for Shells, or Wool for a sparkling Pebble or a Diamond, and keep those by him all his Life, he invaded not the Right of others, he might heap up as much of these durable things as he pleased.

Locke marks the transition to this form of activity with a complete change of language which evinces his moral disapproval. Shells, diamonds and pebbles are grouped together and termed 'things', in opposition to the useful but perishable products which are called 'goods', 'good things', or 'things really useful' (2.37, 46, 47). Things which people heap up are acquired neither for use nor enjoyment, but because they are pleasing. They are not used, but 'hoarded up' (2.50); not acquired to use for convenience, but for the selfish desire to 'keep those by him all his life'. Like Aristotle, Grotius and Pufendorf, Locke identifies the emergence of covetousness as an outgrowth of barter (*Pol*: 1257a 19–30; 2.2.2.4; 4.4.6). Locke stigmatises it, but allows that it is permissible within the spoilage limit: 'the *exceeding of the bounds of his* just *Property* not lying in the largeness of his Possession, but the perishing of any thing uselessly in it' (2.46).

Money is introduced as a continuation of the hoarding of useless but permanent metals: 'thus *came in the use of Money*, some lasting thing that Men might keep without spoiling, and that by mutual consent Men would take in exchange for the truly useful, but perishable Supports of Life' (2.47). Locke's account of money is the same as Aristotle's in three essential respects: it follows from barter, it is introduced by consent in pre-political society, and it caters to and extends the unnatural desire to accumulate more than one needs (*Pol*: 1257a 19–40). As soon as money is introduced, some men begin to put more land under cultivation than is necessary for their natural uses and exchange the products they cannot use for money. This leads to an increase in the amount of land used by some men and hence to unequal possession of land (2.50):

it is plain, that Men have agreed to disproportionate and unequal Possession of the Earth, they having by a tacit and voluntary consent found out a way, how a man may fairly possess more land than he himself can use the product of, by receiving in exchange for the overplus, Gold and Silver, which may be hoarded up without injury to any one, these metalls not spoileing or decaying in the hands of the possessor.

Since gold and silver do not perish, they may be hoarded without transgressing the spoilage limit which acts as a natural check on the amount a person may acquire.

Why should a person desire to accumulate more than he needs for support and convenience? Locke answers that this acquisitive desire is a concomitant of the introduction of money and that it transforms the value of things: 'in the beginning, before the desire of having more than Men needed, had altered the intrinsick value of things, which depends only on their usefulness to the Life of Man; or [Men] had *agreed, that a little piece of yellow Metal*, which would keep without wasting or decay, should be worth a great piece of Flesh, or a whole heap of Corn' (2.37). Now things are valued not for their usefulness, but for their ability to be exchanged for money which can be hoarded. Without money, men laboured and created useful products for both support and convenience (2.36, 40, 41, 48). The increase of industry and agriculture is explained by man's natural desire to produce useful goods for these ends (2.37). This natural desire increases man's possessions somewhat (2.48), but only because his needs increase (2.38). The desire to accumulate more than one needs, therefore, is not the motor of technological advance and a more refined form of life; the only change which money explains is the enlargement of possessions: 'Find out something that hath the *Use and Value of Money* amongst his Neighbours, you shall see the same Man will begin presently to *enlarge* his *Possessions*' (2.49). The sole end this acquisitiveness serves is hoarding: 'Where there is not something both lasting and scarce, and so valuable to be hoarded up, there Men will not be apt to enlarge their *Possessions of Land*' (2.48). Without money man would work only for the sake of convenience: 'we would see him give up again to the wild Common of Nature, whatever was more than would supply the Conveniences of Life to be had there for him and his Family'. The only reason Locke gives for acquisition beyond convenience is the miser's reason: 'to draw *Money* to him by the Sale of the Product'.

2

Locke shows that the consequences of work and industry he wishes to endorse accrue to mankind without the use of money. The productivity of cultivating and using land, once agriculture and handicraft are introduced, is such that a family can satisfy their needs and convenience with one-tenth the land required in a hunting and gathering society (2.37). Therefore, 'he who appropriates land to himself by his labour, does not lessen but increase the common stock of mankind'. The person who industriously puts ten acres under cultivation 'may truly be said, to give ninety acres to Mankind'. I see no evidence for Macpherson's interpretation that 'the greater productivity of the appropriated land more than makes up for the lack of land available for others' (1972: p. 212). Locke explicitly states and repeats that, through increasing productivity, less land is used and more is left for others. He also specifies that this inverse ratio between increasing productivity and decreasing amounts of land required to provide comfort and support, would ensure that even with double the present world population, appropriation could still take place in the natural manner without 'prejudice [to] the rest of Mankind' (2.36).

Macpherson concludes that the motive which emerges with the introduction of money is the 'desire to accumulate land and money as capital' (1972: p. 208). Land, however, is not used as capital; it is possessed, and only as long as it is being used. Land cannot be exchanged; only the products of it are alienable (2.46, 50). There is no evidence in the *Two Treatises* that money functions as capital: it is simply hoarded (cf. Ryan, 1965: p. 222). Macpherson derives his conclusion mainly from Locke's account of money in the *Considerations of the lowering of interest, and raising the value of money*. Aside from the fact that this is a letter of advice and not a theory about the introduction of money, money is not treated here as capital. It is treated as a component of the polity and there is no independent category of the 'economy' in which it could be considered as capital. Locke's considerations on money are part of the seventeenth-century mercantilist discourse in which there is, Tribe concludes, no 'economy': 'That is, the terrain on which contemporary economic concepts and forms of explanation exist is undiscovered, or more precisely is not constituted' (1978: p. 35; cf. Hundert, 1972: p. 17f; 1977: p. 39f). There is no economic analysis, but rather an 'indistinction of economy and polity in the transitional epoch which produced mercantilist theories' (Anderson, 1977: pp. 35–6).[4]

Locke draws a series of contrasts between men's desires before and after the introduction of money in order to highlight the disruptive change in human activity. In the first ages of man 'the Inhabitants were too few for the Country, and want of People and Money gave Men no Temptation to enlarge their Possessions of Land, or contest for wider extent of Ground' (2.108). Pre-monetary society knew 'but few Trespasses, and Few Offenders' (2.107). 'The equality of a simple poor way of liveing confineing their desires within the narrow bounds of each mans smal proprietie made few controverseries and so no need of many laws to decide them.' It was a *'Golden Age* (before vain Ambition, and *amor sceleratus habendi*, evil Concupiscence, had corrupted Mens minds into a Mistake of true Power and Honour)' (2.111). Locke emphasises 'the Innocence and Sincerity of that poor but vertuous Age' (2.110). Here men's desires are natural and confined to the needs and conveniences enjoined by natural law (1.86; 2.36). There was 'little matter for Covetousness or Ambition' (2.107). Money ends the golden age by creating the unnatural desire to seek more than one needs. The temptation to accumulate beyond need, ambition and covetousness emerge. Things once valued for their usefulness are now valued for their capacity to be exchanged for inutile, yet hoardable money. This transformation of values is unnatural and purely of man's own making: 'For as to Money, and such Riches and Treasure. . ., these are none of Natures Goods, they have but a Phantastical imaginary value: Nature has put no such upon them' (2.184).

Men, therefore, bring upon themselves a state of contention, covetousness and acquisitive desire by consenting to the introduction of money. Locke proclaims, in *Some Thoughts Concerning Education*, that 'Covetousness, and the Desire of having in our Possession, and under our Dominion, more than we have need of,. . .[is] the Root of all Evil' (1968: p. 213). In the *Essay* Locke explains that men come to pursue these evil desires and cease to act for the sake of the moral good. Men become motivated by 'the fantastical *uneasiness*, (as itch after *Honour, Power*, or *Riches*, etc.) which acquir'd habits by Fashion, Example, and Education have settled in us, and a thousand other irregular desires, which custom has made natural to us' (2.21.45). Pufendorf offers a similar account of the disastrous result of currency (5.1.14).

The acceptance of money brings with it the fall of man. Prior to its appearance men were motivated by need and convenience; now they are driven by the most corrupt of human motives: the desire for more than one needs (cf. Dunn, 1969: p. 248). A state without quarrels or contentions becomes one of contention for more ground, trespassing and enlargement of possessions. Some men's desires are no longer coincident with the law of nature but, rather, drive them to overstep it. Instead of the meek inheriting the earth through their Christian labour, the covetous people whom Locke inveighs against threaten to engross it. God gave the World 'to the use of the Industrious and Rational, (and *Labour* was to be *his Title* to it;) not to the Fancy or Covetousness of the Quarrelsom and Contentious' (2.34).

Locke's analysis of money furnishes the most powerful motive for entering into political society. It answers his initial question: why should anyone want to leave the state of nature. 'To which 'tis obvious to Answer, that though in the state of Nature he hath such a right, yet the Enjoyment of it is very uncertain, and constantly exposed to the Invasion of others' (2.123). Locke stresses that 'the greater part [are] no strict Observers of Equity and Justice'. Therefore, to 'avoid these Inconveniences which disorder Mens Properties in the state of Nature, Men unite into Societies' (2.136). This is the reason why God 'appointed Government' (2.13). The same theme is taken up in *A Letter concerning Toleration*, written in 1685 and published in 1689 (Montuori, 1963: pp. xx–xxi). Following a precis of his theory that the production of things necessary for support and comfort requires labour, Locke concludes, 'the pravity of mankind being such that they had rather injuriously prey upon the fruits of other men's labour than take pains to provide for themselves, the necessity of preserving men in the possession of what honest industry has already acquired, and also of preserving their liberty and strength, whereby they may acquire what they further want, obliges men to enter into society with one another' (1963: p. 83).

3

The final task Locke undertakes in chapter five is to explain the way in which natural individuation becomes disfunctional once money is accepted. When he states that the introduction of money leads some men fairly to possess more land, in accordance with the natural rules, he immediately reiterates his commitment that the possession of property is fixed by civil law in a polity. 'For in Governments the Laws regulate the right of property, and the possession of land is determined by positive constitutions' (2.50; see above, pp. 98–9). That is, although property is governed by natural regulations in the state of nature, thus permitting unequal possessions after money appears, property is regulated by civil law in a commonwealth. This is what Locke says here and in the earlier editions of the *Two Treatises*: 'it is plain, that the consent of Men have agreed to disproportionate and unequal Possession of the Earth, I mean out of Society and Compact; for in Governments the Laws regulate it' (collation to 2.50: p. 477). Since unequal possession is a creation of a monetarised state of nature and may be superseded by the determinations of civil law, an important clarification is required. Locke needs to discriminate between the transitional and conditional measures of appropriation and use, which govern property in the state of nature, and those which are eternal and non-conditional, and, therefore, remain as background principles in accordance with which government regulates and determines property. Locke's answer is already known because men enter into the state of nature with their three natural and non-conditional claim rights. The only additional natural right they acquire is the right in the products of their labour. The transitional regulations operative in the state of nature are demarcated and dropped in preparation for the move to political community in section thirty-six.

His clarification begins with a restatement of how acquisition and use, prior to the introduction of money, are bounded by nature such that the claim rights of others are not transgressed (2.36):

The measure of Property, Nature has well set, by the Extent of Mens *Labour, and the Conveniency of Life:* No mans Labour could subdue, or appropriate all: nor could his Enjoyment consume more than a small part; so that it was impossible for any Man, this way, to intrench upon the right of another, or acquire, to himself, a Property, to the Prejudice of his Neighbour, who still have room, for as good, and as large a Possession (after the other had taken out his) as before it was appropriated.

The combination of labour entitlement and the inability of man to make use of large amounts of land insures that the claim rights of others are not violated. The situation is equitable also because the world is sparsely populated: 'Men were more in danger to be lost, by wandering from their Company, in the then vast Wilderness of the Earth, than to be straitned for want of room to plant in.' As in present-day Spain, a man's title to land rests, without prejudice to others, on no other title 'but only his making use of it'. These measures would work today and even for double the present population, if money had not been introduced:

This I boldly affirm, That the same *Rule of Propriety,* (*viz.*) that every Man should have as much as he could make use of, would hold still in the World, without straitning any body, since there is Land enough in the World to suffice double the Inhabitants had not the *Invention of Money,* and the tacit Agreement of men to put a value on it, introduced (by Consent) larger Possessions, and a Right to them; which, how it has done, I shall, by and by, shew more at large.

Once money is present, men can and do enlarge their possessions of land by trading the surplus for money (2.48–50); they claim to be entitled to their enlarged possessions because they make use of them. With the increase in population, this rapidly leads to the situation in which others are excluded from exercising their natural claim right. The only solution, therefore, is to remove the rule that every man should have as much as he can make use of, thereby undermining the legitimacy of 'larger Possessions, and a Right to them'. Some other rule must now confine the possession of land such that the inclusive rights of everyone can be exercised. The new rule is civil law (2.50).

Macpherson interprets this section as a transcendence of natural law limits and a justification of unlimited appropriation: 'Hence an individual is justified in appropriating land even when it does not leave enough and as good for others' (1972: p. 211; cf. p. 203). This contradicts what Locke says. Once the rule that every man should have as much as he could make use of is rescinded, no appropriation is justified. The rule suited appropriation in the pre-monetary state of nature because its application could not prejudice the position of any other, thus proving Locke's crucial point that appropriation did not require consent. Applying it in a post-monetary world would 'straitn' others; therefore it must be repealed and other conventional rules, based on consent, must be constructed (cf. Cherno, 1958: pp. 52–3). God gave the world to man to make use of it for the support and comfort of mankind (2.26) and originally no manmade limits were required; each man could have as much as he could use. Now this is impossible without breaking the conditions under which God gave the world to mankind, so now new constraints on 'making use' must be applied in order for man to act within the bounds of the law of nature. It seems to me remarkable to suppose that Locke should attempt to dismantle the Thomist framework of positive natural law which constitutes the basis of his theory. For he clearly could not do away with this without destroying exclusive rights as well. If he had wished to justify unlimited accumulation he surely would have employed a negative community, like Grotius and Pufendorf, rather than reasserting, with Cumberland, positive community.

Locke explains what removal of this rule of property entails by returning to appropriation on the English Common. If a man attempts to move into the Common and enclose a part of it, his making use does not create a title. Consent is now required (2.35):

> 'Tis true, in *Land* that is *common* in *England*, or any other Country, where there is Plenty of People under Government, who have Money and Commerce, no one can inclose or appropriate any part, without the consent of all his Fellow-Commoners: Because this is left common by Compact, *i.e.* by the Law of the Land, which is not to be violated. And though it be Common in respect of some Men, it is not so to all Mankind; but is the joint property of this Country, or this Parish.

Now the law of the land specifies how appropriation takes place. Consent of the commoners is required because the common is their property and 'the remainder, after such inclosure, would not be as good to the rest of the Commoners as the whole was, when they could all make use of the whole'. The original proviso, that there is enough and as good left in common for others, no longer obtains and, therefore, natural appropriation without consent is invalid. Locke immediately contrasts post-monetary, conventional appropriation with appropriation prior to the introduction of money: 'whereas in the beginning and first peopling of the great Common of the World, it was quite otherwise. The Law Man was under, was rather for *appropriating*.'

Locke's illustration not only clarifies the difference between property in the pre-monetary state of nature and conventional property under government; it also makes an important practical point – perhaps the most important point in the chapter. Wealthy landowners were attempting to enlarge their estates by enclosing the Commons without the consent of

the commoners. Their justification was that they could make better use of
the land than could the commoners. Three Bills to legalise enclosure
without consent were introduced in the House of Commons, 1664, 1661
and 1681, but they were defeated (Gonner, 1912: pp. 56–8). Locke's
theory serves explicitly to legitimate the rights of the commoners against
the enclosing landlords. It cannot be the case, therefore, that Locke
intended his theory to exclude all but landholders, as Macpherson assumes
(1972: p. 238). For in justifying the properties of commoners, servants and
day-labourers, Locke refutes Filmer's argument that only landholders
possess rights.

The ground is now cleared for an analysis of property in political
society. Locke notes that men's natural inclusive right, which referred
originally to the whole world, refers only to the whole of one's country
when men enter into polities. Men then individuate this property conventionally (2.45):

the Leagues that have been made between several States and Kingdoms, either
expressly or tacitly disowning all Claim and Right to the Land in the others
Possession, have, by common Consent, given up their Pretences to their natural
common Right, which originally they had to those Countries, and so have, by
positive agreement, settled a Property amongst themselves, in Distinct Parts and
parcels of the Earth.

He also foreshadows that the determination and regulation of property
under government is in accordance with natural principles of justice: '*by
Compact* and Agreement, [they] *settled the Property* which Labour and
Industry began'. It is worth noting that Locke's account is opposite to
laissez-faire theories. According to these, the introduction of money
creates a market which operates naturally or with an invisible hand.
For Locke, social relations naturally conduce to a just society only when
money is absent. Money disrupts this natural order, and government is
required to constitute a new order of social relations which will bring the
actions of men once again in line with God's intentions (2.135).

PART THREE

Conventional Rights

CHAPTER SEVEN

Property in political society

i. Making a polity

1

Locke writes, 'Governments must be left again to the old way of being made by contrivance, and the consent of Men ('Ανφρωπίνη κτίσις) making use of their Reason to unite together into Society' (1.6). In calling the production of government by human reason 'the old way', Locke emphasises the point that theories of divine institution of government, such as Filmer's, are of recent origin. Locke's project is conservative: to reassert the traditional view that men make their own political organisations against the new wave of divine right theories. Ever since Aquinas, it has been a conventional assumption amongst natural law writers that government is a human artifact. In his *Commentary on Aristotle's Politics* Aquinas states, '[t]he commonwealth is, in fact, the most important thing constituted by human reason' (1974: p. 197). It is difficult for us, in the light of post-seventeenth-century political history, to see Locke as a conservative and Filmer as an innovator. Divine right theories of kingship, however, appeared in continental Europe only in the sixteenth century and in England in the seventeenth.[1] The movement in England was, as Locke admonishes, a novelty: 'In this last age a generation of men has sprung up among us, who would flatter princes with an Opinion, that they have a Divine Right to absolute Power' (1.3). Filmer is thus seen by Locke as 'a Reformer of Politicks' (1.106).

When Locke wrote and published the *Two Treatises*, divine right was the new orthodoxy and *Patriarcha* 'the canonical scripture of political obedience' (Laslett, 1949: p. 37).[2] Locke's allegiance to 'the old way' is a radical conservatism – a call for a return to the older, fundamental principles of politics. This seems to be a correct description of his place in the natural law tradition as well, for he reconstructs constitutionalism in opposition to the innovative use of natural law by Grotius and Pufendorf to establish absolutism. Certainly Locke saw himself in this light. In a letter to Edward Clarke on 8 February 1689, expressing his disgust with the superficiality of the form of revolution settlement adopted by the Convention Parliament, Locke describes his position with uncompromising honesty. He writes, 'the settlement of the nation upon the sure grounds of peace and security...can no way so well be done as by restoring our ancient government; the best possible that ever was, if taken and put together all of a piece in its original constitution' (1927: p. 289). The *Two Treatises*, Dunn comments, 'aimed to restore a previous political health; not to initiate but to revert' (1971: p. 137).

2

Locke's construction of political society is in the form of the four Aristotelian causes: material, efficient, formal and final.[3] Commonwealth, independent community and *civitas* are names given to the finished product (2.133). The material out of which a community is constituted is the natural power men have in the state of nature. A man's natural power is comprised of two kinds, the first of which 'is to do whatsoever he thinks fit for the preservation of himself and others within the permission of the *Law* of *Nature*' (2.128). The second is 'the *power to punish the Crimes* committed against that Law'. When a man incorporates into a commonwealth he 'gives up' both these powers. The manner in which natural power is given up is different for each of the two kinds. The first power, '*of doing whatsoever he thought fit for the Preservation of himself*, and the rest of Mankind, *he gives up* to be regulated by Laws made by the Society, so far forth as the preservation of himself, and the rest of that Society shall require' (2.129). Thus, man's power to appropriate, produce, consume, assist others, own, use and enjoy, give, barter and exchange – economic and social power – becomes part of the political power of the society (2.130). Now society determines how a man is to exercise this natural power; his natural liberty to act in any of these ways is thereby confined (2.129). Locke's analysis exhibits the 'indistinction' of economy and polity which we have seen to be typical of seventeenth-century thought. '*Secondly*, the *Power* of *punishing* he wholly *gives up*', and it is exercised by the executive branch of his society (2.130). The two types of power, given up in these two ways, becomes 'the joynt power of every Member of the Society' (2.135).

Consent to give up one's natural power is the efficient cause of a polity.[4] That 'which begins and actually *constitutes any Political Society*, is nothing but the consent of any number of Freemen capable of a majority to unite and incorporate into such a Society' (2.99). Consent is a necessary constituting condition because it is a man's own power which is given and, being his own, it cannot be taken without his consent. In addition to constituting a commonwealth, it is also the act of '*Consent which makes any one a Member* of any Commonwealth' (2.122). Locke uses the concept of a member in the sense of a part of an organic whole. Becoming a member means transforming oneself into a constituent element of a political body (2.121):

> Whereas he, that has once, by actual Agreement, and any *express* Declaration, given his *Consent* to be of any Commonweal, is perpetually and indispensably obliged to be and remain unalterably a Subject to it, and can never be again in the liberty of the state of Nature; unless by any Calamity, the Government, he was under, comes to be dissolved; or else by some publick Act cuts him off from being any longer a Member of it.

By these two means, men make a political body of which they are the parts and their two powers its power: 'when any number of Men have, by the consent of every individual, made a *Community*, they have thereby made that *Community* one Body, with a Power to Act as one Body' (2.96). The unanimous consent which constitutes any political society includes the agreement to be bound 'by the will and determination of the *majority*', which moves the political body or 'acts any Community'. The members 'make one *Body Politick*, wherein the *Majority* have a Right to act and conclude the rest' (2.95).

    'The Majority having, as has been shew'd, upon Mens first uniting into Society, the whole power of the Community, naturally in them', the ground is clear for discussion of the formal element of political society (2.132). This step is the fundamental question of politics (1.106):

> The great Question which in all Ages has disturbed Mankind, and brought on them the greatest part of those Mischiefs which have ruined Cities, depopulated Countries, and disordered the Peace of the World, has been, Not whether there be Power in the world, nor whence it came, but who should have it.

Locke's answer is that the majority decides who should have it. After the unanimous consent which constitutes a commonwealth, 'the *first and fundamental positive Law* of all Commonwealths, *is the establishing of the Legislative* Power' (2.134). By 'legislative' Locke means the law-making body, analytically distinct from the 'legislature' or power of law-making (2.88, 94; cf. Laslett, 1970: p. 347n). The legislative is the community's continuing form of decision procedure which transforms its power into law-making power: 'the power of the Society, or *Legislative* constituted by them' (2.131; cf. Dunn, 1969: pp. 128–9; 1971: p. 141). Because a society is composed of this power, the legislative is, in this sense, the society, and a man who becomes a member 'authorizes the Society, or which is all one, the Legislative thereof to make Laws for him' (2.89). Men, 'when they enter into Society, give up the Equality, Liberty, and Executive Power they had in the State of Nature, into the hands of the Society, to be...disposed of by the Legislative' (2.131).

    The '*Legislative*' is 'derived from the People by a positive voluntary Grant and Institution' (2.141). This consists in a majority decision of all

the commonwealth men to a fundamental constitution or form of legislative or government (2.132, 157). The legislative power is then entrusted
to those whose duty it is to govern in accordance with the constitution
(2.149).[5] Thus, the power of the community is never alienated but entrusted only, and it reverts to the people when governors act contrary to
the constitution: 'the Legislative being only a Fiduciary Power to act for
certain ends, there remains still *in the People a Supream Power* to remove
or *alter the Legislative,* when they find the *Legislative* act contrary to the
trust reposed in them' (2.149). In such a case, 'the Power devolve[s] into
the hands of those that gave it' (2.149), and 'the People have a Right to
act as Supreme, and continue the legislative in themselves, or erect a new
Form, or under the old form place it in new hands, as they think good'
(2.243).[6]

Power, which begins as each man's two natural powers, passes through
two phases: it is given up (in two ways) by consent to make a community;
and it is entrusted to governors as legislative power to be disposed in
accordance with the agreed-upon constitution (2.243). In terms other than
those of power, this is a distinction between society or commonwealth and
government (2.211). Because, however, the legislative holds the power of
the community, the constitution or form of government is necessarily,
apud Aristotle, the form of the community (2.132):

For the *Form of Government depending upon the placing* the Supreme Power,
which is the *Legislative,* it being impossible to conceive that an inferior Power
should prescribe to a Superior, or any but the Supreme make Laws, according as
the Power of making Laws is placed, such is *the Form of the Common-wealth.*

If the constitution specifies a democratic or oligarchic formation of power
in government, then the community is democratic or oligarchic in form
as well (2.132). Consequently, when government dissolves, the people do
not revert to the state of nature but remain members of their society,
lacking only a form (2.211).

The commonwealth is, in terms of the *Essay,* a mixed mode, and the
form of legislative its constitution or real essence (above, pp. 8–27): 'the
Essence and Union of the Society consist[s] in having one Will, the Legislative' (2.212). In making a form of government men are close to imitating
God's making of man, for they make the soul and life of their society:

'tis in their *Legislative,* that the Members of a Commonwealth are united, and
combined together into one coherent living Body. This *is the Soul that gives
Form, Life and Unity* to the Commonwealth: From hence the several Members
have their mutual Influence, Sympathy, and Connexion.

One of the many disanalogies with God's making is that men become
members of the 'living body' they make. Locke's constitution theory of

political society is similar to Hooker's, which he quotes (2.135; Hooker: 1.1.10).

The way in which the legislative acts as the will and soul of a society is to direct its actions, giving form and unity to the movement of its members (1.93; above, p. 134). Since each man gives up his power to act in order to make the society, each man, as a member, derives his power to act from the legislative (2.150; cf. 2.219):

the Legislative is no otherwise Legislative of the Society, but by the right it has to make Laws for all the parts and for every Member of the Society, prescribing Rules to their actions, and giving power of Execution, where they are trans-gressed, the *Legislative* must needs be the *Supream*, and all other Powers in any Members or parts of the Society, derived from and subordinate to it.

The relation of member to society is that of part to whole; or like servant to master because members' actions are directed and the legislative has its power from an agreement (2.152). Locke derives the rights and obligations from the two constitutive acts in the way he prescribes in his analysis of instituted relations in the *Essay* (above, pp. 10–11).

Political society is different in kind from the state of nature. Each man has his own natural power in the state of nature to direct in accordance with natural law. On entering a community, men 'give up all their Natural Power to the Society which they enter into' (2.136) to be regu-lated and directed in concert by the legislative or will of the community of which they are now a part. This explains why, *inter alia*, natural appro-priation ceases to be legitimate. Locke's analysis of the creation of a polity also exhibits the absence of an economic sphere distinct from the political. Again, this is typical of seventeenth-century thought: 'the very idea of a self-regulating market was absent...The economic system was submerged in general social relations; markets were merely an accessory feature of an institutional setting controlled and regulated more than ever by social authority' (Polanyi, 1957: pp. 55, 67).

3

The final step in the construction of such a tightly knit community is to ascertain its end or final cause. When society's power is in each man's hands in the state of nature, it has as its end the preservation of mankind. It has the same end, therefore, when it becomes political power in the hands of the legislative: 'the *end and measure of this Power*, when in every Man's hands in the state of Nature, being the preservation of all of his Society, that is, all Mankind in general, it can have no other *end or measure*, when in the hands of the Magistrate, but to preserve the Mem-bers of that Society' (2.171). This natural end is thus the aim of legislative power, 'a *Power to make Laws*, and annex such *Penalties* to them, as may tend to the preservation of the whole'. Since government is the essence of community, the ends of government and community are one and the same: 'The *Legislative* Power is that which has a right *to direct* how *the Force of the Commonwealth* shall be imploy'd for preserving the Community and the Members of it' (2.143). The preservation of men and of society are, as has been shown, the two basic laws of nature. The result of Locke's conceptual analysis of power is the production of a polity directed toward and bounded by natural law: 'The Obligations of the Law of Nature, cease not in Society, but only in many Cases are drawn closer, and have by Humane Laws known Penalties annexed to them, to inforce their observation' (2.135; cf. Suarez: 1.9.10). Therefore, the '*Rules* that they [legislators] make for other Men's Actions, must, as well as their own and other Mens Actions, be conformable to the Law of Nature, i.e. to the Will of God'. Political authority, Dunn concludes, 'does not extend beyond those actions of the authority which are correctly described as executions of the purposes of God' (1969: p. 127).

Locke redescribes the natural end of political society as the public good: 'Their Power in the utmost Bounds of it, is *limited to the publick good* of the Society. It is a power, that hath no other end but preservation' (2.135). Common good, good of society or community and good of the public are various synonyms he uses to describe the purpose for which a commonwealth is instituted.[7] The common good is the conventional goal of legislation and, as such, of society (Suarez: 1.7.1–4; Hooker: 1.1.10; Cumberland: p. 16). This, in turn, completes Locke's definition of political power (2.3):

Political Power then I take to be *a Right* of making Laws with Penalties of Death, and consequently all less Penalties, for the Regulating and Preserving of Property, and of employing the force of the Community, in the Execution of such Laws, and in the defence of the Common-wealth from Foreign Injury, and all this only for the Publick Good.

This definition comprises the two kinds of power at the legislative's disposal: the power to execute the law of nature, by the death penalty and war if necessary (2.7–12); and the power to regulate the means of preservation (property). It also provides the first description of the principle in accordance with which property is regulated, but not determined, in political society – the public good.

In his definition of political power, Locke places the regulation of property as the means to an end of the public good. He analyses this means–end relationship from two perspectives: by examining the public good and by analysing property. The public good can be considered as a principle of justice governing society in either of two ways: as an aggregative principle it refers only to the total amount of good enjoyed by a particular group; as a distributive principle it refers to the share of that good which different members of the group have for themselves (Miller, 1976: p. 19). Like Cumberland and Suarez (1.7.7), Locke uses the public good as a distributive principle. Since the public good is the natural end of preservation as it applies to political society, it is equivalent to the good or preservation of each (2.6). We have seen that the preservation of each, including comfort as well as support, entails three natural rights: to preservation, to the liberty of preserving oneself and others, and to the material possessions necessary for preservation. These claim rights to life, liberty and possessions are completed and regulated naturally in the state of nature and, by this means, preservation is realised. In political society, then, bringing about the public good is also equivalent to securing the life, liberty and possessions of each (2.135). Political power 'can have no other *end or measure*. . .but to preserve the Members of that Society in their Lifes, Liberties, and Possessions' (2.171).

By equating the public good with preservation and so with the good or preservation of each, Locke ensures that the aim of legislation is identical to the end for the sake of which men enter into and construct political society. Man 'seeks out, and is willing to joyn in Society with others who are already united, or have a mind to unite for the mutual *Preservation* of their Lives, Liberties and Estates, which I call by the general Name, *Property*' (2.123). Preserving life, liberty and possessions is how the legislative discharges its duty to achieve the common good. Men give up their natural powers and enter political society 'only with an intention in every one the better to preserve himself his Liberty and Property;. . .the power of Society, or *Legislative* constituted by them, *can never be suppos'd to extend farther than the common good*; but is obliged to secure every ones Property by providing against those. . .defects. . ., that made the State of Nature so unsafe and uneasie' (2.131). Having exhibited the means–end relation between preservation of property and the public good, Locke continues to use the two interchangeably as the final cause of political community: 'the end of Government it self. . .is the publick good and preservation of Property' (2.239).

ii. Conventional property

1

Once the lineaments of a commonwealth are constructed, Locke addresses the questions left unanswered in chapter five: how 'the Laws regulate the right of property' and how 'the possession of land is determined by positive constitutions' (2.50; above, pp. 98–9, 151). Although a man enters into a polity to preserve his liberty, as a condition of membership he abjures to the community his *natural* liberty – the power of doing whatsoever he thinks fit for the support and comfort of himself and others. This is necessary because he is not now an independent individual but, rather, an interdependent member of an unified whole, orchestrated by government. 'For being now in a new State, wherein he is to enjoy many Conveniencies, from the labour, assistance, and society of others in the same Community, as well as protection from its whole strength; he is to part also with as much of his natural liberty in providing for himself, as the good, prosperity, and safety of the Society shall require' (2.130). The 'Laws of the Society in many things confine the liberty he had by the Law of Nature' (2.129). Such a *quid pro quo* 'is not only necessary, but just; since the other Members of the Society do the like' (2.130). Locke is nonetheless correct to say that a man's liberty is preserved, for, by definition, it is 'a *Liberty* to dispose, and order, as he lists, his Person, Actions, Possessions, and his whole Property, within the Allowance of those Laws under which he is' (2.57). He is now immediately under civil rather than natural law; his new, conventional liberty is formally identical yet materially different from natural liberty.

It follows, *a fortiori*, from his liberty or natural power to dispose and order his person, action and possessions being yielded to, and under the direction of, the community, that his possessions also belong to the community. For what he relinquishes is his power to come to have and to possess these goods. 'To understand this the better', Locke explains, 'it is fit to consider, that every Man, when he, at first, incorporates himself into any Commonwealth, he, by his uniting himself thereunto, annexed also, and submits to the Community those Possessions, which he has, or shall acquire, that do not already belong to any other Government' (2.120). All the possessions a man has in the state of nature, or shall acquire in his commonwealth, become the possessions of the community. As with liberty, men preserve their possessions by exchanging natural possessions for conventionally defined ones:

For it would be a direct Contradiction, for any one, to enter into Society with others for the securing and regulating of Property: And yet to suppose his Land, whose Property is to be regulated by the Laws of the Society, should be exempt from the Jurisdiction of that Government, to which he himself the Proprietor of the Land, is a Subject.

Thus, 'they become, both of them, Person and Possession, subject to the Government and Dominion of that Commonwealth, as long as it hath a being'. This submission of possessions to the community and hence to the control of the government is not only entailed by the yielding of one's natural power over them; it is also necessary if government is to determine the possession of lands. The distribution of property is now conventional and based upon man's agreement to enter political society (cf. Scanlon, 1976: p. 24; Schochet, 1975: p. 253; Nozick, 1974: p. 350; Olivecrona, 1974b: p. 229; Kendall, 1965: p. 104; Cherno, 1958: pp. 52–3).

This is one of the major turning points in Locke's argument. It is foreshadowed by his conclusion in the *Essays on the Law of Nature* that all goods must become common when one man's interest conflicts with another. Men seek political community as a solution to this situation, generated by the introduction of money in the state of nature, and so their possessions must be submitted to the community. The crucial point, however, is that community ownership of all possessions is the logical consequence of the premisses of Locke's theory in the *Two Treatises*. Natural acquisition and possession are legitimate in the state of nature as long as the 'enough and as good for others' proviso is satisfied. With the introduction of money, land becomes scarce and men's claim rights conflict; then the theory of natural appropriation and use has no application. The basic premiss that God gave the earth to all men in common for all time, and at any particular time, necessarily invalidates all exclusive rights once the proviso is no longer met. 'Therefore', to employ the conclusion of Mackie's excellent commentary, 'when the vital proviso is no longer satisfied, goods once legitimately acquired can no longer be retained in exclusive possession, but revert to common ownership' (1977: p. 176).

2

The members of a commonwealth are in a similar position to men in the state of nature: things necessary for comfort and support, including land, belong to all and must be individuated. Civil law now determines what is mine and thine. 'Men unite into Societies, that they may have the united strength of the whole Society to secure and defend their Properties, and may have *standing Rules* to bound it, by which every man may know what is his' (2.136). Men 'have such a right to the goods, which by the Law of the Community are theirs' (2.138). This is a reiteration of Locke's earlier statement that men make 'positive laws to determine Property' (2.30). The necessary condition of the legitimacy of such laws is the consent of the members which they give on entering a political community. He makes this point in his journal, on 21 May 1678: 'a civil law is nothing but the agreement of a society of men either by themselves, or one or more authorised by them: determining the rights, and appointing rewards and punishments to certain actions of all within that society' (MS. Locke, f.2, fo. 241; 1830: I, p. 217). According to Kendall, this means that, 'the individual's rights (including his rights of property) are merely those vouchsafed to him by the positive law of his society' (1965: p. 104).

Kendall fails to remember that the legislative is constrained by the sufficient condition for the legitimacy of any civil law: that it 'be conformable to the Law of Nature' (2.135).

Locke states, 'the *Municipal Laws* of Countries. . .are only so far right, as they are founded on the Law of Nature, by which they are to be regulated and interpreted' (2.12). Natural law is a fixed standard in accordance with which civil rights or properties are determined. We have seen that natural law is a guide, rather than a plan for legislation because there is a wide degree of 'latitude' between natural law and its application (above, p. 48). Legislators exercise their 'prudential' ability to analogise from experience and history, to make laws approximately conformable to natural laws in the given situation (above, pp. 28–30). This is 'the art of government', and as such, it is outside the avowed theoretical scope of the *Two Treatises*. Yet, nonetheless, it is possible and appropriate to recapitulate the natural guidelines governing legislation.

In addition to the natural duty to preserve mankind, the three resulting natural and inclusive claim rights remain as eternal standards for fashioning civil rights. Indeed, each man retains these rights to life, liberty and the means to preserve himself and others (above, p. 154), although the reference of the third right is now restricted to one's own society. When God gives man the substratum right in common out of which the three claims rights are formed, it is distinguished from the capacity for dominion or natural power to exercise the rights. To use Pufendorf's terminology, the right is a moral quality and the ability to exercise it is a natural power. Entering political society consists in foregoing the natural power but not the right; legislators are entrusted to regulate this power in accordance with natural law (2.135). If they do not so regulate it, but abuse it arbitrarily, they transgress the law of nature, and men regain the natural power to exercise their natural rights (2.149):

For no Man, or Society of Men, having a Power to deliver up their *Preservation*, or consequently the means of it, to the Absolute Will and arbitrary Dominion of another; whenever any one shall go about to bring them into such a Slavish Condition, they will always have a right to preserve what they have not a Power to part with; and to rid themselves of those who invade this Fundamental, Sacred, and unalterable Law of *Self-Preservation*, for which they enter'd into Society.

Government is obligated to distribute to each member the civil rights to life, to the liberty of preserving himself and others, and to the requisite goods or 'means of it'. This is a governmental duty from natural law and the public good, and it is now backed up with the threat of legitimate revolution if it is not discharged.

Each member is thereby assured of his comfortable subsistence in approximately the same manner as in the state of nature. He has the civil right and duty to work and the civil right to his share of the community's possessions for support and comfort. Locke draws the same conclusion in his briefer analysis in *A Letter Concerning Toleration*. Here he calls the public good the 'civil interest' and writes that it consists in 'life, liberty, health and indolency of body; and the possession of outward things, such as money, lands, houses, furniture and the like' (1963: p. 15). The extempore list of outward goods and goods of the body are covered by the term 'estates' in the *Two Treatises*. As in the *Two Treatises*, it is the duty of government to ensure that each law-abiding member has these items (p. 17):

It is the duty of the civil magistrate, by the impartial execution of equal laws, to secure unto all the people in general, and to every one of his subjects in particular, the just possession of these things belonging to this life. If any one presume to violate the laws of public justice and equity, established for the preservation of these things, his presumption is to be checked by the fear of punishment, consisting in the deprivation or diminution of those civil interests, or goods, which otherwise he might and ought to enjoy.

A similar argument is presented by Locke in his comparison of civil and ecclesiastical power, 1673–4 (MS. Locke, c.27, fo. 29; 1830: II, pp. 108–16). 'The end of civil society is present enjoyment of what this world affords' (p. 111). This is taken distributively as 'the preservation of society and every member thereof in a free and peaceable enjoyment of all the good things of this life that belong to each of them' (p. 109). Locke's argument at this point is strikingly similar to the one we have seen employed by Cumberland (above, pp. 93–4).

3

The remaining question is how the legislative is to ensure a just and equitable distribution of the common goods to each member. In chapter five Locke anticipates and answers this question by saying that members of society agree to settle their properties which 'Labour and Industry began' (2.45). The fundamental principle of justice is, to each the products of his honest industry (1.42), and all of chapter five stands as a normative model to guide a society in the prudential application of this law of reason. Need, where labour is for some reason impossible, and inheritance, function as two natural principles which ensure that each man shall have enough for comfortable subsistence. In addition, and primarily, the products of one's labour are the only material possessions in which men have natural property, and are, therefore, the property protected by legislation where men 'seek *the preservation of their Property*' (2.127). As he concludes in the *Two Treatises* (2.130) and *A Letter Concerning Toleration*, 'the necessity of preserving men in the possession of what honest industry has already acquired, and also of preserving their liberty and strength, whereby they may acquire what they farther want, obliges men to enter into society with one another, that by mutual assistance and joint force they may secure unto each other their properties, in the things that contribute to the comfort and happiness of this life' (p. 83). (Health is of course a concern of government because it is part of man's natural power.)

The society Locke envisages, in which the share of the goods of the community belonging to each is determined by the labour of each for the public good, is adumbrated by Pufendorf in his discussion of distributive justice (1.7.9). Locke also presents the outline in his letter to William Molyneux on 19 January 1694: 'I think everyone, according to what way Providence has placed him in, is bound to labour for the publick good, as far as he is able, or else he has no right to eat' (1823: IX, p. 332). Although men now work together in mutual assistance, it is not, as has been shown, impossible to apply the fundamental distributive principle (above, pp. 135–45). In addition, a worker is not entitled to the whole product of his labour, since enough must be left for the 'Necessities of the publick' (2.219) or, as he terms it in *A Letter Concerning Toleration*, 'the peace, riches and public commodities of the whole people' (p. 83).

The 'Phansies and intricate Contrivances of Men' which constitute the body of laws in any society (2.12) cannot be accounted for solely in terms of the natural claims rights and the distributive principle. When men enter society, what their 'property *now* is is what the legal rules specify' (Dunn, 1971: p. 140). The legitimacy of conventional property rests in the first instance on the consent of the citizens. No matter how complex and artificial the relations of property are, however, the natural rules stand as an eternal guideline to, and ultimate justification of, legislation (2.135). The gap between theory and practice permits a large amount of latitude in which various and different polities may be legitimately constructed, but the range is not arbitrary nor unconstrained. Any justifiable commonwealth must embody in its fundamental constitution an approximation to the normative structure of natural law and rights.

The result of Locke's theory is the opposite of Filmer's, Grotius' and Pufendorf's. For Filmer, unlimited private property in land is natural; for Grotius and Pufendorf, it is conventional, but since it precedes the constitution of a polity, the sovereign has a duty to protect it. According to Locke's argument, if men agreed to private property in land it would be purely conventional and it would be justified only if it were a prudential means of bringing about a just distribution of property in accordance with the natural right to the product of one's labour and the three claim rights. If it did not conduce to this end it would lose its justification and would have to be abolished, either by legislation, or failing that, by revolution. Locke might have thought some private property in land was justifiable according to his theory, but he did not say so. His undermining of primo-geniture clearly would have the effect of redistributing landed property into much smaller estates. The only form of property in land which he endorses in the *Two Treatises* is the English Common. Locke's theory is consistent with the proposals put forward by John Lilburne (1615–67) in *England's Birth-Right Justified* (1645) and by Richard Overton (?1600–?1660) in *An Arrow Against all Tyrants* (?1646). Overton grants to man a property in his person and a natural right to the means to preserve him-self (Aylmer, 1975: pp. 68–9). In 'The Levellers and the franchise', Thomas concludes, '[t]hey wanted to preserve (or rather create) a world in which every man was an independent proprietor. Hence their attempt to ensure the widest possible distribution of private property by abolishing monopolies, banning primogeniture and throwing open the commons' (Thomas, 1972: p. 77; cf. Brailsford, 1976: pp. 417–55).

The crucial point for Locke in any distribution of property is twofold: that everyone has the means necessary for comfortable subsistence; and that everyone is able to labour in, and enjoy the fruits of, his calling in a manner appropriate to man, and analogous to God's activity as a maker. These are the explicit premisses of the argument and the normative frame-work in terms of which a system of property relations is assessed. The validity of any distribution is conditional upon the fulfilment of these two social functions. Ryan correctly concludes that, 'talk of "absolute" property is seriously misleading and...no sort of absolute ownership is involved in either life, liberty or goods, on all of which there can be claims' (Ryan, 1965: pp. 225–6). The consequence is that 'there seems less reason than ever to suppose that Locke...is engaged in an attempt to deprive the proletariat of all property rights for the benefit of the employ-ing class [as Macpherson proposes]' (p. 226).

Locke's view of the just arrangement of property is, as his letter to Edward Clarke suggests, a conservative appeal for the institution of the 'ancient constitution'. By the Statute of Artificiers (1563) and the Act of Settlement (1662) the government organised labour such that each man had the right and duty to work. The Elizabethan Poor Law (1597/1601) prescribed that the parish poor be given not simply welfare, but the material on which they could work to produce their own means of sub-sistence (Holdsworth, 1926: IV, pp. 375–9). The 'economic' arrangements of society were considered to be an integral and inseparable part of political policy. 'The establishment of a completely free labour market was hardly discussed until the third quarter of the eighteenth century, and the legal, although not the practical restraints to its operation were fully removed only in 1834' (Hundert, 1977: p. 39; cf. Holdsworth, 1926: IV, p. 378; Polanyi, 1957: p. 55; Tribe, 1978: pp. 35–52). Locke did not have to look farther than the tightly knit English constitutional polity to find a comprehensive political body, 'each of whose parts and Members are taken care of, and directed in its peculiar Functions for the good of the whole, by the Laws of the Society' (1.93). Macpherson states that a necessary condition for a 'possessive market society' is 'no authoritative allocation of work' (1972: p. 53). Yet in Locke's theory as well as in law this condition is falsified. It is the duty of the governments to organise the community's possessions and strength for the public good (2.39). In his letter to Richard King on 15 August 1703 Locke defines the arts of government as those which 'comprehend all the arts of peace and war; the management of trade, the employment of the poor; and all those other things, that belong to the administration of the public' (1823: x, pp. 309–10).

Analogous to natural rights in the state of nature, exclusive civil rights exist within a framework of inclusive civil rights and common ownership, and are conditional upon the fulfilment of social functions. Private property and Filmer's absolute right of private dominion have no place. It is remarkable that Locke has been depicted as a defender of unconditional private property in land. Any distribution which conduces to the performance of the form of activity he saw as a duty to God; which ensures the means of preservation for each, and which protects each man in the enjoyment of the fruits of his labour, is a just arrangement. These natural restraints disqualify some forms of communism and the capitalist forms of property described by Braverman and Macpherson. It is a system in which private and common ownership are not mutually exclusive but mutually related: private ownership is the means of individuating the community's common property and is limited by the claims of all other members. What particular legal form this might take in a given commonwealth is not a problem of theory but of prudence.

iii. Property and revolution

1

Once a society passes laws determining what is mine and thine, the civil rights specified by these laws cannot be transgressed by the legislative.[8] Locke makes this argument by repeating that property is the natural right to exercise one's consent over anything which is in any way one's own: 'The *Supream Power cannot take* from any Man any part of his *Property* without his own consent' (2.138; cf. above, pp. 114–15). A *reductio ad absurdum* argument is employed to establish that this right must be logically prior to political society:

For the preservation of Property being the end of Government, and that for which Men enter into Society, it necessarily supposes and requires, that the

People should *have Property*, without which they must be suppos'd to lose that by entring into Society, which was the end for which they entered into it, too gross an absurdity for any Man to own.

It follows that the natural right or property of exercising one's consent over any things which are one's own will necessarily be the one common element in all civil rights:

Men therefore *in Society having Property*, they have such a right to the goods, which by the Law of the Community are theirs, that no Body hath a right to take their substance, or any part of it from them, without their own consent.

The particular rights men have in society are conventionally determined, albeit in accordance with natural principles, and then underpinned by man's natural right or property to exercise moral sovereignty over his own. The point is usually made by saying that property is conventionally determined; the natural law precept to abstain from that which belongs to another then comes into play. Grotius and Pufendorf use this device prior to political society, and then exempt the sovereign in constituting an absolutist state (2.14; 7.6.3). Suarez anticipates Locke in placing the distribution of property posterior to the formation of society and in the hands of government. Following this, the conventional distribution is given natural protection: 'although division of property may not be prescribed by natural law, nevertheless, after this division has been made and the spheres of *dominium* have been distributed, the natural law forbids theft, or undue taking of another's property' (2.14.17). In all these cases the natural law precedes civil law, but its object, mine and thine, is a creation of civil law. Locke makes the same distinction in his journal entry of 26 February 1676: 'the rule and obligation is antecedent to human laws, though the matter about which the rule is, may be consequent to them, as property in land, distinction, and power of person' (MS. Locke, f.1; 1830: 1, p. 114). Locke integrates this natural and negative duty into his active rights theory as the right of an individual to exercise his consent over his own goods. Redescribing the natural precept in this way, he highlights the area of moral sovereignty every agent enjoys no matter how small or large his possessions (2.194). Once a man has his properties by civil law, then his sovereignty is inviolable and he uses it against a government which attempts to place itself above the law (2.139):

But *Government* in whatsoever hands it is put, being...intrusted with this condition, and *for this end*, that Men might have and secure *their Properties*, the Prince or Senate, however it may have power to make Laws for the regulating of *Property* between the Subjects one amongst another, yet can never have a Power to take to themselves the whole or any part of the Subjects *Property*, without their own consent. For this would be in effect to leave them no *Property* at all.

This rule holds of course for any of man's properties, whether they are rights to have or to do something; that is, whether the goods in question are life, liberty or material possessions (1963: p. 17).

Locke's doctrine of property as a natural right to exercise sovereignty over what is legally one's own defeats the unlimited right of Filmer's absolute sovereign. It would equally hold against Hobbes' absolute sovereign, as Laslett notes (1970: p. 379n). Indeed, in *Religious and Civil Polity* (1660) George Lawson (d.1678) develops a refutation of Hobbes that is much briefer but nonetheless similar to Locke's argument (pp. 15–17; cf. MacLean, 1947; Franklin, 1978). In general terms Locke's theory overthrows all his absolutist adversaries – Grotius and Pufendorf as well as Filmer. The ideological target is, however, much closer at hand. One aspect of royal policy in 1680 and 1685–8 was non-parliamentary taxation and confiscation of freeholds in order to consolidate executive authority (Dunn, 1969: p. 216). One conclusion Locke immediately draws from his account of natural property is that taxation without consent is invalid (2.140). His practical intention at this point is to delegitimise the court's action. Also, the standard means the court used to legitimate its action was to describe it in absolutist and Filmerian terms (Kenyon, 1977: pp. 5–8); hence one of the major focal points of Locke's refutation of Filmer and positive theory of natural property in this practical political issue. He undermines the justification of Crown policy and places the right to resist illegal acts of the Crown in the hands of each citizen. His audience could hardly fail to understand the practical implication of his theoretical re-description of the traditional negative duty in terms of an individual and active natural property or right to exercise sovereignty over their civil rights. It is an unequivocal incitement to revolution: 'whenever the *Legislators endeavour to take away, and destroy the Property of the People*, . . .[they] are thereupon absolved from any farther Obedience, and are left to the common Refuge, which God hath provided for all Men, against Force and Violence' (2.222).

It is essential to see that Locke is protecting individual civil rights from arbitrary interference of the Crown by giving the ultimate right to enforce the law to the citizenry. A kind of historical foreshortening is required to impute to Locke, as Macpherson does, the attempt to preserve capitalist property against the proletariat (1972: pp. 220–1). Indeed, Locke explicitly denies that property in land holds against any person who has no materials of production available to him (1.42; above, pp. 131–8). Locke's manifesto, Polanyi corroborates, is 'directed only against arbitrary acts from above. . .at excluding high-handed acts of the Crown. . .A hundred years later. . .industrial property was to be protected, and not against the Crown but against the People. Only by misconception could seventeenth-century meanings be applied to nineteenth-century situations' (1957: p. 225; cf. Dunn, 1969: p. 216).

2

With the right to resist arbitrary interference from above firmly established, Filmer's reduction of the subject of a government to the status of a slave is quite literally 'overthrown'. The argument holds for illegal governmental interference with any civil rights, irrespective of their content. Locke is no less concerned to refute Filmer's absolute right of private dominion in its univocal manifestation throughout social relations *within* society (1.1; 2.2). This second type of Filmerian slavery is denied application by Locke's fundamental conclusion that each man, as God's workmanship, has natural claim rights to life, liberty and the goods necessary to preserve himself. These inalienable properties render immoral Filmer's despotical lords (and landlords) who exercise absolute power over their servants, reducing them to slaves and stripping them of all property. (Filmer, 1949: p. 188; above, pp. 56, 135–46.) Such absolute power within society is illegal because the sovereign is obligated to create civil rights which approximate to each man's three inalienable rights (as well as the natural right to the products of one's labour). This substantive condition of a legitimate polity, in addition to the formal condition of government under law, also is enforced by the right of revolution (2.149, 171–2, 222; above, pp. 165–7). Revolution is the ultimate defence against the emergence of absolute power of one member of society over another, which, because it denies the servant his property, is inconsistent with civil society (2.174; above, p. 138; cf. Ryan, 1965: p. 226). The right of revolution is the final rampart of government by law and of a constitution of society conformable to natural law.

The political issue involved in this second revolutionary dimension of Locke's theory of property is at least as important as the first. The conventional criterion for the right to vote in the seventeenth century was the possession of property. Filmer's theory systematically denies property, and therefore suffrage, to all but independent landholders. In demonstrating that every man has property in his life, liberty, person, action and some possessions, Locke extends the franchise to every adult male. He does not explicitly state the criterion in the *Two Treatises*; he simply assumes it as the basis of his discussion of various kinds of representation: 'whenever the People shall chuse their *Representatives upon* just and undeniably *equal measures* suitable to the original Frame of Government, it cannot be doubted to be the will and act of the Society' (2.158). The equal measures suitable to the original constitution cannot but be the natural equality of all men (2.5). Locke's theory thus serves to justify the Exclusion strategy of the Whigs to make representation as broadly based as possible (Dunn, 1969: pp. 44–57; Plumb, 1967: pp. 31–65).

The contest between Filmer and Locke over two opposing views of property represents one of the most important political issues in the seventeenth century: does property mean property fixed in land and so restricted to a few, as in Filmer, Grotius and Pufendorf; or does it mean any sort of right, and thus include everyone, as in Cumberland and Locke? For example, J. Bullokar in *An English Expositour* (1688) and E. Coles in *An English Dictionary* (1676) restrict 'property' to 'the highest right a man can have to a thing' as the 'sole owner of it'; whereas John Rastell in *Les termes de la ley* (1667), following Coke, and J. Kersey in *A New English Dictionary* (1702), extend 'property' to 'a right or rightful use of a thing'. The two views are nowhere more trenchantly advanced and vigorously debated prior to Locke's confrontation with Filmer than in the revolutionary situation of the army debates at Putney in 1647.

Commissary-General Ireton, like Filmer, argues that property means fixed property in land and that it is wholly conventional (Woodhouse, 1974: pp. 62–3, 66–7, 68–9). It follows that only those with landed property should have the franchise: 'the law...is made by those people that have a property, a fixed property, in the land' (p. 66). Colonel Rainborough responds that this would be to exclude five parts out of six of the population and so to enslave them (pp. 67, 71). Both Rainborough and Edward Sexby proclaim that men have a natural property in their person and liberty and hence have an interest in determining the law of the kingdom (pp. 67–9). Ireton responds that this would entail the destruction of all (conventional) property because each man would claim a natural right to goods necessary for preservation (pp. 69, 72–3). Maximilian Petty retorts that far from destroying property, 'it is [on the contrary], the only means to preserve property' (p. 61). What Petty means by property is man's natural liberty and right to preservation. He declares that men 'choose representatives, and put themselves into forms of government that they may preserve property' (p. 62). With the *Two Treatises* the theoretical foundation for the view advanced by Petty is firmly laid; and revolution to reconstitute society accordingly is equally firmly justified. Indeed, men have their property to gain and nothing to lose but their Filmerian chains.

iv. Conclusion

To conclude, I wish to replace Locke's explanation of property in the context of his thought as a whole. Although Chapters One and Two are designed to explicate the constitutive and regulative beliefs in which his views on property belong, a brief recapitulation will help to redress the imbalance caused by concentrating on one aspect of his philosophy. If there is one leitmotiv which unites Locke's works it is surely a philosophy of religious praxis. He writes in the *Essay*, 'Our Business here is not to know all things, but those which concern our Conduct' (1.1.6). The central quest is to 'find out those Measures, whereby a rational Creature put in that State, which Man is in, in this World, may, and ought to govern his Opinions, and Actions depending thereon'. Completion is possible because men 'have Light enough to lead them to the Knowledge of their Maker, and the sight of their own Duties' (1.1.5). The duties which constitute man's conduct are of two general kinds: the use and organisation of things necessary for support and convenience; and the activity which is prerequisite to an afterlife in heaven.

Locke's explanation of property comprehends the first set of duties; duties which are directed towards and organised in accord with the preservation of mankind. The fundamental and undifferentiated form of property is the natural right and duty to make use of the world to achieve God's purpose of preserving all his workmanship. A commonwealth which arranges men's action accordingly is the complementary kind of society. Property and political society thus stand as the means necessary for the practice of man's other set of moral duties, those religious duties over and above supporting and comforting oneself and others. Locke lays out this plan in his journal on 8 February 1677. He summarises: 'Besides a plenty of the good things of this world and with life, health and peace to enjoy them', it is 'certain...that there is a possibility of another state when this scene is over, and that the happynesse and misery of that depends on the ordering of our selves in our actions in this time of our probationership here' (1936: p. 87). The form of organisation for the performance of these duties is a religious society. In 'Civil and Ecclesiastical Power' (1673–4) he compares and contrasts the two kinds of duties and societies. 'The end of civil society is present enjoyment of what this world affords; the end of church communion, future expectation of what is to be had in another world' (MS. Locke, c.29, fo. 29; 1830: II, p. 111). Locke assumes that most men will be members of both kinds of society (p. 116). The reason that the goods of civil society are basically common and those of an ecclesiastical society private is, 'one man's good is involved and complicated with another's, but in religious societies every man's concerns are separate, and one man's transgressions hurt not another' (p. 114). *A Letter Concerning Toleration* is his finest discussion of the two spheres of religious praxis and the epitome of his life's work.

These two types of duties intermingle at various points, but nowhere do they do so in a more morally important manner than in the case where men have more than they need. When men have only enough, they use their provisions as the means to achieve subsistence; when they have more than enough, they enjoy the end achieved (Suarez: 7.1.2). God gave all things richly to enjoy; men enter into society not only for preservation, but to enjoy it (2.77) and for 'the enjoyment of their Properties' (2.134).

Enjoyment, however, consists not in the sin of acquisitiveness, as Macpherson suggests, nor in the modern activity of consumption. It consists in the Christian duty of liberality or charity and it is the first thing to teach children about property. 'As to having and possessing of Things', Locke instructs in *Some Thoughts Concerning Education*, 'teach them [children] to part with what they have easily and freely to their Friends' (1968: p. 213). 'Covetousness, and the Desire of having in our Possession, and under our Dominion, more than we have need of, being the Root of all Evil, should be early and carefully weeded out, and the contrary Quality of a Readiness to impart to others, implanted' (pp. 213–14). The way to 'understand Property', as well as justice and honesty, 'is to lay the Foundations of it early in Liberality, and an Easiness to part with to others whatever they have or like themselves' (pp. 214–15). This is Locke's last and consistent word on the subject.

Notes

PREFACE

1. I adopt this methodological commitment from Wittgenstein, 1974: s. 130.
2. This point also is adapted from Wittgenstein's work in *On Certainty*.
3. For a partial list of their publications refer to the bibliography.
4. See Thompson, 1976; Goldie, 1977, 1978; and Kenyon, 1977.
5. For the Lockeian socialists, see Beer, 1921 and Driver, 1928.
6. The reinterpretation begins with Stocks, 1933 and changes to unlimited private property with Macpherson, 1972.

CHAPTER ONE

1. See Locke, 1823: x, pp. 306, 308; 1968: pp. 294, 395, 400.
2. I owe this point to Dr Richard Tuck of Jesus College, Cambridge.
3. Locke sometimes calls the idea a mixed mode and at other times the action or 'object' the idea stands for. This is less a confusion in Locke than a fundamental feature of this kind of concept. Since the idea is the essence of the object there is a fundamental identity between the two. I follow Locke in using 'mode' or 'relation' for both, but signal whether the terms refer to ideas or their objects if this is not clear from the context.
4. Examples of mixed modes: 2.12.4–5; 2.22.4, 7, 9; 2.27.9; 2.28.3, 7; 2.32.11; 3.5.3, 6; 3.6.40, 49; 3.11.16; 4.3.18, 26; 4.5.4. Examples of relations: 2.25.2, 3, 7, 10; 2.26.6; 2.28.2, 3, 7; 4.3.18; 1970a: 1.98; 2.2; 2.3.
5. Compare Locke, 1936: pp. 3, 4, 11, 17, 18, 21–6; 1931: pp. 99–100; 148–51; 153–60.
6. The similarity may not be a coincidence. See Toulmin and Janik, 1973: p. 123.
7. Compare 3.43; 3.5.14; 3.11.15; 4.12.8.
8. Compare Bacon, 1874: I, p 385; Boyle, 1660: p. 2.
9. See 2.31.5, 2.38.8–14; 3.6.2, 3.6.51, 3.9.6, 3.10.22, 3.10.32, 3.11.6, 3.11.11.
10. I therefore demur to Laslett's suggestion that the discussion of the empirical aspect of politics, in Locke's journal of entry of 26 June 1681, refers to the *Two Treatises* (1970: pp. 84–5). I have attempted to show in this section that Locke places the *Two Treatises* unquestionably in the category of theory.
11. See Pocock, 1967; Skinner, 1965; Kenyon, 1977; Thompson, 1976; and Goldie, 1977, 1978.

CHAPTER TWO

1. This quotation encapsulates the central expository theme of Dunn's account of Locke's political thought. See 1969: p. 1.

2. See Aquinas, *ST*: II.II.93.1; Bacon, 1874: 1, p. 342; Barbeyrac, 1729: p. 1; Cumberland, 1727: p. 128; Grotius, 1950: 2.1; Hooker, 1717: 1.1.3; Newton, 1962: p. 107; Pufendorf, 1729: 1.1.1; Suarez, 1944: 2.2.10; Whichcote, 1685: p. 91.
3. Compare 1975: 1.3.4, 1.3.12, 2.28.6; 1970a: 1.86, 2.59, 2.60, and Suarez, 1944: 1.5.10–13.
4. See: 1970a: 1.86, 2.6, 2.7, 2.11, 2.16, 2.23, 2.60, 2.79, 2.129, 2.135, 2.138, 2.149, 2.155, 2.159, 2.168, 2.171, 2.200; 1970b: pp. 157, 173, 181. Compare: Aquinas, *ST*: I.II.94.2; Hooker, 1717: 1.1.5; Pufendorf, 1729: 2.3.15; Suarez, 1944: 2.7.7.
5. See below, pp. 101–5.

CHAPTER THREE

1. For the seventeenth- and sixteenth-century background to these two aspects of the *Two Treatises* respectively, see Franklin, 1978 and Skinner, 1978: II.
2. See Laslett, 1949; Straka, 1962; Dunn, 1969: pp. 43–58, 84; Bennett, 1976; Kenyon, 1977: pp. 3–10, and Goldie, 1977, 1978.
3. The contributors to the debate are Driver, 1928, Laslett, 1970, Hinton, 1974 and 1977, Olivecrona, 1976 and Kelly, 1977.
4. This seems to be the common element in the interpretations of Laslett, 1949: p. 13 and Dunn, 1969: p. 66.
5. The fundamental law of nature is set out in terms of preservation of 1.86, 2.129, 2.135, 2.149, 2.159, 2.170, 2.182 and 2.209; and in terms of to preserve at 1.88, 2.6, 2.8, 2.11, 2.159, 2.220.
6. I regret that Parry, 1978, which concentrates on Locke's rights and duties, appeared too late for me to include discussion of it.
7. I am greatly indebted to the studies of these writers by Tuck, 1979 and Skinner, 1978: II.
8. An excellent analysis of Grotius' argument is provided by De Pauw, 1965: pp. 35–7.
9. Although Pufendorf does not mention Filmer by name, Barbeyrac suggests that the critique refers to an 'English knight, named Robert Filmer' (4.4.3n).

CHAPTER FIVE

1. Locke himself suggests that the conclusions of the First Treatise are pre-misses of the Second Treatise (2.1).
2. I therefore agree with Laslett and Cranston that the *Two Treatises* consti-tutes, as Locke himself states, 'a Discourse concerning Government' and not two separate and unconnected treatises. See Laslett, 1970: pp. 45–66 and Cranston, 1957: p. 207. For the contrary view, see Olivecrona, 1976 and Hinton, 1974, 1977.
3. Tyrrell, in *The Patriarch un-monarched*, also misinterprets Grotius (pp. 108–9²). This error has been repeated more recently by Schlatter, 1951: pp. 127, 196; and Kelly, 1977: p. 82. For Grotius' community as a negative com-munity, see Green, 1927: p. 214, and Gierke, 1934: I, p. 103.
4. This is the view of Laslett, 1970: p. 304 (but see p. 103); Gough, 1973: p. 84, and Kelly, 1977: p. 82.
5. This is the view of Schlatter, 1951: p. 152, and Olivecrona, 1974b: p. 152.

6. He analyses this conceptual relationship in his later writing. See *Morality*: MS. Locke, c.28, fo. 139 and *Essay* 2.21.28–47.
7. It is arguable that the failure to make this distinction is the reason for the confusion concerning Locke's alleged hedonism. See Yolton, 1970: pp. 144–7.
8. The *locus classicus* of this argument is Cicero, *Of Duties*, 2.3, 3.3. Compare Pufendorf, 2.3.9 and the discussion of Suarez's similar defence of natural law moral theory against Machiavellian morality in Skinner, 1978: II, pp. 171–3.
9. I see no evidence to support Kelly's suggestion that Locke abandons his Thomist concept of positive community and embraces a negative community in section twenty-six, or in any other section. See Kelly, 1977: p. 90. Positive community is the conventional scholastic starting point: Gierke, 1934: I, p. 103.
10. See Overton, 1646: p. 1; Parker, 1652: p. 36; Lawson, 1660: p. 80; Baxter, 1659: p. 69; Penn, 1726: II, p. 679 and Macpherson, 1972: pp. 137–42.
11. For a recent discussion of this view, see Hintikka, 1975.
12. Compare 2.27.14, 16, 17, 18, 25.
13. See above, p. 7.
14. For an excellent analysis of the emergence of the concept of an inalienable right, see Tuck, 1979.
15. Laslett, 1970: pp. 100–2 surveys this debate.
16. Olivecrona, 1974b: p. 226 also rejects the value-added interpretation.
17. The model of God and man making things in accordance with their ideas is the historical root of the term 'idea': Aquinas, *ST*: 1.15.1.
18. I see no evidence for Day's claim that Locke failed to distinguish these two senses of 'work' or 'labour' (1966: p. 109). Locke seems rather to analyse the conceptual connections underlying these equivocal terms.
19. For a monumental survey of this movement see Webster, 1976.
20. The right to enforce the law of nature is not quite as 'strange' as Locke implies. See Gierke, 1934: I, p. 99 and Skinner, 1978: II, pp. 340–5.

CHAPTER SIX

1. Compare Polanyi, 1957, Finley, 1973: pp. 20–1 and Brunner, 1956.
2. This is the 1925 translation.
3. Compare Ryan, 1965; Dunn, 1969: pp. 203–67; Hundert, 1972 and 1977.
4. For an attempt to develop an explanatory model of the pre-capitalist yet post-feudal mode of production in the seventeenth and eighteenth centuries, see Anderson, 1974: pp. 43–59, 420–31. A discussion of the methodological issues involved and a presentation of a structuralist explanation, which situates the emergence of capitalist theory and practice in the early nineteenth century, is provided by Tribe, 1977 and 1978. Pocock carefully reconstructs the ideological debate in the eighteenth century out of which arose capitalist thought and action: 1975a: pp. 423–506, 1975b and 1979. A complementary survey is advanced by Hirschmann, 1977.

CHAPTER SEVEN

1. For sixteenth-century absolutism, see Skinner, 1978: II.
2. See Straka, 1962; Bennett, 1976; Thompson, 1976; Goldie, 1977, 1978 and Kenyon, 1977.
3. I am greatly indebted to Dunn's scholarly elucidation of Locke's creation of a legitimate polity (1969: pp. 120–48).

4. For an excellent study of Locke's concept of consent, see Dunn, 1971.
5. Laslett's analysis of Locke's concept of trust is unsurpassed (1970: pp. 112–14).
6. For the similarity between Locke and George Lawson on the construction of a legislative, see MacLean, 1947 and Franklin, 1978.
7. See 2.3, 2.131, 2.132, 2.135, 2.137, 2.142, 2.143, 2.147, 2.150, 2.151, 2.156, 2.157, 2.158, 2.159, 2.162, 2.163, 2.165, 2.167, 2.200, 2.216, 2.217, 2.222.
8. For a comprehensive analysis of Locke on legitimate resistance see Dunn, 1969: pp. 165–86.

Bibliography

PRIMARY SOURCES

Aquinas, St Thomas. 1964. *Summa theologica*. Latin and English edition, 60 vols., ed. T. Gilby, O.P. London.

Aquinas, St Thomas. 1974. *Selected Political Writings*. Latin and English edition, ed. A. P. d'Entrèves. Oxford: Basil Blackwell.

Aristotle. *EN. Nicomachean Ethics*. Ed. W. D. Ross. Oxford: Clarendon Press, 1972.

Aristotle. *Met. Metaphysics*. Ed. W. D. Ross. Oxford: Clarendon Press, 1972.

Aristotle. *Pol. Politics*. Ed. W. D. Ross. Oxford: Clarendon Press, 1972.

Aristotle. *An. Po. Posterior Analytics*. Tr. Jonathan Barnes. Oxford: Clarendon Press, 1975.

Aylmer, G. E., ed. 1975. *The Levellers in the English Revolution*. London: Thames and Hudson.

Bacon, Francis. 1874. *Works*. 17 vols., ed. R. L. Ellis, J. Spelding and D. D. Heath. London.

Barbeyrac, Jean. 1729. An historical and critical account of the science of morality. *In the Law of Nature and Nations, by Samuel Pufendorf*. Ed. Jean Barbeyrac. Tr. Basil Kennett. London.

Barbeyrac, Jean, ed. 1729. *The Law of Nature and Nations, by Samuel Pufendorf*. Tr. Basil Kennett. London.

Barbeyrac, Jean, ed. 1738. *The Rights of War and Peace, by Hugo Grotius*. Tr. W. Innys and R. Manby. London.

Baxter, Richard. 1659. *A Holy Commonwealth, or Political Aphorisms upon the True Principles of Government*. London.

Bellers, John. 1696. *Proposals for Raising a College of Industry of all Useful Trade and Husbandry*. London.

Boecler, Johann Henrich. 1633. *In Hugonis Grotii, & C., Commentatio*. Strasburg.

Boyle, Robert. 1660. *The Origins of Forms and Qualities*. London.

Bullokar, J. 1688, 1697. *An English Expositour*. London.

Cabet, Etienne. 1842. *Voyage en Icarie, roman philosophique et social*. Paris.

Chamberlen, Peter. 1649. *A Poor Man's Advocate*. London.

Coles, E. 1676. *An English Dictionary*. London.

Coste, Pierre, ed. 1735. *Essai philosophique concernant l'entendement humain*. Third edn. Amsterdam.

Cumberland, Richard. 1672. *De legibus Naturae disquisitio philosophica*. London.

Cumberland, Richard. 1727. *A Treatise of the Laws of Nature*. Tr. John Maxwell. London: R. Phillips. (All quotations from this edition unless otherwise specified.)

Descartes, René. 1967. *The Philosophical Works of Descartes.* 2 vols., tr. E. Haldane and G. R. T. Ross. Cambridge: Cambridge University Press.

Filmer, Robert. 1949. *Patriarcha and Other Political Works.* Ed. Peter Laslett. Oxford: Basil Blackwell.

Fleetwood, William. 1705. *The Relative duties of Parents and Children, Husbands and Wives, and Masters and Servants.* London.

Grotius, Hugo. 1738. *The Rights of War and Peace.* Tr. Basil Kennett with the notes of Jean Barbeyrac. London. (All quotations from this edition unless otherwise specified.)

Grotius, Hugo. 1916. *Of the Freedom of the Sea 1609 [Mare Liberum].* Latin and English edition, tr. Ralph van Deman Magoffin. Oxford: Oxford University Press.

Grotius, Hugo. 1925. *De Iure Belli ac Pacis 1625.* Latin and English edition, 4 vols., tr. F. W. Kelsey. Oxford: Clarendon Press.

Grotius, Hugo. 1950. *De Jure Praedae commentarii 1604.* Latin and English edition, 2 vols., tr. G. L. Williams and W. H. Zeydel. Oxford: Clarendon Press.

Hartlib, Samuel. 1641. *A description of the Famous Kingdom of Macaria.* London.

Hobbes, Thomas. 1642. *De Cive.* London.

Hobbes, Thomas. 1650. *De Corpore Politico.* London.

Hobbes, Thomas. 1651. *Leviathan.* London.

Hobbes, Thomas. 1845. *The English Works of Thomas Hobbes.* 11 vols., ed. Sir William Molesworth. London.

Hooker, Richard. 1717. *Of the lawes of the Ecclesiastical Politie.* London.

Kersey, J. 1702. *A New English Dictionary.* London.

Lawson, George. 1660. *Politica Sacra & Civilis.* London.

Leibniz, Gottfried. 1717. *A Collection of Papers which passed between the late learned Mr. Leibnitz and Dr. Clarke in the year 1715 and 1716, relating to the Principles of Natural Philosophy and Religion.* London.

Leibniz, Gottfried. 1916. *New Essays Concerning Human Understanding.* Tr. A. G. Langley. Chicago: Open Court.

Lilburne, John. 1645. *Englands Birth-Right Justified.* London.

Locke, John. MS. The Lovelace Collection of the papers of John Locke in the Bodleian Library, Oxford.

Locke, John. 1789. *A Report to the Board of Trade to the Lords Justice 1697, Respecting Relief and Unemployment of the Poor.* London.

Locke, John. 1823. *The Works of John Locke.* 10 vols. London.

Locke, John. 1830. *The Life of John Locke with extracts from his Correspondence, Journals and Common-place books by Lord King.* 2 vols. London.

Locke, John. 1931. *An Essay Concerning the Understanding, Knowledge, Opinion and Assent.* Ed. B. Rand. Cambridge, Mass.: Harvard University Press.

Locke, John. 1936. *An Early Draft of Locke's Essay together with excerpts from his Journals.* Ed. R. I. Aaron and J. Gibb. Oxford: Clarendon Press.

Locke, John. 1963. *A Letter Concerning Toleration.* Latin and English texts, ed. Mario Montuori. The Hague: Martinus Niijhoff.

Locke, John. 1967. *Two Tracts on Government.* Ed. Philip Abrams. Cambridge: The Cambridge University Press.

Locke, John. 1968. *The Educational Writings.* Ed. James Axtell. Cambridge: Cambridge University Press.

Locke, John. 1970a. *Two Treatises of Government.* Ed. Peter Laslett. Cambridge: Cambridge University Press.

Locke, John. 1970b. *Essays on the Law of Nature*. Latin and English edition, ed. W. von Leyden. Oxford: Clarendon Press.

Locke, John. 1975. *An Essay Concerning Human Understanding*. Ed. Peter Nidditch. Oxford: Clarendon Press.

Locke, John. 1976. *The Correspondence*. 8 vols., ed. E. S. de Beer. Oxford: Clarendon Press.

Nelson, William, ed. 1717. *John Manwood's Treatise of the Forest Laws*, 1598. London.

Newton, Isaac. 1704. *Opticks, or a Treatise of the reflexions, refractions, inflexions and colours of light*. London.

Newton, Isaac. 1729. *The Mathematical Principles of Natural Philosophy*. 2 vols., tr. A. Matte. London.

Newton, Isaac. 1962. *Unpublished Scientific Papers of Sir Isaac Newton*. Ed. A. R. Hall and M. B. Hall. Cambridge: Cambridge University Press.

Overton, Richard. ?1646. *An Arrow Against all Tyrants*. London.

Parker, Henry. 1652. *Jus Populi*. London.

Penn, William. 1726. *Works*. 2 vols. London.

Perkins, William. 1618. *Christian Oeconomie or a short survey of the right manner of erecting and ordering a family, according to Scripture*. London.

Pufendorf, Samuel. 1660. *Elementa Jurisprudentiae Universalis*. Amsterdam.

Pufendorf, Samuel. 1672. *De Jure Naturae et Gentium libri Octo*. Amsterdam. (A copy signed by John Locke is in the Osler Library, McGill University, Montreal.)

Pufendorf, Samuel. 1673. *De Officio Hominis et Civis juxta legem naturalem libri duo*. Amsterdam.

Pufendorf, Samuel. 1729. *Of the Law of Nature and Nations*. Tr. Basil Kennett with the notes of Jean Barbeyrac. London. (All quotations from this edition unless otherwise specified.)

Pufendorf, Samuel. 1934. *De Jure Naturae et Gentium libri Octo 1688*. Latin and English edition, 2 vols., tr. C. H. Oldfather and W. A. Oldfather. Oxford: Clarendon Press.

Rastell, John. 1667. *Les termes de la ley, or certain difficult and obscure words and terms of the common law and statutes of this realme now in use expanded and explained*. London.

Selden, John. 1636. *De dominio maris juribusque ad dominium*. London.

Selden, John. 1652. *Of the Dominion or Ownership of the Sea*. Tr. Marchamont Nedham. London.

Strauch, Johannes. 1674. *Dissertatio de Imperio Maris*. Jena.

Suarez, Francis. 1944. *Selections from Three Works*. Latin and English edition, 2 vols., tr. G. L. Williams. Oxford: Clarendon Press. (All translations from *De legibus ac Deo legislatore* and *Defensio Fidei Catholicae et Apostolicae adversus Anglicanae sectae errores* are taken from this translation.)

Suarez, Francis. 1878. *Opera omnia*. 28 vols., ed. M. André. Paris.

Toland, John. 1751. *Pantheisticon, or the form of celebrating the Socratic Society*. London.

Tyrrell, James. 1681. *The Patriarch un-monarched*. London.

Tyrrell, James. 1694. *Bibliotheca Politica*. London.

Velthuysen, Lambert. 1651. *Dissertatio de principiis justi et decori*. Amsterdam.

Vico, Giambattista. 1970. *The New Science of Giambattista Vico*. Tr. T. G. Bergin and M. H. Fisch. New York: Cornell University Press.

Welwood, William. 1613. *An Abridgement of all Sea Laws*. London.
Whichcote, Benjamin. 1685. *Select Notions*. London.
Wollaston, William. 1724. *The Religion of Nature Delineated*. London.
Woodhouse, A. S. P., ed. 1974. *Puritanism and Liberty*. London: J. M. Dent.
Ziegler, Caspar. 1662. *In Hugonis Grotii...*Amsterdam.

SECONDARY SOURCES

Anderson, Perry. 1977. *Lineages of the Absolutist State*. London: New Left Books.
Anscombe, G. E. M. 1972. *Intention*. Second edition. Oxford: Basil Blackwell.
Arendt, Hannah. 1973. *The Human Condition*. Chicago: University of Chicago Press.
Arendt, Hannah. MS. Unpublished Manuscripts. New York.
Axtell, James, ed. 1968. *The Educational Writings of John Locke*. Cambridge: Cambridge University Press.
Becker, Lawrence C. 1977. *Property Rights: Philosophic Foundations*. London: Routledge & Kegan Paul.
Beer, Max. 1921. *The History of British Socialism*. London: The National Labour Press.
Bennett, G. V. 1976. *The Tory Crisis in Church and State*. Oxford: Clarendon Press.
Brailsford, H. N. 1976. *The Levellers and the English Revolution*. Manchester: C. Nicholls and Company.
Braverman, Harry. 1974. *Labor and Monopoly Capital. The Degradation of Work in the Twentieth Century*. New York: Monthly Review Press.
Brunner, O. 1956. 'Das "ganze Haus" und die alteuropäische ökonomick'. In *Neue Wege der Sozialgeschichte*. Gottingen.
Cavell, Stanlay. 1976. *Must We Mean What We Say?* Cambridge: Cambridge University Press.
Cherno, Melvin. 1958. 'Locke on property'. *Ethics*, 68, pp. 51–5.
Child, A. 1953. 'Making and knowing in Hobbes, Vico and Dewey'. *University of California Publications in Philosophy*. Los Angeles: University of California Press.
Copleston, F. 1963. 'Late medieval and renaissance philosophy: the revival of platonism to Suarez'. In *A History of Philosophy*, III, 2. New York: Image Books.
Copleston, F. 1964. 'Modern philosophy: The British philosophers, Hobbes to Paley'. In *A History of Philosophy*, v, 1. New York: Image Books.
Cranston, Maurice. 1957. *John Locke, A Biography*. London: Longmans, Green.
Daumbauld, Edward. 1969. *The Life and Legal Writings of Hugo Grotius*. Oklahoma: University of Oklahoma Press.
Day, J. P. 1966. 'Locke on property'. *Philosophical Quarterly*, 16, pp. 207–21.
De Pauw, Francis. 1965. *Grotius and the Law of the Sea*. University of Brussels: Editions de l'institut de sociologie.
Dobb, Maurice. 1947. *Studies in the Development of Capitalism*. London: Routledge.
Driver, Charles. 1928. 'John Locke'. In *The Social & Political Ideas of Some English Thinkers of the Augustan Age 1650–1750*, ed. F. J. C. Hearnshaw. London: G. G. Harrap.

Dunn, John. 1968. 'Justice and the interpretation of Locke's political theory'. *Political Studies.* 16, 1, pp. 68–87.

Dunn, John. 1969. *The Political Thought of John Locke.* Cambridge: Cambridge University Press.

Dunn, John. 1971. 'Consent in the political theory of John Locke'. In *Life, Liberty and Property; Essays on Locke's Political Ideas,* ed. G. Schochet, pp. 129–61. Belmont, California: Wadsworth.

Dunn, John. 1977. Review of *Anarchy, State, and Utopia. Ratio,* 19, 1, pp. 88–95.

Dunn, John. 1978. 'Practising history and social science on "realist" assumptions'. In *Action and Interpretation,* ed. C. Hookway and P. Pettit. Cambridge: Cambridge University Press.

Euchner, Walter. 1969. *Naturrecht und Politik bei John Locke.* Frankfurt am Main.

Finley, M. I. 1973. *The Ancient Economy.* Berkeley: University of California Press.

Fletcher, Eric. 1969. *John Selden 1584–1654.* London: Selden Society, Bernard Quaritch.

Forbes, Duncan. 1975. *Hume's Philosophical Politics.* Cambridge: Cambridge University Press.

Franklin, Julian. 1978. *John Locke and the Theory of Sovereignty.* Cambridge: Cambridge University Press.

Fruin, Robert J. 1925. 'An unpublished work of Hugo Grotius's'. *Bibliotheca Visseriana,* v, pp. 3–74.

Fulton, T. W. 1911. *The Sovereignty of the Sea.* Edinburgh: William Blackwood.

Gierke, Otto von. 1934. *Natural Law and Theory of Society.* 2 vols., tr. Ernest Barker. Cambridge: Cambridge University Press.

Gierke, Otto von. 1939. *The Development of Political Theory.* Tr. Bernard Freyd. New York: W. W. Norton.

Gilby, Thomas. 1958. *The Political Thought of Thomas Aquinas.* Chicago: University of Chicago Press.

Goldie, M. 1977. 'Edmund Bohun and *ius gentium* in the revolution debate, 1689–93'. *Historical Journal,* 20, 3, pp. 569–86.

Goldie, M. 1978. 'Tory Political Thought 1689–1714'. Cambridge University Ph.D. dissertation.

Gonner, E. C. K. 1912. *Common Land and Inclosure.* London: Macmillan.

Gough, J. W. 1973. *John Locke's Political Philosophy.* 2nd edn. Oxford: Clarendon Press.

Gough, J. W. 1976. 'James Tyrrell, whig historian and friend of John Locke'. *Historical Journal,* 19, 3, pp. 581–610.

Green, Thomas Hill. 1927. *Lectures on the Principles of Political Obligation.* London: Longmans, Green.

Grene, Marjorie. 1963. 'Causes'. *Philosophy,* 38, pp. 149–59.

Habermas, Jurgen. 1974. *Theory and Practice.* Tr. John V. Viertel. London: Heinemann.

Hacking, Ian. 1975. *Why Does Language Matter to Philosophy?* Cambridge: Cambridge University Press.

Hintikka, J. J. 1975. 'Theoretical and practical reason: an ambiguous legacy'. In *Practical Reason,* ed. S. Körner. Oxford: Basil Blackwell.

Hinton, R. W. K. 1974. 'A note on the dating of Locke's Second Treatise'. *Political Studies,* 22, 4, pp. 471–8.

Hinton, R. W. K. 1977. 'On recovering the original of the Second Treatise'. *The Locke Newsletter*, pp. 69–76.

Hirschmann, Albert O. 1977. *The Passions and the Interests*. Princeton: Princeton University Press.

Hohfeld, W. N. 1964. *Fundamental Legal Conceptions as Applied in Judicial Reasoning*. New Haven: Yale University Press.

Holdsworth, William. 1926. *A History of English Law*. 9 vols., 3rd edn. London.

Hundert, Edward J. 1972. 'The making of homo faber: John Locke between ideology and history'. *Journal of the History of Ideas*, 33, 1, pp. 3–22.

Hundert, Edward J. 1977. 'Market society and meaning in Locke's political philosophy'. *Journal of the History of Philosophy*, 15, January 1, pp. 33–44.

Jardine, Lisa. 1975. *Francis Bacon: Discovery and the Art of Discourse*. Cambridge: Cambridge University Press.

Joachim, H. H. 1970. *The Nicomachean Ethics*, ed. D. A. Rees. Oxford: The Clarendon Press.

Kelly, Patrick. 1977. 'Locke and Filmer: was Laslett so wrong after all?' *The Locke Newsletter*, pp. 77–86.

Kendall, Willmoore. 1965. *John Locke and the Doctrine of Majority-rule*. Urbana: University of Illinois Press.

Kenny, Anthony. 1975. *Will, Freedom and Power*. Oxford: Basil Blackwell.

Kenyon, J. P. 1977. *Revolution Principles: the politics of party 1689–1720*. Cambridge: Cambridge University Press.

Klein, Jacob. 1968. *Greek Mathematical Thought and the Origin of Algebra*. Tr. Eva Braun. Cambridge, Mass.: MIT Press.

Knight, W. S. M. 1925. *The Life and Works of Hugo Grotius*. London: Grotius Society Publications no. 4, Sweet and Maxwell.

Kosman, L. A. 1964. 'The Aristotelian Backgrounds of Bacon's "Novum Organum"'. Ph.D. dissertation, Harvard University.

Krieger, Leonard. 1965. *The Politics of Discretion: Pufendorf and the Acceptance of Natural Law*. Chicago: University of Chicago Press.

Lamprecht, Sterling Power. 1918. *The Moral and Political Philosophy of John Locke*. New York: Columbia University Press.

Landes, David S. 1969. *The Unbound Prometheus*. Cambridge: Cambridge University Press.

Laslett, Peter, ed. 1949. *Patriarcha and Other Political Works of Sir Robert Filmer*. Oxford: Basil Blackwell.

Laslett, Peter. 1964. 'Market society and political theory'. *Historical Journal*, 7, 1, pp. 150–4.

Laslett, Peter, ed. 1970. Locke, *Two Treatises of Government*. Cambridge: Cambridge University Press.

Liddell, Henry and Scott, Robert. 1845. *Greek–English Lexicon*. London.

Loemker, Leroy. 1972. *Struggle for Synthesis. The Seventeenth-Century Background of Leibniz's Synthesis of Order and Freedom*. Cambridge, Mass.: Harvard University Press.

Long, Philip. 1959. *A summary catalogue of the Lovelace collection of the papers of John Locke in the Bodleian Library*. Oxford: Oxford University Press.

Lyons, David. 1970. 'The correlativity of rights and duties'. *Nous*, 4, pp. 45–55.

Mabbott, J. D. 1973. *John Locke*. London: Macmillan.

MacIntyre, Alasdair, 1962. 'A mistake about causality in social science'. In *Philosophy, Politics and Society*, ed. P. Laslett and W. G. Runciman, series II. Oxford: Basil Blackwell.

MacIntyre, Alasdair. 1974. *A Short History of Ethics.* London: Routledge & Kegan Paul.

Mackie, J. L. 1976. *Problems from Locke.* Oxford: Clarendon Press.

Mackie, J. L. 1977. *Ethics: Inventing Right and Wrong.* Middlesex: Penguin.

MacLean, A. H. 1947. 'George Lawson and John Locke'. *Cambridge Historical Journal,* 9, 1.

Macpherson, C. B. 1963. 'A rejoinder to Viner'. *Canadian Journal of Economics and Political Theory,* 29, 4.

Macpherson, C. B. 1972. *The Political Theory of Possessive Individualism.* Oxford: Oxford University Press.

Macpherson, C. B. 1975. *Democratic Theory.* Oxford: Clarendon Press.

Macpherson, C. B., ed. 1978. *Property.* Toronto: University of Toronto Press.

Marx, Karl. 1970. *Critique of Hegel's Philosophy of Right.* Tr. Joseph O'Malley. Cambridge: Cambridge University Press.

Marx, Karl. 1973. *Grundrisse.* Tr. Martin Nicholas. Middlesex: Penguin.

Marx, Karl. 1976. 'The German Ideology'. In *Collected Works.* 50 vols., 5. London: Lawrence and Wishart.

McKeon, Richard. 1937. 'The development of the concept of property in political philosophy: A study of the background of the constitution'. *Ethics,* 48, pp. 297–366.

Miller, David. 1976. *Social Justice.* Oxford: Clarendon Press.

Montuori, Mario, ed. 1963. *A Letter Concerning Toleration.* The Hague: Martinus Nijhoff.

Nozick, Robert. 1974. *Anarchy, State, and Utopia.* Oxford, Basil Blackwell.

Olivecrona, Karl. 1974a. 'Appropriation in the state of nature: Locke on the origin of property'. *Journal of the History of Ideas,* 35, 2, pp. 211–30.

Olivecrona, Karl. 1974b. 'Locke's theory of appropriation'. *Philosophical Quarterly,* 24, 96, pp. 220–34.

Olivecrona, Karl. 1975. 'The term "property" in Locke's *Two Treatises of Government*'. *Archiv fur Rechts und Sozialphilosophie,* 61, 1, pp. 109–15.

Olivecrona, Karl. 1976. 'A note on Locke and Filmer'. *The Locke Newsletter,* 7, pp. 83–93.

Olsen, Christopher. 1969. 'Knowledge of one's own intentional actions. *Philo- and Public Affairs,* 6, 1, pp. 3–25.

Parry, Geraint. 1978. *John Locke.* London: George Allen & Unwin.

Plumb, J. H. 1967. *The Growth of Political Stability in England 1675–1725.* London: Penguin.

Pocock, J. G. A. 1967. *The Ancient Constitution and the Feudal Law.* New York: W. W. Norton.

Pocock, J. G. A. 1975a. *The Machiavellian Moment.* Princeton: Princeton University Press.

Pocock, J. G. A. 1975b. 'Early modern capitalism: the augustan perception'. In *Feudalism, Capitalism and Beyond,* ed. E. Kamenka and R. S. Neale. London: Edward Arnold.

Pocock, J. G. A. 1979. 'The mobility of property and the growth of eighteenth-century sociology'. In *The Theory of Property in the Western Tradition,* ed. Anthony Parel. Waterloo: Wilfred Laurier University Press.

Polanyi, Karl. 1957. *The Great Transformation: the political and economic origins of our time.* Boston: Beacon Press.

Pompa, Leon. 1975. *Vico.* Cambridge: Cambridge University Press.

Ritchie, D. G. 1893. 'Locke's theory of property'. In *Darwin and Hegel*. London: Sonnenschein.

Ryan, Alan. 1965. 'Locke and the Dictatorship of the Bourgeoisie'. *Political Studies*, 13, 2, pp. 219–30.

Sargentich, Thomas, ed. 1974. 'Locke and ethical theory: two MS pieces'. *The Locke Newsletter*, 5, pp. 24–31.

Scanlon, Thomas. 1976. Nozick on rights, liberty, and property. In *Philosophy and Public Affairs*, 6, 1, 3–25.

Schlatter, Richard. 1951. *Private Property. The History of an Idea*. London: Allen & Unwin.

Schochet, Gordon. 1969. 'The family and the origins of the state'. In *John Locke: Problems and Perspectives*, ed. J. W. Yolton, pp. 81–98. Cambridge: Cambridge University Press.

Schochet, Gordon, ed. 1971. *Life, Liberty and Property; Essays on Locke's Political Ideas*. Belmont, California: Wadsworth.

Schochet, Gordon. 1975. *Patriarchalism in Political Thought*. Oxford: Basil Blackwell.

Sidgwick, Henry. 1906. *Outlines of the History of Ethics*. London: Macmillan.

Skinner, Quentin. 1965. 'History and ideology in the English revolution'. *Historical Journal*, 9, pp. 151–78.

Skinner, Quentin. 1969. 'Meaning and understanding in the history of ideas'. *History and Theory*, 8, pp. 3–53.

Skinner, Quentin. 1970. 'Conventions and the understanding of speech acts'. *Philosophical Quarterly*, 20, pp. 113–38.

Skinner, Quentin. 1971. 'On performing and explaining linguistic actions'. *Philosophical Quarterly*, 21, pp. 1–21.

Skinner, Quentin. 1972. ' "Social meaning" and the explanation of social action'. In *Philosophy, Politics and Society*, ed. P. Laslett, W. G. Runciman and Q. D. R. Skinner, series IV. Oxford: Basil Blackwell.

Skinner, Quentin. 1974. 'Some problems in the analysis of political thought and action'. *Political Theory*, 2, pp. 277–303.

Skinner, Quentin. 1978. *The Foundations of Modern Political Thought*. 2 vols. Cambridge: Cambridge University Press.

Steiner, H. 1977. 'The natural right to the means of production'. *Philosophical Quarterly*, 21, pp. 41–9.

Stocks, J. L. 1933. 'Locke's contribution to political theory'. In *John Locke: Tercentenary Address*, ed. J. L. Stocks and Gilbert Ryle. Oxford: Oxford University Press.

Straka, Gerald M. 1962. 'The final phase of divine right theory in England'. *English Historical Review*, 77, pp. 305, 638–58.

Strauss, Leo. 1953. *Natural Right and History*. Chicago: The University of Chicago Press.

Thomas, Keith. 1972. 'The Levellers and the franchise'. In *The Interregnum: The Quest for Settlement 1646–1660*, ed. G. E. Aylmer, pp. 57–97. London: Macmillan.

Thompson, M. B. 1976. 'The reception of Locke's Two Treatises of Government 1690–1705'. *Political Studies*, 24, 2, pp. 184–91.

Toulmin, Stephen and Janik, Allan. 1973. *Wittgenstein's Vienna*. New York: Simon and Schuster.

Tribe, Keith. 1977. 'The "histories" of economic discourse'. *Economy and Society*, 6, 3, pp. 314–43.

Tribe, Keith. 1978. *Land, Labour and Economic Discourse.* Routledge and Kegan Paul.

Tuck, Richard. 1979. *Natural Rights Theories: Their Origin and Development.* Cambridge: Cambridge University Press.

Unger, Richard. 1975. 'Technological and industrial organization: Dutch shipbuilding to 1800'. *Business History,* 17, 1, pp. 56–73.

Vaughn, C. E. 1925. *Studies in the History of Political Philosophy.* 2 vols. Manchester: Manchester University Press.

Viner, Jacob. 1963. ' "Possessive individualism" as original sin'. *Canadian Journal of Economics & Political Theory,* 29, 4.

von Leyden, Wolfgang. 1956. 'John Locke and natural law'. *Philosophy,* 31, pp. 23–35.

von Leyden, Wolfgang. 1968. *Seventeenth-Century Metaphysics.* London: Duckworth.

von Leyden, Wolfgang, ed. 1970. *Essays on the Law of Nature.* Oxford: Clarendon Press.

Walzer, Michael. 1974. *The Revolution of the Saints: A Study in the Origins of Radical Politics.* New York: Atheneum.

Webster, Charles. 1976. *The Great Instauration.* London: Duckworth.

Weisheipl, J. A. 1965. 'Classification of the sciences in medieval thought'. *Medieval Studies,* 27, pp. 54–90.

Wittgenstein, Ludwig. 1974. *Philosophical Investigations.* Tr. G. E. M. Anscombe. Oxford: Basil Blackwell.

Yolton, John W. 1970. *Locke and the Compass of Human Understanding.* Cambridge: Cambridge University Press.

Yolton, John W. 1977. *The Locke Reader.* Cambridge: Cambridge University Press.

Index

of labour, 115–30; man's, 105;
servant's, 135–45; 169; *see also*:
making; property in
rights of fatherhood, 57–9
rights of private dominion, 55–7, 59–64,
68, 70, 75, 96, 133, 136–45, 169–70
rights to means of preservation
charity, 132, 137–8; civil rights'
foundation, 163, 166–7; Cumberland,
78–9, 92–4; family, 133–5; from law
of nature, 62–4; from Scripture,
60–1; in use, 115–30; are common
property, 64; not renounced in
political society, 151–4, 166–70;
rights of revolution, 170–4; *see also*:
law of nature; preservation; rights,
inclusive
Ritchie, D. G., 135–6, 145
robbery, 97, 125–8
Ryan, Alan, 116, 131, 136, 138, 142–3,
149, 169, 173, 179

Sargentich, Thomas, 105
Saxby, E., 174
Scanlon, Thomas, 99, 165
Schlatter, Richard, 100, 178
Schochet, Gordon, 56, 133–4, 165
Selden, John, 77–9, 88, 91–2, 95, 97–9,
113
self-interest, 47–50, 101–4
servant and slave, 56–7, 82, 92, 111–14,
135–46, 154, 161, 173–4
Shaftesbury, first Earl of, 146
Sidgwick, Henry, 92
Skinner, Quentin, ix, 33, 63, 66, 82,
177–9
slave, *see* servant
Socrates, 97
*Some Considerations of the Lowering of
Interest and Raising the Value of
Money*, by John Locke, 140, 149
Some Thoughts Concerning Education,
by John Locke, 103, 150, 176
*Some Thoughts Concerning Reading
and Study for a Gentleman*, by John
Locke, 28
Soto, Domingo de, 66
Spinoza, B., 12
Steiner, H., 63
Stillingfleet, Edward, 4
Stocks, J. L., 177
Straka, Gerald M., 178–9
Strauch, Johann Heinrich, 75–6
Strauss, Leo, 63
Suarez, Francisco
common property, 67–8; contrast
with Pufendorf, 76–7; distribution of

property, 171; end of government,
162–3; *ius ad rem* and *ius in re*, 67;
justice, 66–7, 84; law of nature, 41–
2; private property is conventional,
98; property defined, 112–14;
property in, 80; rights, active, 84;
rights, subjective, 66–8; 23, 49, 58,
71, 74, 88, 111, 137, 175, 178–9
suum, 80–1, 83, 85–6, 90, 112–14

Thomas, Keith, 138, 141, 169
Thompson, M. B., 177, 179
Toland, John, 35
Toulmin, Stephen, 177
traductionism, 58
Tribe, Keith, 134, 136, 140, 143, 149,
169, 179
Tuck, Richard, 65, 177–9
Tyrrell, James, 6, 53, 97–8, 126, 178

Unger, Richard, 141

value, 116, 144–5
Vaughn, C. E., 117
Velthuysen, Lambert, 87, 125
Vico, G., 12, 23–4, 27, 32, 58
Viner, Jacob, 116
Vitoria, Francisco, 66
von Leyden, W., 6, 38, 48, 66, 121

Wallis, John, 6
Walzer, Michael, 109
Webster, Charles, 179
Weisheipl, J. A., 12
Welwood, William, 77
Whichcote, Benjamin, 178
Wittgenstein, L., 16, 177
Wollaston, William, 58, 117, 120
Woodhouse, A. S. P., 113, 174
workmanship
analogy between God and man, 9,
109–10, 116–17, 140–1, 170; Aquinas,
121; basis of natural laws and
natural rights, 4, 7–9, 34–50, 59, 62,
175; conceptual analysis of, 10, 11,
14, 16–27, 34–5; defended against
Filmer, 55, 57–9; God as maker, 35–
8; man as God's property, 4, 37, 39;
55, 131, 160–1; *see also*: making;
property in; right, maker's

Yolton, John, 3, 8–9, 13, 15–17, 21–2,
24–6, 32–3, 38, 41, 47, 100, 106–8,
126, 179

Ziegler, Caspar, 97, 126